COLOR SYMBOLISM

Six Excerpts from the Eranos Yearbook 1972

Adolf Portmann □ Christopher Rowe □ Dominique Zahan
Ernst Benz □ René Huyghe □ Toshihiko Izutsu

1977
Spring Publications
Postfach
8024 - Zürich
Switzerland

ACKNOWLEDGEMENTS

These six papers were delivered at the annual Eranos Conference, Ascona Switzerland, August 1972. They were then published in the tri-lingual volume *Eranos 41 – 1972, The Realms of Colour (Die Welt der Farben, Le Monde des Couleurs)* together with papers by Gershom Scholem, Henry Corbin, Peter Dronke, S. Sambursky, and P. A. Riedel. We are grateful to the editors of the yearbook, Adolf Portmann and Rudolf Ritsema, as well as its publisher, E. J. Brill, Leiden. We especially thank the four translators for having accomplished almost impossible tasks. This volume was composed by Susan Haule, editorially aided by Robert Weening who also made the index.

Cover by Rhoda Kassof Isaac.

ISBN 0-88214-400-6

Composed and Manufactured in Switzerland
by Buchdruckerei Schrumpf, 8123 Ebmatingen-Zürich
for Spring Publications, Postfach, 8024-Zürich
Spring Publications are also centrally distributed in the United States from:
Box 1, University of Dallas Station, Irving, Texas 75061

CONTENTS

ADOLF PORTMANN

COLOUR SENSE AND THE MEANING OF COLOUR FROM A BIOLOGIST'S POINT OF VIEW

The garden at Casa Eranos is a tempting distraction for the biologist, yet it makes me mindful of the need for brevity if I am to speak about the world of colour. The abundant green of its foliage has its chief meaning for the biologist as a sign of the grand metabolism of nature, the formation of organic substances in plants through the action of sunlight. If I were to go into this aspect of the colour problem, I would have to deal too with the role of our red blood pigmentation, and this would mean entering upon a vast field which is the proper concern of physics and chemistry. All that would have no place in today's survey. The theme of this conference is the experience of colour. Thus I must put aside the problems connected with green leaves and red blood. The green of this garden must thus serve merely as a background for the flowers and fruits whose striking colours attract the searching eyes of insects and birds. We are concerned with the sense for colours and the sense which colours have in the interrelated lives of organisms which, like ourselves, live in a world full of colour.

I

There are two theories which have attempted for more than a century to explain, each in its way, the processes and structures that enable us to perceive colour. Both of them take their origin in the wave theory, which has been the basis of all interpretations of the effect of light since Christian Huyghens worked out its details in the approximate years of 1678-1690.

One of the theories was proposed by Thomas Young around 1801 and modified by Hermann Helmholtz a half-century later. Young was able to build on the concept of a three-colour basis of our colour vision, since the physicist Mariotte had already proposed this in the seventeenth century; the engraver LeBlon had reduced from seven to three the number of plates required for colour prints as early as 1722. In the updated Helmholtz-Young formulation the theory assumes the presence of three processes, ultimately involving three elementary colour perceptions (red, green, and violet) through the agency of special retinal cells called cones. The colours seen, however, are further influenced by the action of a second type of retinal cell, the rods, which are responsible for shades of grey. The interaction of rods and cones results in our richly varied colour perception.

In contrast to this theory we have one proposed by Ewald Hering (1875), in its original form involving three opposing pairs of biochemical processes, red-green, yellow-blue, and white-black. The gradual confirmation of the role played by the rods and cones, culminating in the "duplicity theory of vision", resulted in the black-white grouping being set apart from this triad as a different kind of phenomenon.[1] In the present theory of complementary colours, the two remaining pairs are seen as the result of two substances in the retinal cones which react differently to different wave lengths of light, as shown in the following table:[2]

Substance A	7000-5800 Å (Red)
Substance A	5800-4700 Å (Green)
Substance B	6900-4900 Å (Yellow)
Substance B	4900-3800 Å (Blue)

We notice at once that Hering's opposing pairs are in fact the so-called complementary colours, a phenomenon we are familiar with from our own experience in the form of simultaneous visual effects in the case of a colour seen against a neutral background or as the aftereffect of a strong colour impression. It should also be noted that colour blindness in man most often affects the ability to distinguish red and green, less often blue and yellow. All of this leads us to suspect close connections between these paired processes, which in their details have not as yet been fully explained.

Even in the early stages, the theorising about colour vision had to reckon with the certainty that the whole brain is involved in the visual process, from the retina of the eye at the periphery, via the diencephalon (the rear of the forebrain) to the cerebral cortex of the occipital region. Since 1880 the analysis of the entire visual process has been intensified by the increasing refinement of research equipment. The retina, by origin a part of the brain projected outward, remains even in its peripheral status a complicated cerebral organ with several strata of differently-structured cells. The innermost layer, that of the visual cells, is the seat of the first transformation of the stimulating processes brought about by light. This cell layer very probably operates largely along the lines of the three-colour theory. But even the other retinal cell layers combine the initial stimuli in complex ways.

In fishes, amphibia, reptiles, and birds it is the twin bodies, corpora bigemina, of the midbrain that act as the seat of further analyses and syntheses of the optical stimuli. In mammals, important regroupings of the stimuli take place in the diencephalon; electrophysiological findings among other primates point to the lateral geniculate (kneelike) bodies of the inner brain-surface as the area in question, and these findings must be accepted as having validity also for man. Six cellular layers are found here, the two thicker ones being at the bottom and the four thinner ones at the top. To put the matter very simply, these layers can be variously related to the theories of colour vision we now have to work with, and their organization points to an increasingly complex process culminating in the experience of seeing. It is possible that the bottom two layers serve primarily for black-white seeing. Of the four uppermost layers, numbers three and four (counting upwards) seem to operate along the lines of Hering's theory, while the functions of numbers five and six bear out rather the view of Young and Helmholtz.

Only those in the most intimate circles of neurological research can appreciate the complexity and strangeness of the processes which, thanks to the syntheses of the cerebral cortex, finally result in our experiencing the colourful world about us. If I might venture a tentative picture of the colour experience as it is currently understood, a very general scheme, still subject to change, of the processes at work, then I should have to outline it as follows: the beginning of this internal transformation of external processes seems to follow more closely the Young-Helmholtz theory, while the further activities within the brain increasingly favour an interpretation along the lines laid down by Hering. Thus, the researching of our colour sense brings us to the standpoint that while a Newtonian analysis of the initial effects of light has its place in our understanding of the process, the situation changes as we seek to understand the ultimate neurological synthesis of the optical system, and we are forced more and more to adopt a view approaching that of Goethe, whose ultimate concern was the experiencing of a world of colour, not the analyses and syntheses of the preceding stages, however necessary it may be to know about these.

The necessary variety of our approach to all manifestations of the living makes it unavoidable that physical and chemical methods are dominant, and indeed achieve impressive results, when we investigate the initial stages of our relation to the environment; here, after all, our concern is the effect on living cells of physical phenomena whose nature has been rather thoroughly elaborated. It is no less true, however, that in the final stages of stimulus-transformation by the higher nerve centers to yield subjective sensory experience the scientist's eye must be directed to the ultimate conscious results of the process. Toward that end he must avail himself of the established methods for investigating mental things, namely those of psychology. The conflicting views of Newton and Goethe are seen today as equally valid alternative approaches to the same thing. The quarrel of bygone days has been resolved by our recognition that different paths to knowledge are necessary. Colours may be "the deeds done and suffered by light" – but we must now stress more than ever that the stage on which these active and passive manifestations take place is the neurological structure of our vision. The interaction of this neurological organ with that segment of reality called light is one of the grand mysteries of higher life as we know it.

I cannot conclude this outline of our knowledge about the colour experience without briefly reporting on some experiments that seem to hint at factors as yet unknown in the relation of organisms to light. In connection with certain experiments on sensitivity of the human eye to light intensity, an attempt was made to discover an annual rhythm of this function. The results at first were inconclusive. Finally, in 1940, the presence not only of a yearly cycle but of a monthly cycle alongside it was conclusively shown; but the explanation was still forthcoming.

More exact measurements have been provided by experiments done on the guppy from 1963 on.[3] The decisive factor in this more precise method is the fact that guppies, like many other fishes, react not only to gravity but also to incident light, which in their normal lives comes from above and thus coincides directionally with the gravitational influence. However, if the light field is altered so that the rays fall in a different direction from that of gravity, the fish is forced by this unaccustomed stimulus to take up a slanting bodily position, whose angle turns out to be a resultant of the gravitational and light effects. This angular "stance" varies, however, with the effects of different-coloured light and with the phases of the moon. At full moon the sensitivity to yellow light is at a maximum and to violet at a minimum. The situation is reversed at new moon, when the sensitivity to violet light is at a maximum. The experimental results are valid even under prolonged illumination; we cannot yet explain what specific factors of lunar influence upon living things are at work in this changing sensitivity. My main purpose in mentioning these experiments was to bring home the complexity of light influence on the various sensory spheres.

Our summation of colour experience would be incomplete, were we not to take into consideration the peculiar fact that light-experiences are possible in total darkness, in the absence of any overt optical stimulus. The visual system can be activated in dreams and religious visions. In his study of visionary phantasies, Johannes Müller ascribed this sensory activity to a central organ, the "Phantastikon". The physicist M. Knoll devoted his last years in Munich to the study of such inner visions and sought to fathom the laws governing them.[4]

We cannot hope to grasp the problem of colour sense in all its profundity unless we leave the world of vertebrates, whose many correspondences to our own colour experience engender a certain feeling of familiarity; we must instead exercise a new caution in making comparisons between man and the higher animal forms.

But how can we ever hope to find out in what manner animals distinguish colours – especially, animals whose organisation is quite at variance with our own, such as the insects – or whether they can distinguish colours at all? That they can indeed do so has much evidence in its favour: the existence of varicoloured flowers in the first place, and the consistency with which some insects visit particular ones. That could, of course, be due to the form or fragrance of the flower; but the assumption of a colour sense on the part of insects has been lent a high degree of probability, even certainty, by the foundation-laying lifelong efforts of Christian Konrad Sprengel, who in 1793 unveiled *Das entdeckte Geheimnis der Natur im Bau und in der Befruchtung der Blumen* (The Secret of Nature Revealed in the Structure and Fertilization of Flowers). To be sure, Sprengel's views seemed suspect to his contemporaries and resulted in his premature retirement from his position as rector of the secondary school in Spandau. It was not until the publication of Darwin's work of 1859 that scientific attention was again focused on Sprengel's achievement.[5]

Sprengel was able to build on the general recognition of the special role played by flowers in the sexual life of higher plants. The flower had been recognised as a sexual organ in the seventeenth century – Carl Linné helped win this battle against theologians – but it remained for Sprengel to demonstrate the necessary role of flower-visitation in the lives of many plants. At a time in which it was generally believed that the splendour of flowers had been created for the delight of human eyes, he ventured the bold conclusion "that in the forget-me-not the yellow ring about the corollary opening, which contrasts so nicely with the sky-blue corollary edge, serves as a signpost for the insects in their quest for nectar". Sprengel goes on to conclude: "If the corolla is coloured a certain way in a certain place, then this colouration is there purely for the sake of insects." This seems to him to be "one of the most admirable and wondrous institutions of Nature".

This was a giant step, a daring conception: the splendour of the plant world is not there for our sake; but the bold conclusion was based on an idea that seemed quite self-evident at that time: that the flower-colours were something objectively given, appearing the same to our eyes as they did to those of other animals. The bold conclusions that Sprengel drew from his observations were as yet no proof for the colour vision of insects. The new biology, trained in physics and chemistry, demanded experimental precision. Sceptical thinking gave rise to doubts which were strengthened by the known fact of human colourblindness. Animals, after all, might very well be colourblind.

The question was settled by experiments of Karl von Frisch around 1914.[6] Bees, he found, can be trained to select different colours, but they are unable to distinguish red, which they confuse with black or dark grey.

In 1924 the proof followed that bees see more than we do at the opposite end of the physical spectrum; they perceive ultraviolet as a colour in its own right. The spectrum of visible light as scattered by a prism extends in our own case over a range of 8000 to 4000 Å, but for bees this range is about 5600 to 3000 Å.

Let us now pursue the course of experimentation in some detail. Toward this end I have chosen the experiments done by F. Knoll on the Istrian peninsula in 1920,[7] as they are less well-known than the studies on bees, whose pioneer Karl von Frisch still remains.

In 1920 Knoll took observations on the bee-fly Bombylius that inhabits the chalky Carsic region of the Istrian peninsula. The observations were made in the spring, when this insect frequents the blue blossoms of the grape-hyacinth Muscari. It was proven that it is indeed the blue colour that guides the bee-flies in their pursuit by placing sealed glass tubes over some of the flowers in order to rule out any effect of fragrance. It was found that Bombylius invariably flies directly to that part of the glass where the blue colour appears. But does it see this colour as "blue"? The biologist, after all, cannot content himself with the first indication of a colour sense that comes along. Might not the flower appear in a particular shade of grey, as indeed it would to a human afflicted with blue-yellow colour-blindness.

The further proof is quite simple. Amidst gradated grey squares on a placard we interpose a blue square that could be confused with certain of the grey ones. Experiments in the open air show that the bee-fly, while approaching Muscari flowers, visits the blue rectangle without fail and without hesitation. This square of paper must thus possess a special attraction, which can only lie in its quality of colour. At the time these experiments were made, the colour sense of bees in the yellow-to-violet segment of our spectrum had been well-established. Here, too, the proof lay in observations of colour-consistency in the visitation of flowers. The experiments began with the bees' being trained to approach certain coloured papers harbouring a food-reward. Then came the crucial test: colour was offered without food, and the bees approached it none the less. Finally, in the main part of the experiment, coloured papers were displayed amidst grey shades and without food-rewards, in order to check on any possibility of confusion. But even then the bees flew to their training-colour and showed no tendency to confuse it with grey.

Many experimental variations have confirmed these findings and have succeeded in convincing us that insects have a colour sense. Paper, of course, cannot be used to test ultraviolet-seeing. This is done by means of an ultraviolet wave-bundle that we cannot see in a dark room but the insect can.

Investigations carried out over a period of years have yielded an impressive picture of the differing colour perception of humans and insects. If in the following I single out bees in order to compare their colour world with our own, it is because these "domestic animals" among the insects are the ones whose colour perception we are best informed about.

However, both the correspondences and the differences between the colour perception of humans and of bees have to be examined more rigorously. It has been mentioned that bees are blind to red. They are able to distinguish orange, yellow, and green, but these colours seem to hold little difference for them. Blue-green, on the other hand, is seen as a quite distinct colour. Sensitivity is quite pronounced to nuances in the blue and ultraviolet regions. Just as our eye registers a blending of colours from the opposite ends of the spectrum, red and violet, as the special colour purple, a blending of the bees' spectral end-colours of yellow and ultraviolet yields for them a discrete colour-quality which has been designated as "bees' purple".

The absence of red in the bees' spectrum and their high sensitivity toward ultraviolet leads us to regard in a new light the world of flowers – a delight to our eyes but a life-and-death matter for many insects. It was noted even in the early stages of investigation, before the role of ultraviolet in bees' vision was known, that many flowers that appear red to us had the same effect as blue on insects, or else they appeared to have an active yellow component. In 1923 it was discovered that countless flowers emit ultraviolet radiation, and as already mentioned the proof followed in 1924 that insects can see ultraviolet. Since then the investigation of just this aspect has been of special importance in our attempts to penetrate the mysteries of insect sight. It points up much more graphically than the negative trait of red-blindness the unique nature of this quite divergent optical system. Even where the actual ultraviolet emission of a flower is not great by our standards, the insects' high sensitivity to it renders it vastly important in their relation to the flower-filled environment.

Some flowers that appear a pure bright yellow to us, such as the evening primrose *Oenothera*, display ultraviolet patches that attract insect visitors to their nectar. In other flowers, the petals are brilliantly ultraviolet but bear similar patches which are not. Knoll observed early in the 1920's that the bee-fly also approaches white flowers (e.g. *Cerastium*), but he never succeeded in getting his experimental subjects to approach white paper. Now we know the answer to this riddle. The role of ultraviolet radiation in "white" flowers was not known at that time, and white paper simply does not reflect the same kind of light that a white flower does.

Vegetational "green" is so rich in ultraviolet, which humans cannot see, that it must have quite a special appearance for bees, and probably for many other insects as well. Careful experimentation and thoughtful comparison seem to indicate that a yellowish light grey is the vegetation colour that a bee sees.[8]

Today there is one important fact that we must try to assimilate into our view of the world: our colour spectrum, which paints such a rich picture of the world about us on the naive level of experience, is in reality nothing but a translation of environmental processes in terms of our retinal and cerebral structures. This translation of an alien reality is every bit as limited in its informational content with regard to our world as is the corresponding achievement of alien eyes and nervous systems. The statement given by our perceptual equipment is quite different from that of flies or bees, and thus it is quite inadequate for true cognition of the world around us, let alone being an objective instrument for constructing a "correct" picture of the world. None the less, this colour world is, in the end, the one that conforms to our immediate experience; it is in the deepest and highest sense "our" world, just as the non-red, ultraviolet-rich world of the insects belongs to them and no one else. I mentioned Goethe's words on colours as the actions and sufferances of light. The investigations into the colour sense of insects bear witness to the varied structures of vision in higher organisms, structures which lend these actions and sufferances of light their unique and vital import in each case. We spoke before of a "stage" on which these transformations of light take place; comparative biology shows us how different the "actors" are who take part in the play of genetic structures involving man and bee.

The great privilege of man is that his spiritual make-up enables him to construct instruments that can expose this limitation of naive experience and break through barriers to gain new insight into the unknown reality. The question as to the origins of this one aspect of our relation to the world represents the crux of all questions about the development of our life-form.

II

We must ask what significance the question of colour vision may have in the overall interplay of life, the coexistence of countless plant and animal species. Many possible roles become evident when we subject the wonder of colour to practical questions of utility and advantage. We may think, for example, of the function of colour as a self-display signal for animals, flowers, and fruits – a function of no less importance than that of camouflage or self-concealment. Both involve the relationship of an animal or plant to an observing eye, except that in the one case the colour image transmits positive information, while in the other case we have to say that appearances are deceptive. We are reminded too of the colours and patterns that announce unmistakably the presence of a butterfly or bird, colours that may contrast sharply with their background – whether this contrast is a signal to others of its kind or the warning of a poisonous or inedible animal to its enemies. And there has been no doubt that flower colours and shapes attract pollinators since Sprengel dared assign this beauty, unintended for human eyes, its rightful place in the living cosmos.

Ever since Darwin directed public attention to the species-preserving significance of colourations and patterns that deceive the eye while concealing the underlying shape, biologists have devoted a great deal of attention to this phenomenon. It ranges from the simplest protective colouration (desert-grey, grass-green, snow-white) to the complex alternation of summer and winter coats, from sophisticated diverting of the glance by means of markings on an animal's non-vital parts to the stonelike camouflage of desert plants. Our schoolbooks and museums abound in illustrations of this kind of natural obfuscation of actual living forms.

Camouflage and signaling colouration are both as effective as they are because the eyes of higher animals are subject to special laws. This inherent constraint upon our seeing was observed early, and many of the more striking deviations from an objective visual orientation were designated as "optical illusions" and were used in all sorts of playful diversions and optical puzzles. An important revaluation of our environmental orientation was achieved, however, when it was realised that illusions are only extreme cases of the basic rules of seeing whereby we are prepared to face our natural surroundings. In our day, artists, having abandoned the replication of everyday life-forms, have begun to concentrate on the play of colour and form called up by these laws of vision and have evoked the techniques of "op art" to stimulate the eye toward pure activity along these lines. André Breton was quite right in calling attention to the autonomy of the visual process at a time when surrealistic revolt was taking up arms in the cause of optical emancipation. "*L'oeil existe à l'état sauvage*" – this was a battle cry against the narrowly rational concept of "correct" seeing then prevalent.

But let us leave for a moment the camouflaging and signaling functions, which in any case are well enough known. Not all optical phenomena can be forced into these categories of limited rational explainability. We must try to arrive at a more comprehensive groundwork for our understanding of organic forms.

Some structures can act upon the eye, and thus "appear", whose form and colour stand in no vital relationship to an observing organism. I shall take as an example the spendour of autumn foliage in our temperate zone. The origin of these red and yellow colours has been largely explained in terms of species-determined metabolism. The mobilisation of reserves gives rise to certain water-soluble pigments, red anthocyanins, which collect in the central reservoirs of cellular fluid (vacuoles) and are sometimes even given names connected with autumn or aging. With the loss of chlorophyll, the non-water-soluble yellow pigments remain in the cell membranes and, together with the cell fluid, bring about the characteristic appearance of the leaf at this late stage. Finally there remains only the leather-brown colour of the dying leaf, which is essentially that of the cell membranes themselves. This well-organised system is thoroughly understood by scientists in its broad outlines. We should bear in mind that blossoming flowers, too, often appear green until they break down the green pigment and thus free the red, blue, and yellow pigments from their green components. Flowers, like autumn leaves, are destined to pass away. Likewise, many fruits are green at first: only on ripening does the leaf-green colour fade and the brilliant red and yellow come into their own.[9]

The autumnal aging colours of green leaves play no role in the theater of life, as far as their "appearance" is concerned. The fall enchantment of our forests rests upon a series of processes important for the self-maintenance of the plant. The fact that the human eye is thereby delighted is of no vital importance to the plant; it is as unhampered by purpose as is the colour of clouds in the morning and evening sky, the nuances of waves, or the glistening of a snowy peak in the rays of the rising or setting sun. Countless optical phenomena of this kind could be mentioned. They are in no way essential to the life of the organism, however they may strike the eye. We shall call them "nonessential appearances".

The contrary example can be found without any trouble in the vegetable kingdom. No one can dispute that the same pigments of the plant serve a definite optical purpose when they appear in the cells of flowers or fruits. Whether they attract pollinating insects or birds or entice animals to eat the fruit, the pigments in this case always perform a necessary function in the life of the plant or animal. They are there "for appearance's sake", that is to say they have some clear connection with an observing eye. For the sake of precise distinction we shall call them "essential appearances". "Essential" and "nonessential" thus refer, in our usage, to a recognisable survival function of the appearing trait or to the lack thereof. In terms of functional morphology, "nonessential appearances" are to be regarded as nonfunctional characteristics.[10]

The validity of this distinction between two types of "appearance" as regards our human way of thinking lies in its application to the role of colours in non-human seeing. Our own manner of observing things goes beyond the dichotomy of "essential" and "nonessential". It is the essence of our own peculiarity that we are able to lavish true interest and concern upon any object that one might choose. Any optical phenomenon, the most unobstrusive as well as the most striking, can become the focus of our most intense concentration. All of our science rests upon this capacity for insatiable and fruitful curiosity; we sometimes neglect to give it full credit as an essential trait when we contemplate just what it is that sets the human species apart amid the totality of living things.

Thus, nonessential appearances such as autumn foliage or the colour of the sky and clouds become "essential" ones for us; they become bearers of roles in our experiencing of the world, or sometimes even symbols of those hidden workings of nature that seem all the more intrinsic to us in their very concealment.

Essential appearances in the structuring of animals and plants have been given their due by science. Though our theme is colour, we should not forget that all the other sensory modes can likewise yield both essential and nonessential stimuli.

Natural scientists are usually quite eager to bear witness to the efficacy of those recognisably functional structures of the organic world that display a survival value confirmed by frequent observation. The miracle of the eye and ear, of heart, liver, and kidney, not to mention the brain – it is confirmed ever anew how astonishingly well-appointed and complex these all are, and the crowning touch to such descriptions is the discovery that all of these wonders arose by minute stages, over vast periods of time, by virtue of the rigourous workings of selection and isolation upon random mutuations, quite apart from any guidance by a long-range *telos*. The organs involved in "appearance" are often accorded this same attentiveness. If we examine a peacock feather, with its iridescence resulting from microscopic and submicroscopic structures, we indeed have to recognise a high degree of genetically ordained complexity and order. Whoever pursues the sophisticated structure of this feather, whose specifically modified barbs give rise to a brilliant blue in the absence of any blue pigment, comes face to face with a wondrous fact. Since on the one hand the optical effect, which may have been subject to selection on the basis of observing eyes, can only proceed from an already optically active structure (such as the blue of the barbs or the iridescence of the radii), but since, on the other hand, these optical structures only become operative by virtue of a quite complex interplay of factors, the initial phase of a selection process cannot be accounted for except on the basis of an already functioning total effect. The origin of the process is hardly explained by the fact that selection plays a role in maintaining it in its final phases.

The origin of these formations in the context of overall evolution cannot

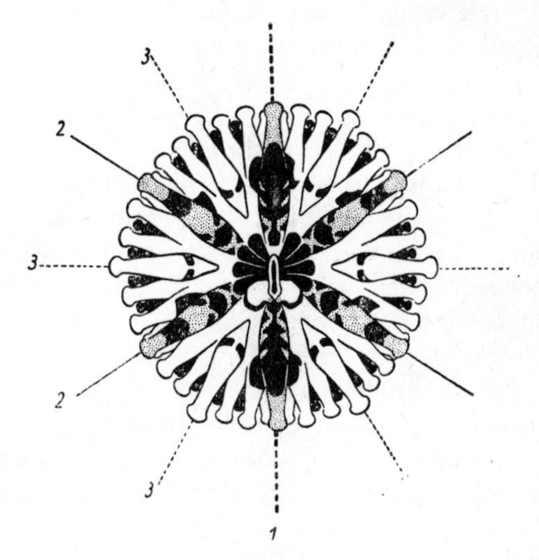

Symmetry planes of the sea anemone *Calliactis*, after T. A. Stephenson.

be explained by the potential survival value of such as yet inactive structures. Whoever seeks to understand appearance structures must find a broader standpoint than the severely limited one of functional and selectional thinking. A survey of the broad realm of nonessential appearances leads us deeper into the question of origins and causes us to focus our attention on the prerequisites for those selection effects dependent on the eyes of higher animals.

Simple levels of organisation such as that of the sea anemone display colour patterns, in its case about the mouth and the surrounding ring of tentacles. The illustration shows a representative of the genus *Calliactis*, with a colour pattern that can be regarded neither as protective camouflage nor as an attention-getting signal. At least no one seems to have thought seriously of relegating it to either category. Some English physiologists have arrived at a conclusion with regard to another sea anemone that can be applied just as well to *Calliactis*: that the often bright colours of these aquatic animals are without any significance and may express not so much a functional adaptation as a freedom from the limitations imposed by environment.[11] Freedom, that is to say, from the exigencies of self-preservation! Notwithstanding this, there are indications of something transcending self-preservation. A more thorough examination of the mouth and tentacle area of *Calliactis* shows that the markings stand in a strict relationship to the symmetry, structure, and phylogeny of the tentacles. The radially arranged tentacles show a hierarchy of the marking pattern in which the buccal disc and the two tentacles of the primary plane occupy first place; beyond this there is a second array clearly comprising two other planes, and a third one comprising the more modestly patterned tentacles. This hierarchy of tentacle markings and colouration contributes a symmetry which elevates the radial arrangement to a two-sided figure. The patterning represents a bilateral organisation which also thoroughly permeates the innermost structure of the sea anemone. A survival value cannot be attributed to this arrangement, but we have been able to confirm the presence of a genetically bound achievement, characteristic of the species, which lends this appearance-configuration a special cast. The colouration of our sea anemone is regarded as "nonfunctional" in orthodox scientific parlance, whose practitioners, captivated by the possibility of explaining the origin of all new forms in terms of natural selection, find themselves confined to the narrow sphere within which only those genetic achievements are recognised that are essential to the life of the organism. This limitation necessarily leads to scant recognition for morphological research, which cannot eschew the discovery of laws transcending the self-preservation function. To be sure, "functional morphology" is still in vogue, but its sole aim is proof of "survival values" in the service of currently prevalent evolution theory. Functional morphology is a subdivision of the study of forms, whose overall task is much more comprehensive; and if this field of study is nowadays relegated, as it were, to the vestibule of biological science, then this relegation has to be regarded in itself as a historically determined orientation whereby certain aspects are necessarily stressed at the expense of others. The intrinsic value of morphology, if its mission is correctly grasped, is not affected by all this. There is a *morphologia perennis* whose continued existence is not in danger. The nonessential appearances of plants and animals provide an unlimited reservoir of structural characteristics of the type mentioned. This superabundance is, of course, subject to frequent utilisation by those mechanisms of selection that may arise with the evolution of image-generating eyes among higher animals.

Nonessential appearances of a high degree of organisation and variety of form are thus the prerequisite for selection, which in turn may favour, preserve, or enhance already active structures. The selective process, however, does not bring appearance-phenomena into existence, and thus it does not explain the enigma of origins and the growth of forms. In order to point up the intrinsic value of nonessential appearance, we shall unite the characteristics already described under the broader heading of "self-presentation". Structures of this type play a large role in the selecting process acting through organisms, and thereby they are continually on the verge of becoming essential appearances.

If the attempt to understand organic forms has diverted the attention of observers toward appearances with life-preserving roles, and if a fascination with the possibility of immediate understanding has caused their gaze to be fixed on this realm of formal abundance, then it is more than ever the task of the biologist to point to the much more comprehensive reality of nonessential appearances, from whose domain the role-bearers among the visual shape and colour structures have issued forth and continue to do so. Such nonessential characteristics, which are nonfunctional from an adaptational viewpoint, have been regarded all too often as "merely taxonomic", as having a purely "systematic value", at best a means of naming plants and animals and not good for much else. As if just this systematic and taxonomic value did not imply the manifestation of broader laws of form and appearance – laws, to be sure, which hold out no promise of practical use, of biotechnical advances, or of "understanding" as conceived by the tool-oriented mentality.

Self-presentation of basic organisational features in the most divergent sensory areas appears to us to be a first-ranking quality of evolution, a quality that is enhanced as the complexity of the environmental relationship increases – a manifestation within the sensory area of the mysterious inner nature of the organism which the eye cannot see.[12] The theme of this Eranos conference is the world of colour; thus it was only natural to make self-presentation in the realm of light the topic of this biological approach to the problem before us. Of chief importance is the insight that colour and pattern stand primarily in the service of this self-presentation, and that the much-observed contributions toward self-preservation and life-maintenance are secondary functional subdivisions.

Since the status of nonfunctional characteristics in organisms is stressed so much here, and since they are lent, as it were, the right of the firstborn in terms of evolutional value, the division into "nonessential" and "essential" make strike some as strange. I have been granting the nonessential appearances a primary value above and beyond all self-preserving adaptation. The term "essential" refers to the fact that appearance (*Erscheinung*) presupposes a receptive organ which finds something "before its eyes" and a receptive sense to which something "appears". Our designation aims at pinpointing the countless characteristics of shape, colour, pattern, and sensory stimuli, wherever they may occur, which attain to significance in the life of some observing organism. Therefore let it be stressed again that the mind of the human organism indeed comprises and recognises a kind of appearance directed toward immediate utility and life-contingencies, but that the narrowness of this category is continually being overcome by the freedom, the magnificant "randomness", of our interests.

We know nothing of the origin of this non-concupiscent "interest". It is a link in the mysterious chain of events that the evolution of mental apprehension of the world still represents for us.

When questions arise about this origin, however, I can do no better than to quote the thoughts and observations contained in A. Kortlandt's studies on chimpanzees:[13]

> The odd thing about wild chimpanzees is that they appear more and more human with advanced age, in contrast to our experience with zoo specimens .... One of the reasons for this is the breadth of their interest in any sort of novel or

> notable thing .... They examined carefully, and collected, surprising objects that I placed in their path. Once I saw a chimpanzee stare attentively at the cloudy sky, which had taken on an unusually beautiful colouration with the setting sun. He stared for fifteen minutes, until it was too late and too dark for him to get his papaya supper that night .... Another reason why chimpanzees in the wild appear so human is their uncertain, hesitant, doubting manner. Everything remains uncertain for them. They take time to weigh everything in their minds, and whenever a dilemma arises they scratch their chest or arm pensively, the way our laboratory chimpanzees do in an experiment .... It is as if that quality that has often been called the "certainty of instinct" had been replaced here by something that in the human realm we would call the uncertainty of intellect, though to be sure it lacks human determination and decisiveness.

Kortlandt's report, restrained as it is, rests on years of familiarity with wild chimpanzees. It is with this in mind that these observations are presented here, amidst our questions as to the hidden origin of a particularly important mental quality of man: the evolution of the non-concupiscent inclination to pursue matters which are chosen at random or which (as the idiom has it) "strike our fancy". The beginnings of mental world-experiencing will forever remain obscure to us, since the event in question must have taken place millions of years ago. But our very knowledge of this obscurity will cause us all the more to pursue all clues which will cast light on this enigma, so that we may say all that can be said about the growth of our form of existence.

III

Six decades of intensive investigation of the colour perception of insects now give us some idea of how very different the bees' colour world is from ours. Let us be reminded once more that the bee sees nothing of the brilliant red of our poppy, the "fire blossoms" (*Feuerblumen*) of my native region. On the basis of experiments we can only make a tentative guess as to how this poppy appears to the insect. Presumably the petals appear whitish, while the four large basal blotches remain black for the bee also but have a brilliantly ultraviolet border – an effect whose quality we cannot grasp in any definitive way because this type of colour experience is denied to us.

The bright red poppy is thus "our" poppy. I am reminded of the countless paintings in which this red is found – those of Van Gogh, for instance, or Monet's meadow scenes. I can sense, too, what a powerful role this brilliant colour plays in our whole experience, and alongside it a world of yellow, white, and blue, about which I now realise how very much it is *our* world, and how different this summer splendour appears to the insect eye. The feeling for one's native landscape that we humans experience (if fortune wills it) from our earliest childhood on has its roots in a world of appearances that manifests itself differently to other living things than it does to us. And all of these colour worlds, with all their differences, remind us how alien to us reality itself is, that actual world that science seeks to fathom beyond the deceptively clear evidence of our senses.

The contrast between our eye's relatively faithful apprehension of form and the more dubious information provided by colour has in some artistic modes of expression led to a dominance of form, as in the radical renunciation of colour in Far Eastern watercolour art. The dominance of colour in some branches of modern painting, on the other hand, arises from a new aversion to all objectivity, an espousal of the individual world of our own vision.

I mentioned the relatively faithful conveyance of form by the eye. We should not forget, however, to what degree form-consciousness is subject to particular laws, rooted in the organisation of the highest nerve centers and capable of calling into being a deformation of the objective reproduction of things; this in turn renders the visual world of man a peculiar world of his own, to be sure to a much lesser extent than is the case with colour perception. It would lead too far afield if we were to discuss also the idiosyncrasy of human hearing or other sensory modes, but we must not lose sight of the general fact that our experiencing of the world via the naive senses is severely limited.

The insight into all these conspicuous sensory limitations and the considerable peculiarity of human colour experience causes us to direct our human gaze once again to the totality of life of which we are a part. We are again brought to face the limited scope of our own naive experience. This limitation is counterbalanced, however, by a high human privilege; there is a path leading away from the naive world-view, namely the specifically human conquest of sensory boundaries by intelligence, which opens up to us a second world-view.

The embarkation upon this secondary way of experiencing the world about us dominates all contemporary life, not only in the West, its place of origin, but even in lands that, though they still pay homage to more ancient ways of life, nevertheless find themselves compelled by a kind of planetary pressure to accept our secondary mode, with all of its rationality, science, and overweening technology.

In previous pages I stressed the narrow scope and peculiar nature of "our" colour world and the severe limitations placed upon its objective informational value as regards true reality. Accordingly I must seek once more to demonstrate the grandeur and dignity of the primary world-view in its bearing upon our existence as a whole.

The need to transcend the limits of sensory experience manifests itself not only, and not even initially, in the boundary-crossing to the secondary world view culminating in present-day scientific thought; it is also strongly active within the reaches of the more primal experience-mode. Before present-day scientific methods could use numerical measurements to develop wholly new forms and to arrive at their present degree of certainty in conveying information about the hidden world, the need to broaden the bounds of the accessible by means of intellectual constructs had already caused people to seek broader perspectives on the world and its origin and passing, and on life and its purpose. The human imagination, in its casting about for the totality of things, has in all ages far transcended immediate experience, being guided by the conviction that we have been created by uncomprehended alien forces, and that we are irrevocably and mysteriously bound to these creating powers. Intuitive insights, ascribed to these presumed powers, have formed the revelatory basis of profound religious approaches to the world around us and have provided us humans over the millennia with a certainty about life situations and our role in the cosmos which is sorely missed today, to judge from the distress of our contemporary life. The fundamental insight that the sky above and the dark earth below constitute a real and formative ground of our existence, that this great Earth is at rest with the heavenly bodies moving around it, that the eternal movement of the sun bestows night and day upon a firmly stationed Earth – all that is the work of a world-view with which every human, even now, begins his life on earth. To be sure, with every passing century we are forced more strongly to form a quite different view. Compared to the broadly ranging primal imagination, this new and second view is beginning to take on the aspect of a constricting asceticism which we Occidentals have imposed upon ourselves by a mighty effort of will after long struggles.

The theme of Eranos 1972 leads us to reflect upon the meaning of the first and primal mode of experience in which colours represent first truths.

The confidence lent by the special truth of our senses, the wealth of emotions and symbols triggered by colour – all this suggests that the emergence of the spirit into a second world-view can by no means be equated with an expulsion from the wondrous original home of man, or with the outgrowing of an early naive approach to the world. The limitation imposed upon all of our orientation by the basic senses is a heritage that we share with all living things. It engenders a special human world which enables our firm and happy anchouring in primal experience no less than it favours the assimilation of insights resulting from a rational delineation of the world and our place in it. The synthesis of our two aspects of reality must be arrived at with a new sense of modesty informed by reverence for the unknown. We dare no longer regard ourselves as the divinely ordained summit of creation, but rather as mortal links of a vast chain, the investigation and contemplation of which is made possible to us by a gift of nature: the very chance of rising to embrace a new view of the cosmos.[14]

A gift of nature – for from whatever aspect we seek to explain the human approach to the cosmos, it is not "we" who brought about the possibility of penetrating the bounds of naive vision. At best we have methodically elaborated, and thus spurred on to greater achievement, a capability bestowed upon us in ways unknown. To be sure, in so doing we have also sown the seeds of mortal peril. But even our ultimate findings about the structure of sense organs and nerve centers will not explain the processes of consciousness and experience, for the instrument that aids us in this effort is incapable of analysing itself.

Whether we will ever succeed in finding out anything definite about the way in which our peculiarly human world came about is a problem for the future, which we of today cannot answer. I see the prospects as very slight, but the natural scientist had best avoid the prophet's role.

One of the goals of the Eranos conferences has been to continually make plain the deeply rooted and fruitful role which the primal approach to the cosmos plays in furthering a life of human fulfillment. It is our concern not only to provide learned commentaries upon the documents of religious experience or upon the spiritual achievements of past ages in which a more intimate relation with the cosmos prevailed, but rather to bear out the prime and immediate necessity of this mode of experience, a necessity that exists for us even here and now. On this very spot C. G. Jung called attention over a period of years to the profound significance, indeed the necessity, of a religious attitude in bringing about a life of fulfillment. It was not by chance that our founder, Olga Froebe-Kapteyn, followed up the clues provided to her and sought out Rudolf Otto, a man whose life had been devoted to things numinous, that is to the relationship of irrational experience to rational thought. Throughout forty Eranos conferences, stress was laid again and again, in the most far-ranging approaches, on the discovery of those spiritual treasures that humanity owes precisely to the penetration of the barrier separating us from the irrational. In an age when the much-admired scientific approach has lent its cast more and more to Western life, it is all the more important to attest that every view making a claim to some broadening of scope must necessarily lead to a high respect for the creative possibilities of the irrational and must further their workings.

In these past days it has been attested from the most divergent viewpoints to what extent the experience of colour is a beneficence from the deepest wellsprings of life, a gift from the innermost structure of our being, destined to increase the subjective wealth of our existence; not, as some might claim, the mere means toward unequivocal orientation within that alien world in which our senses find a home from childhood on. We must maintain our awareness of the distant origins of our attempts to find our station in an unknown and partially veiled world; and this awareness must help to determine the ways in which we experience this world. Our existence cannot but be enhanced by our intuitive grasp of the mystery of hidden being.

Translated by Lee B. Jennings

NOTES

1 Y. Galifret, ed., *Mechanisms of Color Discrimination. International Symposium*, London 1960, pp. 296 ff.; H. Autrum, "Die biologischen Grundlagen des Farbensehens", Naturwissenschaft und Medizin I, 1964, No. 4, pp. 3-15.

2 Å = angstrom unit, one ten-millionth of a millimeter.

3 H. -J. Lang, "Mondphasenabhängigkeit des Farbensehens", *Die Umschau*, 1970 No. 14, pp. 445-46.

4 M. Knoll, "Die Welt der inneren Lichterscheinungen", *Eranos*-34, 1965.

5 Christian Konrad Sprengel, *Das entdeckte Geheimnis der Natur im Bau und in der Befruchtung der Blumen*, Berlin 1793, reprinted in Ostwald's Klassiker LI, Leipzig 1894.

6 Karl von Frisch, "Der Farbensinn und Formensinn der Bienen", *Zoologisches Jahrbuch*, Abteilung: Allgemeine Zoologie und Physiologie 35, 1914, No. 1.

7 Friedrich Knoll, "Bombylius fuliginosus und die Farbe der Blumen", in: *Insekten und Blumen,* Abhandlungen der Zoologischbotanischen Gesellschaft Wien XII, 1926, pp. 19-119.

8 K. Daumer, "Blumenfarben, wie die Bienen sie sehen", *Zeitschrift für vergleichende Physiologie* XLI, 1958, pp. 49-110.

9 W. H. Pearsall, "Herbstfarben", *Endeavour*, Vol. 8. No. 32, 1949, pp. 157-62; A. Seybold, "Die Pflanzenpigmente als physiologisches Problem", *Jahrbuch der Akademie der Wissenschaften und der Literatur,* Heidelberg 1957, pp. 213-229.

10 Adolf Portmann, *Entlässt die Natur den Menschen?* , München 1970, pp. 13-136. In Part I of this work my earlier studies on the problem of "appearance" are collected, along with the bibliographical references.

11 T. A. Stephenson, "Die Farben der Meerestiere", *Endeavor*, October 1947.

12 Adolf Portmann, "Zur Philosophie des Lebendigen", in: F. Heinemann, *Die Philosophie im 20. Jahrhundert*, Stuttgart 1959, pp. 410-440.

13 A. Kortlandt, "Observing Chimpanzees in the Wild", *Scientific American*, May 1962. Cited from the English text provided by the author in the form of proofs.

14 To this point see also K. Löwith, *Der Weltbegriff der neuzeitlichen Philosophie*, Heidelberger Akademie der Wissenschaften, Sitzungsberichte, Phil. -hist. -Kl. 1960, Abh. 4, pp. 7-23.

CHRISTOPHER ROWE

CONCEPTS OF COLOUR AND COLOUR SYMBOLISM IN THE ANCIENT WORLD

A great deal has been written in the last 150 years about colour-terms in Greek literature, and much of it begins from, and centres around, the colour-vocabulary of the monumental Homeric poems, the *Iliad* and the *Odyssey*. William Gladstone, the great British statesman, in his book *Homer and the Homeric Age*, saw "signs of immaturity" in Homer's use of colour: the relative rarity of colour-terms; "the use of the same word to denote not only different hues or tints of the same colour, but colours which, according to us, are essentially different"; "the description of the same object under epithets of colour fundamentally disagreeing one from the other"; "the vast predominance of the most crude and elemental forms of colour, black and white, over every other, and the decided tendency to treat other colours as simply intermediate modes between these extremes"; and finally, "the slight use of colour in Homer, as compared with other elements of beauty, for the purpose of poetic effect, and its absence in certain cases where we might confidently expect to find it". [1] In its assumptions and in its conclusions, Gladstone's book was in many ways typical of nineteenth-century literature on the topic, although in general it betrays a sharpness of mind not always shared by his contemporaries. Homer's supposed deficiencies led some scholars of the time, under the influence of Darwinian theory, to suggest that the Greeks as a race suffered from a form of colour-blindness. [2] Somewhat similarly, Gladstone argued that "the organ of colour and its impressions were but partially developed among the Greeks of the heroic age", because colours, both natural and artificial, played a less prominent role in the visual environment of early Greece: "the olive hue of the skin kept down the play of white and red. The hair tended much more uniformly, than with us, to darkness. The sense of colour was less exercised by the culture of flowers. The sun sooner changed the spring-greens of the earth into brown ... The art of painting was wholly, and that of dyeing was almost, unknown ... [3] The artificial colours, with which the human eye was conversant, were chiefly the ill-defined, and anything but full-bodied, tints of metals. The materials, therefore, for a system of colour did not offer themselves to Homer's vision as they do to ours. Particular colours were indeed exhibited in rare beauty, as the blue of the sea and of the sky. Yet these colours were, so to speak, isolated fragments; and, not entering into a general scheme, they were apparently not conceived with the precision necessary to master them. It seems easy to comprehend that the eye may require a familiarity with an ordered system of colours, as the condition of its being able closely to apprehend any one among them". [4] The "ordered system" which Gladstone has in mind is "our own list of primary colours, which has been determined for us by Nature", that is, the colours of the Newtonian spectrum, together with white and black. [5]

There is a fundamental confusion here, which Gladstone shares with other nineteenth-century scholars. The absence of a fixed term for a certain colour does not necessarily signify an inability, either of a psychological, or of any other kind, to distinguish that colour from others. To take the example cited by Gladstone, the striking absence of any reference in Homer to the *blueness* of the sky (or, with one possible exception, of the sea): can we really suppose that "the Greeks of the heroic age" were unable to distinguish the colour of the sky in summer from the colour of blood or of snow? Such a conclusion is clearly untenable. We must look for a different explanation; and the explanation is to be found in a facet of Homeric colour-usage noticed by Gladstone himself. Most of the Homeric epithets connected with colour refer not so much to "colour proper", but to "the modes and forms of light, and of its opposite, or rather negative, darkness". [6] Homer's world is a world of brightness and darkness, of the gleam of weapons and the dark lustre of a swelling sea. The fault in Gladstone's account is that he regards this automatically as a sign of primitiveness and inferiority. Rather, we should think simply in terms of a different kind of sensitivity to visual stimuli; but if value-judgements are to be made, the apparently lesser sensitivity of the Homeric poets to Gladstone's "primary colours, determined for us by Nature" must be weighed against their heightened sensitivity to an aspect of the visual field to which we, in our turn, are relatively blind.

This explanation seems to resolve the remaining difficulties listed by Gladstone: the apparent confusion over the application of colour-terms is the result of a simple misunderstanding on our part of the nature of those terms; and similarly, the relatively infrequent use of colour-vocabulary in situations where we might expect it to play a leading role, as in the description of feminine beauty, or of the landscape, can be seen merely as symptomatic of a different way of seeing the world.

Müller-Boré, writing in 1922, argued that the lack of emphasis on colour was characteristic of epic style. Epic style, he says:

> "... nowhere seeks after intimate emotional effects, which seem inappropriate to its subject matter. The relative absence of colour can be thought of as betraying a typically archaic stiffness; but it can also be seen simply as the result of a feeling for style, which matches the grandeur of the subject with an equal grandeur of expression, and which never uses artistic devices to bring the figures of an earlier heroic age down to the level of contemporary man. To this choice of style is to be ascribed also the complement of the playing down of colour: the predominance of words denoting brightness, and of similes of the sun, moon, and stars. An epithet of brightness raises the object being described to a higher level than a term indicating colour: the colour-word carries suggestions of the concrete and prosaic, the brightness word of the ideal. There are powerful and noble effects, too, in the light-similes – wonder, awe, and fear. Similar effects can certainly also be conjured up by the use of colours, but they are not bound up in the same way with the concepts themselves; most strongly by white and black, since they often do no more than to express the presence or absence of light, and next by red, the colour of blood and killing. After red one might put the penetrating gleam of yellow, which in poetic diction is rendered by "golden". Blue and green, on the other hand, the colours of lyrical expression, fall completely into the background." [7]

I quote this passage from Müller-Boré in full because of its value as a counterweight to Gladstone's view, that Homer's use of colour is somewhat deficient. Müller-Boré suggests, by contrast, that Homer's preference for terms whose primary reference is to brightness or lustre is a matter of deliberate *choice*. Yet this view too is open to serious doubt. A choice presupposes alternatives; and even apart from his known tendency to rely on descriptions embedded in the formulae of a long-standing tradition, it is highly questionable whether the author of the *Iliad* and *Odyssey* had such alternatives before him. [8] In other words, it is at least uncertain, and to my mind extremely unlikely, that there existed at the time of the composition of the poems any developed means for describing colour beyond what we find in the poems themselves. Thus I argue that one important limiting factor in Homeric colour-usage was *the availability of terms in the language*. It is highly significant that the philosophers of the the fifth and fourth centuries, when dealing with colour, mention few terms which are not also found, if with a rather different meaning, in Homer. Had there been a fund of colour-terms in current use, which Homer chose to neglect, we would certainly expect to find these appearing in the accounts of the philosophers; but we do not. It would be unnatural to suppose that a Democritus or a Plato would choose to take over and adapt a Homeric term in preference to using an already existing term with an identical meaning. Moreover, completely new colour-terms rarely appear in any later period of Greek literature, except for a large number of formations of the type "the colour of ...", e.g. "the colour of a leek", "the colour of ash". The tendency, as we shall see, is towards the development of a colour-vocabulary resembling our own, based largely on the vocabulary found in the Homeric poems.

It is possible, of course, that the formulaic epithets of the Homeric poems merely preserve archaic meanings from an earlier period, and that by the time at which the monumental poems themselves took their final shape, their colour-epithets had already developed new meanings in ordinary language. [9] Quite certainly, there cannot *always* have been a gulf between epic and ordinary usage. It is Gladstone, again, who seems to me to make the decisive point. "Are we", he says, "to reject altogether the idea of defect, and to treat [Homer's] use of colour as one concerned in the spirit which, with even the most perfect knowledge, would properly belong to his art? ... Our answer ... must ..., I think, be in the negative. It is true, indeed, that much of merely literal discrepancy as to colour might be understood to appertain to the license of poetry. There is high poetic effect in what may be called straining epithets of colour. But it seems essential to that effect, (1.) That the straining should be the exception, and not the rule. (2.) That there should be a fixed standard of the colour itself, so that the departures from it may be measured. Otherwise the result is not license, but confusion." Gladstone goes on to quote Shakespeare's lines from *Macbeth*: "Here lay Duncan, His silver skin laced with his golden blood". "Here the idea is not that silver is of the same colour as skin, nor gold as blood; but that the relation of colour between silver and gold may be compared with that between skin and blood: the skin throws the blood into relief, as a ground of silver would throw out a projection of gold. In license of this kind we can always trace both a rule and an aim. The rule is relaxed only for the particular occasion. The effect produced is that of tenderness, dignity and purity." [10] The formulaic nature of the Homeric poems makes such an argument in itself ineffective for the last stage in their formation, that stage in which they achieved their final and unified shape through the agency of the "real" Homer; [11] but it is clearly applicable to the beginnings of the epic tradition. As Gladstone says, "straining epithets", if they are to be effective, must be the exception, not the rule. Indeed, the earliest poets would have been unable to communicate with their audience at all, unless there existed some connection between their language and that of the audience. Thus we may justifiably suppose that the way in which colour-terms were used at least by these early poets corresponded closely with the way in which they were used in ordinary language. But it is also probable that, by and large, the same correspondence still existed at the time of the "real" Homer; for the evidence is that the development of Homeric terms – generally into colour-terms in the strict sense, with a gradual elimination of the primary Homeric connotations of brightness and darkness – was by no means complete even in the fourth century.

Thus the Homeric poems can, in general terms, be used as evidence for the type and extent of the colour-vocubulary possessed by the Greek language as late as the eighth century B.C. [12] The two main features of Homeric colour-language, the rarity of straightforward colour-terms like our "yellow", "blue", or "brown", and the predilection for terms referring to brightness and lustre (or its absence), were, I suggest, also general features of ordinary Greek language in the pre-classical period; and it was the existence of those features in ordinary language which helped to determine the nature of Homeric colour-usage. Their effect was to suggest a relative lack of interest in what Gladstone calls the "proper colour" of objects, and a far greater interest in "modes and forms of light, and of its ... negative, darkness".

There are probably two words in Homer which at least sometimes approximate to straightforward colour-terms: *leukos*, "white", and *melas*, "black". *Leukos* is used, for example, of milk, teeth, and wool, *melas* of black lambs and sheep. To these two I would also add *eruthros*, "red". It is true that the word is only used of bronze (*chalkos*), of nectar, and of wine, and, as Müller-Boré remarks, [13] these cases are not enough in themselves to allow conclusions to be drawn about the general use of the word (*chalkos eruthros*, "red bronze", may refer to the *glow* of bronze; the attributes of nectar are unknown; and "red wine" may be a special term). But the cognate verbs *ereuthō* and *eruthainō*, "to redden", are used, always in the context of blood, as for example in the following passage from the *Iliad*:

> "At Odysseus' words, filled with fury by Athene of the gleaming eyes, Diomedes killed men right and left. Hideous groans arose from them as his sword cut through them, and the earth was *reddened* with blood."

It is at first sight strange that *eruthros* itself is never used of blood, the commonest epithet for which is *melas*, "black", "dark" (presumably in origin an epithet of *dried* blood, but then transferred for formulaic reasons even to freshly spilled blood). But there is enough to suggest that there are here at least the beginnings of a process towards the isolation of *eruthros* as a simple colour-term with the meaning of our "red". Müller-Boré implies that the process is already complete, and argues that the rarity of its use in Homer stems from its "prosaic" quality. The conclusion is possible, but probably derives too much from comparison of later poetic usage, where there is clear evidence of such divergence between the vocabulary of poetry and prose. For the Homeric period, we have practically no independent evidence about non-poetic usage. The fact that blood is not called *eruthros* may be seen as reflecting Homer's general lack of interest in "colour proper"; although metrical considerations are also relevant, since *eruthros* cannot be juxtaposed to *haima*, "blood", in the Homeric hexameter. That lack of interest, as I have argued, was not peculiar to the Homeric poets. Differences of colour might be of importance in the technical sphere, or in ritual: white animals, for example, were sacrificed to the Olympians, black to the chthonian deities. But outside these contexts, colour itself was not the primary distinguishing feature of objects.

Again, it is the contrast between Homer's colour-usage and our own which strikes us, not the similarities between them. It is only rarely that *leukos* and *melas* can be translated simply as "white" and "black"; in the great majority of cases, their essential reference is still to the bright and the dark. Reiter has pointed out the obvious connection between brightness and whiteness. [15] White reflects light better than any other colour; white objects thus represent the paradigm of brightness. This should make us cautious about distinguishing too sharply between the two meanings (or even, perhaps, about distinguishing two *meanings* at all); even in cases which appear to involve a clear colour-reference, the primary meaning of brightness may still be more important. One of the most remarkable examples mentioned by Reiter is the description of Rhesus' horses in *Iliad* X as *leukoteroi chionos*, not so much "whiter than snow", as "brighter than snow" (" 'strahlender' als Schnee"), since later in the same book Nestor is to describe them as "like the rays of the sun". [16] A corresponding point also holds for *melas*, "black", "dark". Conversely, specific terms for brightness, e.g. *phaeinos, lampros, sigaloeis,* may sometimes also contain a colour-reference. [17] This two-sidedness is a general feature of Homer's colour-terms.

We thus reach a compromise between the positions represented by Gladstone and Müller-Boré. The sparing use of colour made by the Homeric poems is not simply the result of artistic choice; but neither is it a sign of "primitiveness", except in a historical sense. It is not a sign of inferiority or defect. The feeling of the early Greeks for the bright, the gleaming, the glowing and the dark, rather than for colour as such, was mirrored in a comparatively undeveloped colour-vocabulary, with remarkably few abstract terms like those which form the basis of our own; and it was against this background that the Homeric poets worked. Yet, as we shall see, the situation was one which, with all its apparent limitations, they were able to turn to positive advantage.

In spite of what I have said, the means at their disposal for visual description display a variety to which I have so far done scant justice. To the three terms for brightness mentioned earlier can be added a host of others: *aglaos, liparos, phaidimos, pamphanoōn* and so on. It is often difficult to make out any difference of meaning between these terms, although more often than not they are tied formulaically to particular groups of nouns. There are also several different words for "dark", but the leading term here is *melas*, "black". *Aithōn, aithops* ("burning", "looking like fire"), both used among other things, of bronze, and possibly also *oinops* ("looking like wine", of the sea), seem to refer to a reddish gleam or glow. Another term apparently more closely connected with colour is *kuaneos*, which Gladstone hesitantly equates with "indigo", but which also frequently seems interchangeable with *melas* in the sense of "dark": the word is derived from *kuanos*, a substance whose nature is still disputed. I mention also three equally difficult words, *glaukos, porphureos,* and *pólios*. *Glaukos*, used once, of the sea, together with the compound *glaukōpis* ,and the related verb *glaukiō,* used of eyes, appears to be connected with "grey", or "blue"; but in none of the three cases is the primary reference obviously to colour. In *Iliad* XVI, where Patroclus in condemning Achilles' refusal to fight, he tells him that he is no son of the sea-goddess Thetis and the gallant Peleus: "only the grey sea (*glaukē thalassa*) with its steep cliffs could have spawned one so pitiless as you". [18] The harshness of the sea is well conveyed to us by the translation "grey", but in the standing epithet *glaukōpis* as applied to the warlike Athena the word *glaukos* seems better taken as referring to the harsh *gleam* of her eyes; and similarly in the image of the wounded lion in *Iliad* XX, glaring (*glaukioōn*) as he charges his hunters. *Porphureos*, "purple", can be applied to the rainbow, a supernatural cloud, clothes and carpets; but also to the sea in motion, the wave of the enraged River Scamander, and to blood and death. In these latter cases it has been doubted whether *porphureos* refers to colour at all, largely because of a supposed connection with the verb *porphurō*, which is used, for example, of the surging movement of the sea. But the connection with *porphurō* is now generally rejected; and we have therefore somehow to treat all the applications of the word *porphureos* on the same footing. Yet the word apparently tends to belong, at least in later literature, to the blue end of the spectrum, and not to the red: [19] how then can it be applied to blood? The probable solution is that we should again think of the word both as a colour-word and as a word for "dark". In its application to blood and death, it serves, perhaps, as no more than a substitute for *melas*: "dark blood", "dark death". Lastly, *polios*. *Polios* is used of hair (in connection with old age), of the sea, of iron, and of the light-coloured wolf's hide which Dolon stupidly wears in the nocturnal expedition in *Iliad* X. Reiter suggests that, as a colour-word, its primary reference is to the white hair, or "grey hair", of old age (we can compare *xanthos*, which in Homer is applied only to horses' manes and to human hair, and is generally regarded as an equivalent to our "blond", although in English it is often translated as "red-haired"; similarly, *glaukos* is the "blue-grey" of eyes). "White-grey iron": this resembles the expression "white tin", and should no doubt be explained in the same way, as describing the *gleam* of iron.

I have here done no more than to single out what are perhaps the most important colour-words in Homer; there are many other words, particularly composites, like *ioeidēs,* "looking like the violet", of the sea, *miltoparēos,* "red cheeked", of ships. But the list which I have given is enough to show the justice of Gladstone's general remarks about the peculiarities of Homeric colour-usage, and the plausibility of the central part of his solution to the problems which they raise: "as a general proposition, then, I should say that the Homeric colours are really the modes and forms of light, and of its opposite, or rather negative, darkness: partially affected perhaps by ideas drawn from the metals, like the ruddiness of copper, or the sombre and dead blue of *kuanos*, whatever the substance may have been, and here and there with an inceptive effort, as it were, to get hold of other ideas of colour". [20]

Among words with a specific colour-reference there are several types: first, compounds like *ioeidēs* ("looking like the violet"); second substantival adjectives like *kuaneos*, "like *kuanos*", or *phoinios*, "red-purple", of blood, probably derived from *phonos*, "slaughter" by analogy with *phoinix*, itself a Homeric colour-word, apparently with the same meaning; third, words like *polios*, "white-grey", *porphureos*, "purple", which may acquire a more general application, but whose primary reference is to one type of object (that of *polios* being to hair, of *porphureos* to dyed objects); and fourth, *leukos*, "white", *melas*, "black", and *eruthros*, "red". These last three, I suggested, approximate most closely to abstract colour-terms, of the kind that predominate in our languages: that is, like our "white", "black", and "red", they do not depend for their colour-meaning on a reference to any particular coloured object, as do *ioeidēs* or *kuaneos*; and they are not special terms, like *polios*, tied to a single object, but can be applied generally to all objects of the same colour. The process of abstraction, of the grouping of the infinitely varied colours of the environment under a limited number of general terms, had as yet only begun. Even *leukos, melas* and *eruthros* themselves cannot, as I have stressed, be regarded as straight-forward colour-terms, carrying as they do the essential connotations of the bright, the dark and the glowing. Nonetheless, we may regard these three as at least resembling abstract colour-terms in the sense defined.

Two of the three may appear in this guise in Mycenaean Greek, on the tablets discovered in the palaces of Crete and southern Greece, which probably predate the earliest stage in the formation of the Homeric poems. [21] Here we find *leukos* used of textiles, oxen, and safflower, which is also described as *eruthros,* "red": the reference is apparently to the pale seeds of the plant, on the one hand, and to its red florets on the other.

Eruthros is also used of leather. Other colour-words are *porphureos*, "violet-purple", and *phoinikeos*, "red-purple", of textiles, and, curiously, also *polios*, used in the same context. [22] But clearly, not much can be drawn from these scanty, fragmentary, bureaucratic lists.

I shall turn next to the development of colour-terminology in the post-Homeric period. There is no doubt that there is such a development; and in this sense, and only in this sense, Homeric colour-usage can be described as "primitive". We have already seen two examples of the subtlety of which it is capable, in the harsh grey-blue gleam of the sea, and the fine contrast between Dolon's name – connected with the word for cunning – and his choice of a white-grey wolfskin for disguise on a night expedition. One may also add, for example, a passage from the end of *Iliad* XIX, where Achilles has ended his feud with Agamemnon after the death of Patroclus, and is preparing for battle once more:

> "As thick as the snowflakes which come flying from the sky, borne on by the sudden chill blast of the north wind, *brightly gleaming* helmets poured from the ships, bossed shields, plated cuirasses and ashen spears. *A flash went up to heaven, and all around the earth laughed with the gleam of bronze*, and rang to the feet of marching men. In the midst of them the noble Achilles fitted on his armour. His teeth gnashed, *his eyes blazed like fire* as intolerable grief sank deep into his heart. Full of fury for the Trojans, he donned the divine gifts which Hephaestus had worked for him; first, he tied round his legs the fine greaves with their silver fittings; next he put the cuirass on his breast. Over his shoulder he threw the silver-studded sword with its bronze blade; then he took the great thick shield, which *flashed into the distance like the moon. As when sailors see the flash of a blazing fire which burns high up in the mountains on a lonely farm, and yet are borne by storm-winds far away from their loved ones out into the fishy sea: such was the flash that went up to heaven from Achilles' finely worked shield.* Then he lifted up the stout helmet, and placed it on his head. The horse-tailed helmet *gleamed like a star*, and around it danced the many golden plumes which Hephaestus had put upon the crest. The noble Achilles tried himself in the armour to see if it fitted and allowed his splendid limbs free movement. It felt like a pair of wings, and lifted him up, ready to lead his people into battle. Then he drew his father's spear from its case ... ". [23]

The richness and literal brilliance of this passage need no comment.

It is in descriptions of the landscape and the countryside that we would most expect to find Homer using colour-terms, and here they are noticeably absent. Just as there are no words for the blue of sky and sea, so there are none for the lush greens of Calypso's island of Ogygia in the *Odyssey*:

> "When Hermes reached the far-off island, he stepped onto the shore from the violet sea and walked along until he reached the great cave where the lovely-haired Nymph lived. He found her inside. A great fire was burning on the hearth, and the scent of split juniper and cedar blazing there was carried far across the island. Inside, Calypso busied at her loom, weaving with her golden shuttle as she sang in her beautiful voice. A luxuriant growth of trees surrounded the cave, alders, poplars, and sweet-smelling cypresses. There long-winged birds roosted, horned owls, falcons, and long-tongued sea-birds which busy themselves around the ocean. Around the mouth of the cave spread a lush vine, covered with bunches of ripe grapes; and four springs in close order ran with crystal clear water, turning this way and that. Around, there flourished soft meadows of violet and parsley. Even an immortal coming there might look at the scene with wonder and pleasure". [24]

The picture is one which appeals to all five senses: we have the smell of the burning logs and of the cypresses, the magical sound of Calypso's voice, the bunches of ripe grapes, soft meadows, and the bright, clear (*leukos*) water of the streams. But it is the visual effect of this ideal landscape which is strongest: and that effect is one of freshness and brightness, not of colour. Yet the picture succeeds, and we are able to share Hermes' admiration.

Before leaving Homer, a word must be said about the quality of one particular group of colour-epithets, epithets for dawn and the sea. Dawn is described as *rhododaktulos*, "rosy-fingered", or as *krokopeplos*, "saffron-robed"; the sea can be *polios*, "white-grey", *oinops*, "wine-dark", "wine-red", *ioeidēs*, "like the violet", *porphureos*, "purple". The range and type of the epithets applied to the sea is partly caused by the frequency of its use in similes; this accounts, for example, for the preponderance of dark colours, which reflects a deeply-embedded fear of the sea. But in both cases, in spite of the fact that the use of the epithets is frequently no more than formulaic, we can detect a sensitivity to colour which we miss elsewhere.

II

One of the major causes of the difficulties in the interpretation of Greek colour-usage is that the evidence is mainly literary; and, as I have frequently suggested, there is always the danger that literary usage may stand at a considerable distance from ordinary language. I shall next consider the technical evidence provided by philosophical discussions of colour in the fifth and fourth centuries B.C.

A late source [25] tells us that Empedocles spoke of four primary colours, white, black, red and yellow; the terms used by the source, but possibly not by Empedocles himself, are *leukos* (white), *melas* (black), *eruthros* (red), and *ōchros* (yellow). Democritus, according to Theophrastus, also chose four primary colours: white (*leukon*), black (*melan*), red (*eruthron*), and *chlōron*, probably "yellowy-green". Other colours are formed by the mixing of these: gold and bronze, from a mixture of white, which gives them their brightness, and red; a "very beautiful colour" formed by the addition of *chlōron*; purple (*porphureon* – here, at least, *red*-purple) from white, black and red, white "giving it its brightness and lustre"; woad-blue (the word used being the name of the plant itself), from "the very black" and *chlōron;* leek-green (*prasinon*, derived from the plant *prason*), from purple and woad-blue, or from *chlōron* and purplish; "indigo" (*kuanoun*) from woad-blue and "the fire-like", "the atoms being rounded and pointed, so that the black should contain brilliance"; and nut-brown, from *chlōron* and the indigo-like (*kuanoeides*). [26]

Only three terms on the list are obviously abstract: those for white, black and red. And it is again striking that at the same time as being treated as a colour, *leukon*, "white" is accorded the role of producing *brightness* in the mixtures, rather than paleness. *Chlōron* in this context is sometimes translated as "yellow", sometimes as "green". The truth probably is that it should be regarded as falling between the two: in Homer, the word sometimes means "fresh", of vegetation, but was also used of honey; in the passage from Theophrastus, it is used of young plants. In post-Homeric poetry, on the other hand, *chlōros* may acquire a general meaning of "green", as a standing epithet of plants and trees.

Plato's account in the *Timaeus* [27] follows a broadly similar pattern, first giving a list of primary colours, then of composite colours. His primaries are white, black, red, and, a curious addition, about which I shall say more in a moment, "bright" (*lampron*). Throughout the passage, Plato is talking about light; all colour is described as "a flame flowing off from objects", and white, red and "bright" are species of fire, or light. A mixture of the three produces *xanthon*, "orange" (the word here being the Homeric word for blond); red with black and white produces purple; with more black added "dark violet" (*orphninon*); orange and grey (*phaion*) produce *purron*, "tawny" (usually the word for "red-haired"), while grey is black mixed with white; *ōchron*, yellow, is produced by white and orange. White mixed with "bright" and "falling into" deep black produces *kuanoun*, "indigo", "deep-blue"; *kuanoun* mixed with white produces *glaukon*, the Homeric blue-grey; tawny with white produces "green" (i.e. leek-green).[28] There are even greater difficulties here than in the case of Democritus in identifying the various colours; the translations, which are mostly Cornford's, are sometimes highly questionable. The position is not helped by the fact that Plato himself acknowledges that there may be differences in his account, when he remarks at the end that "only divinity has knowledge and power sufficient to blend the many into one and to resolve the one into many".[29]

One noticeable difference between Plato's list of colours and Democritus' is that Plato's seems, at least at first sight, to contain a far higher proportion of abstract terms (two clear exceptions are perhaps "leek-green", and purple, the word for which is *halourgon*, literally "sea-worked", "sea-purple"). One obvious explanation is that Plato has chosen different terms; but there is, I think, more to it than that. From his analysis of the uses of the word *phaios* ("grey") in non-philosophical contexts, Reiter suggests that, if *phaios* does stand here, and in other similar passages in Aristotle, as a general, abstract term for grey, it had no such status in non-philosophical writing.[30] Not only is its own range of meaning relatively wide, covering dull browns, greens and blues; but there are several other words for grey existing side by side with it. In Reiter's view, the frequency with which the term appears as an epithet of clothes, and especially of woollen clothes, points to a technical origin.[31] Again, the word translated "yellow" elsewhere tends to preserve its Homeric meaning of "pale", "wan". Even more significant, at least two of Plato's terms have an essentially specialised reference: *glaukos*, "blue-grey", of eyes, *purros*, "red-haired". We may thus justifiably assume that Plato's list of terms owes more than a little of its apparent abstractness and fixity to Plato himself. It is, perhaps, simply the inevitable result of an attempt to deal with the phenomenon of colour in and by itself. Thus Plato's account does little to alter our general picture of Greek colour-vocabulary at this period. The standard Greek way of expressing colours seems still to be by reference to particular objects; to the green of the leek, or to the blue-grey of eyes. Undoubtedly there is progress towards the development of an abstract colour terminology; but the process is slow.

The most interesting aspect of Plato's theory of colour lies in his choice of primaries: white, black, red, and "bright". What is primary for Plato is just what was primary for Homer, the brightness, glow and lustre of objects. Perception of colour, on his account, involves the active participation both of observer and of object: a "pure fire" issues from the eyes and coalesces with a fire flowing from the object (its "colour"); the result is "a single homogeneous body" between eyes and object, which passes on information about the object. Daylight is merely a condition of sight: without it, "the visual ray is cut off; for issuing out to encounter what is unlike it [i.e. darkness] it is itself changed and put out, no longer coalescing with the neighboring air, since this contains no fire". [32]

In the context of this general theory of colour-perception, the inclusion of the "bright" among the primaries is no longer surprising. What Plato is referring to here is a dazzling brilliance, which makes the eyes water: "itself consisting of fire, it meets fire coming from the opposite quarter, and this leaps out as if from a lightning flash, while the in-going fire is quenched in the moisture (of the eye); and in this confusion all manner of colours arise. The effect we call 'dazzling'; the agent which produces it 'bright' and 'flashing' ". [33] Red is placed between "bright" and white: "then there is the variety of fire intermediate between these two, which reaches the moisture of the eyeballs and is mixed with it, but is not flashing. The radiance of the fire through the moisture with which it is mingled yields blood-colour, which we call 'red' ".

Thus the supposedly "primitive" sensitivity of the Homeric period is built into and forms the foundation of a complex and sophisticated – if mistaken – colour-theory of the fourth century. No doubt Plato's choice of primary colours was encouraged by his confusion over the role which light plays in vision; but it was also a choice which reflected a traditional way of looking at the world.

To complete this brief account of philosophical discussions of colour, we turn finally to Aristotle. Aristotle's discussion is the most complex and difficult of the three. He rejects the Platonic theory of vision (so also the Democritean, which I have not discussed). The primary condition of vision is the presence of an actualised transparent medium, by which he means, for example, air in daylight. Colour sets this medium in motion, and the motions instantaneously reach the eye. Light it, he says, "a sort of colour of the transparent", [34] i.e. of the transparent medium; and similarly the colours of definite objects are said to arise from the presence of "the transparent" in bodies. "Hence", he tells us in the *De sensu*, "it is clear that that in [air and water and in bodies] which is susceptible of colour is in both cases the same. It is therefore the transparent, according to the degree to which it subsists in bodies (and it does so in all more or less), that causes them to partake of colour. But since the colour is at the extremity of the body, it must be at the extremity of the transparent in the body, whence it follows that we may define colour as the limit of the transparent in determinately bounded body ... Now that which when present in air produces light may be present also in the transparent which pervades determinate bodies; or again, it may not be present, but there may be a privation of it. Accordingly, as in the case of air the one condition is light, the other darkness, in the same way the colours white and black are generated in determinate bodies."[35] Other colours, we are told, are formed by the mixing of these two. A list of seven species of colour is given:[36] white, black, *xanthon* ("golden-yellow"[37]), crimson, purple (i.e. sea-purple), leek-green, and *kuanoun* (Gladstone's "indigo", "deep-blue"). Grey seems finally to be regarded as a species of black. The remaining colours (and there is, Aristotle says, only a limited number of colours) are formed by the mixture of these. The seven are regarded as the only truly distinct colours. Here, perhaps, for the first time we find a list of colours which bears some resemblance to our own. But the choice of terms seems strange: why, for example, "golden-yellow" for yellow, "crimson" for red? I shall return to this presently.

The primacy of white and black, and the explicit connection of these two colours with light and darkness suggests a close resemblance between Aristotle's account and Plato's. But this resemblance is, I think, deceptive. Two factors alone account for the whole range of colours: the transparency or opacity of the object, and "that which produces light in the air", which actualises the transparency of the object. This mysterious agent is probably the "colour of what we would call the light-source, which becomes indirectly the colour of the medium which transmits it (in the pseudo-Aristotelian treatise *De coloribus*, light is explicitly said to be the colour of fire).[38] The complexity of Aristotle's discussion is the result of his uncertainty about the physical basis of light: for him, it is not bodily, nor does it move. The term "light" is reserved for the actualised state of the medium, the state in which it is "actually" and not merely "potentially" transparent. The interaction, then, of the sun, or fire (or their "colour", light) and transparency in bodies produces colour. The presence of light in the transparent in bodies produces white; its absence, presumably in the case of an opaque body, produces black; different degrees of transparency or opacity produce the other colours (quite how they do this, Aristotle does not say). Colour effects in the atmosphere are explained in the same way: for example the three colours which he attributes to the rainbow, crimson, leek-green and purple, are explained as a progressive weakening of light.[39] Since in his account of colour he begins from an analysis of the causes of light and darkness, it seems probable that that account is built up on observation of and reflection on meteorological phenomena, and not *vice versa*. Aristotle's reasons for choosing his primary colours, black and white, were thus different from Plato's. Plato's primary colours were those which fitted in with his general theory of vision; but that theory of vision was in part derived from a common Greek attitude towards the visual world, in which "differences of tone and brilliance"[40] played a far greater part than differences of hue. Aristotle's account shows no such reliance on common attitudes, characteristically attempting to give an independent analysis of observed phenomena.

But the contrast between the two accounts goes still deeper. The ideas of brightness and darkness, so important to the "primitive" Greek attitude, and which figured so prominently in Plato, are absent from Aristotle. The Janus-like nature of colour-terms in Homer, Democritus and Plato is little in evidence; all terms, including those for white and black, appear to refer straightforwardly to colour.

Aristotle thinks of his list of seven colours as a list of the basic colours given by nature; the five intermediate colours are, he suggests, the results of mixtures of white and black "in determinate numerical ratios",[41] like the major musical intervals. Again, three of them, the colours of the rainbow, recur with a constancy which is not found, for instance, in the changing hues of plants and animals – and he adds elsewhere that these three are almost the only colours which cannot be reproduced on the painter's palette, thus again suggesting that they are somehow basic and primary.[42] If, as I argued, Aristotle's theory is founded on observation of atmospheric effects, it may be that we should assume similar motives behind the choice of the other two intermediate colours, golden-yellow and deep-blue: golden-yellow is said in the *De coloribus* to be the colour of the sun,[43] and is also "often" a colour of the rainbow, produced by contrast, because of the juxtaposition of crimson and leek-green,[44] while deep-blue is, for example, the colour of the sea-depths.[45] (Interestingly enough, "deep-blue", or rather a related term, with the literal meaning "looking like *kuanos*", is also apparently applied, in the *De coloribus*, to the *sky*: "air seen close at hand appears to have no colour, for it is so rare that it yields and gives passage to the denser rays of light, which thus shines through it; but when seen in a deep mass it looks practically dark blue" (or deep-blue: literally, "it appears to have a colour like *kuanos*"). "This again is the result of its rarity, for where light fails the air lets darkness through." [46] The term *kuanous* itself normally in Aristotle means a blue bordering on the black; but the *De coloribus* passage suggests the possibility that in the list in the *De sensu* it covers not merely blue-black, but sky-blue. The basis of Aristotle's list, then, is provided by particular colours observed in nature, not by any system of abstract terms. But it is surely in just this context, of a discussion of the species of colour, that we would expect to find such a system.

Aristotle's evidence thus points to two things: a greater interest in colour as such, rather than in Homer's "modes and forms of light"; and the continuing dependence for colour-description on reference to particular coloured objects. At the same time, there may again be some signs of a progression towards an abstract colour-vocabulary: in addition to the already existing terms for white, black and red, there is now apparently a general yellow-word (Plato's *ōchros,* used by Aristotle of the yolk of an egg); and I have also argued that Aristotle's *kuanous* may be an attempt to express the idea of blue. In this case, the broadening of meaning would have weakened the original connection with *kuanos*. Similarly, it is arguable that *prasinos*, "leek-green", used by Democritus and Plato as well as Aristotle, may already be used as a general green-word, as it certainly is in later Greek. But even if this is so, it still remains highly questionable how far all these terms would have been used in the same way in ordinary language.

III

The evidence of Greek poetry after Homer is even more difficult to disentangle than that of Homer himself. (The prose-writers, other than the philosophers, refer only rarely to colour, and may safely be ignored in the present context.) Later Greek poetry is more consciously artistic; and in particular, it shows a peculiar love for reminiscence and imitation, especially of Homeric material. The Hellenistic poet Apollonius Rhodius, for example, refers to blood as *kuaneos*, not "deep-blue", but "dark";[47] on the same model, the Roman poets can apply the word *caeruleus* e.g. to a storm-cloud. [48] Again, there is a natural tendency towards idealisation in the application of colour-words: for example, in Euripides, heroic figures are automatically *xanthoi*, "blond", although the same is generally true, at least of Greek heroes, in Homer. [49] Because of these difficulties, post-Homeric poetry can provide us with little which is of use towards tracing the development of colour-terminology. Only two facts emerge: first, that the post-Homeric poets make much greater use of colour in their descriptions, and second, that the Homeric colour-vocabulary undergoes modifications of meaning broadly similar to those found in the philosophical discussions of colour, with a lessening emphasis on brightness and darkness, and a correspondingly greater reference to "colour proper".

At the same time, a comparison of the two types of post-Homeric evidence, philosophical and literary, suggests that we must allow for the independent development of two different kinds of colour-vocabulary, a poetic and a prosaic. The growing separation between poetic and prose usage is illustrated by the words for green and yellow: in poetry, the standard word for green (if we can talk of standard words at all) is *chlōros* though this is also used by Democritus; Plato and Aristotle use *prasinos*, "leek-green", Theophrastus *poōdēs*, "grass-green". In the case of yellow, the poets tend to use *chruseos*, "golden", while Plato and Aristotle use *ōchros*. *Prasinos* is never used in poetry, and *ōchros* never with the unambiguous meaning "yellow".

The most outstanding feature of Greek colour-usage at all periods in the ancient world is its *imprecision*. Precise colour-references could in general only be made by means of direct comparison with familiar objects; and this also provided the chief means of extending the range of colour-terms available, by the formation of new composite words. The relative tidiness of the picture presented by the philosophers is in large part, as we saw, of their own making. It can easily be forgotten how much nearer the Greeks stood to the beginnings of language. But again, Greek literature itself is far from primitive: the fine effects of Homer's use of brightness and darkness is paralleled by the richness of association of later poetry, which, paradoxically, is forced by the apparent poverty of the language to rely on analogy. Even outside the literary context, the so-called "primitiveness" of Greek colour-terminology can be seen as a reflection of a greater awareness of the changeability of colours in the natural environment; an abstract vocabulary is in a real sense artificial, and in reducing the world of colour to a few simple categories, over-simplifies it, and robs it of its subtlety.

For Latin, we have little or no evidence for the pre-classical period. By the first century B.C., when evidence begins to be available in any quantity, the Latin language had reached a stage of development comparable with that of the Greek language of the fourth century. It was usual for the Romans to admire the greater richness of expression available to the Greeks: Lucretius, the Epicurean poet-philosopher, bewails the *patrii sermonis egestas*, [50] the poverty of his mother tongue, while Cicero, for his part, is at some pains to defend the Latin language against its detractors: "I have often declared", he says, "under some protest not only from Greeks, but from those who would rather be regarded as Greeks than Romans, that our vocabulary is not only not inferior to the Greek in richness, but even superior". [51] In both cases, what is in question is only the capacity of Latin to express the technicalities of Greek philosophy; but later Aulus Gellius extends Lucretius' complaint explicitly to colour-vocabulary. [52] In this, he was probably mistaken: as André argues, his real complaint is a general one, that the range of variations of colour will always be greater than the number of terms available in a language. [53] The evidence which André has collected suggests that Latin colour-vocabulary was at least as rich as Greek.

Latin possesses roughly the same number of abstract terms for colour as fourth century Greek: such terms exist for white, black, red, yellow, green, and possibly blue. *Caeruleus*, "blue", was probably borrowed by prose from poetry, [54] just as Plato and Aristotle may borrow the Homeric *kuaneos*. In poetry, *caeruleus* is a standing epithet of sky and sea, a fact which makes the infrequency of blue skies and seas in Greek poetry even after Homer all the more surprising. The word itself derives from *caelum*, "sky". Just as *kuanous*, "indigo", "deep-blue", may have tended to develop from the meaning "dark", "dark blue", to "blue", so *caeruleus*, by analogy with it, could be used, for example, by Virgil, as a synonym for "black". [55]

Beyond these abstract terms, as in Greek, there is a large number of words of the type "the colour of ..."; e.g. *niueus*, "the colour of snow", *sanguineus*, "the colour of blood". These words may be formulated by the poets, as synonyms for the basic terms, or else they may be used to give greater precision of reference. There is the same imprecision in many terms, and the same divergence between poetic and prose usage, a divergence which is again encouraged by the imitative habits of the poets. Almost all genres of Roman poetry stand in a close connection with their Greek counterparts; and the colour-usages of Greek poetry have a particularly marked influence on them.

The development of Greek and Latin colour-terminology is nicely illustrated by the lists given in various periods of the colours of the rainbow. Homer described it merely as *porphureos*, perhaps "violet-purple", "violet", [56] Xenophanes, the sixth century poet-philosopher, as violet, yellowy-green and crimson; [57] in Aristotle, the colours were violet, leek-green, "often" golden-yellow, and crimson; for the first century Stoic philosopher Posidonius, according to Schultz (though this is at best doubtful), they were violet, blue (*kuanous*), leek-green and red; [58] Seneca gives them as violet, blue, green, yellow-orange, and "the colour of fire", i.e. red; [59] and finally Ammianus Marcellinus, the Roman historian of the fourth century A.D., lists violet, blue, green, yellow, "golden-yellow or tawny", [60] and crimson. [61] Of Newton's list of the seven colours of the spectrum, Ammianus' list only omits indigo, which, as Gipper remarks, more than anything reflects Newton's predilection for the number 7. [62] The phenomenon of the rainbow was the same in all periods; and the Greeks and Romans of all periods possessed precisely the same capacities for distinguishing between colours. What accounts for the lacunae in the earlier lists is essentially the existing resources of the language. The point is worth repeating, that *distinguishing* between colours and *naming* them are two quite different processes. Any observer of normal vision will be able at least to separate objects of strongly contrasting colours, whatever those colours may be; but if he is to name those colours, terms for them must exist in the language. At the same time, it seems reasonable to suppose that the number of terms available will tend to limit the number of colours which he regards as "really distinct". Aristotle identifies only three, or four, colours of the rainbow because those colours are, as it were, singled out for him by the language. Later, as language develops, so more colours are separated off from their neighbors and given an identity of their own. (The two poets, Homer and Xenophanes, should probably not be included in this particular discussion: neither, in a poetic context, is bound to give a complete list of the rainbow's colours, whether they were capable of doing so or not.)

IV

Classical colour-symbolism is in many ways a much less complex and sophisticated phenomenon than that of other periods and cultures; but for all that it is well worth considering in the general context of ancient ideas about colour.

In many primitive societies we find basic pairs of opposites to which there belongs some special symbolic significance: such pairs as up and down, right and left, and light and dark. Up, right, and light, are generally associated with goodness and life; their opposites with the bad and with death. [63] White and black, closely connected with light and darkness, represent another of these pairs. In both Greek and Roman society, these primitive associations were preserved remarkably well; but particularly those of the two pairs light-dark, white-black.

The connection between the two pairs is so close that it is difficult to separate them. Historically speaking, light-dark is no doubt the original pair; the associations of white and black stem just from their identification with light and darkness. As we have seen, in early Greek literature, whiteness and lightness, blackness and darkness are conveyed by the same words; but as the colour-reference of these words gradually increases, so they lose none of their symbolic meaning. Not only in poetry, but in ordinary life, and particularly in ritual tradition, the associations remain.

Homer described death as "dark", *melas*; in the *Odyssey*, the souls of Penelope's slaughtered suitors obey Hermes' summons

> "gibbering like bats that squeak and flutter in the depths of some mysterious cave when one of them has fallen from the rocky roof, losing his hold on his clustered friends. With such shrill discord the company set out in Hermes' charge, following the Deliverer down the dark paths of decay. Past Ocean Stream, past the White Rock, past the Gates of the Sun and the region of dreams they went, and before long they reached the meadow of asphodel, which is the dwelling-place of souls, the disembodied wraiths of men". [64]

The transition from life to death is one from light to darkness: past the white rock, past the gates of the setting sun, beyond the shadowy world of dreams. The contrast is heightened by the long simile: the suitors are now creatures of the night, dislodged like bats from life.

No one, then, can doubt the strength of the associations in Homer between darkness and death, and light and life. More important, we find what looks like a clear example of *symbolic* use of a colour-term. Scholars have been unable to agree about the precise significance of the white rock, and have put forward various different explanations of it, which share only a common rationalism: the rock is white, we are told, because it is struck by the rays of the setting sun; or else it is to be identified with the promontory of Leucas in Epirius, north-west of Ithaca. Neither explanation carries any conviction. Like the ocean which rings the earth, and like the gates of the sun, the rock marks the boundary between this world and the world beyond; and it is white because that boundary is also the boundary of light and life. Similarly, white animals are sacrificed to the Olympian gods, black to the powers of the dead: so, in *Odyssey* XX, on Circe's instructions, Odysseus promises the soul of the dead seer Teiresias an all-black sheep in return for advice about his journey home. White for the Olympians, black for the chthonian deities was apparently the general rule in ancient ritual. [65]

White, in the poets, is a mark of divinity and beauty: Hera is *leukōlenos*, "white-armed", Venus *candida*. Whiteness is also particularly an epithet of deities friendly to mankind, of the Dioscuri, the patron gods of sailors, regularly described as *leukippoi*, *leukopōloi*, "riding on white horses", and of Pax and Concordia. The Fates are sometimes *candidae sorores*, "the white sisters", when they spin white, or lucky, threads; sometimes *sorores nigrae*, "the black sisters", when their threads are "dark threads of misery". [66]

So the words for white and black develop connotations of "lucky", "unlucky", "happy", "unhappy": a lucky day is *leukē hēmera*, *albus* (or *candidus*) *dies*, an unlucky day *dies ater*. In such cases, the original symbolic associations were doubtless lost, as the expressions were hardened by common usage; and a hardening of a similar kind no doubt took place in the ritual uses of white and black. Plutarch, writing in imperial times, can only guess at the reason why the dead are wrapped in white; his explanation is straightforward rationalisation, based on Platonic and Pythagorean dogma: "they adorn the corpse in this way because they cannot do so to the soul, which they wish to send off bright and clean, as one that has now come off victorious from a great and difficult struggle ... " [67] Radke believes that white is used as a magical protection against evil, but the guess may be no better than Plutarch's.

Plutarch is at least right in associating whiteness with cleanliness and purity of a religious kind, even if this may not be relevant to the case he discusses. The white dress worn by Greek and Roman religious officials almost certainly symbolised their stainlessness and so their fitness for their functions. But quite possibly we should not look for any connection with *light* here: white is perhaps as obvious a symbol of purity as black is of death. There is always a danger that we may attempt to introduce too much rationality and order into a phenomenon which is by its very nature irrational: it has its own kind of logic, but that logic has a closer relation to feeling and emotion than to reason.

It has been shown that the opposition between light and darkness has little to do with a moral dualism. [68] Rather, light symbolises *well-being*, good in a non-moral sense, darkness, evil in the sense of what is harmful. Indeed, moral goodness and badness in our sense have little place in early Greek society. "The word *agathos*, ancestor of our *good*, is originally a predicate specifically attached to the role of the Homeric nobleman ... *Agathos* is not like our word *good* in many of its Homeric contexts, for it is not used to say that it is 'good' to be kingly, courageous and clever – that is, it is not used to commend these qualities in a man, as our word *good* might be used by a contemporary admirer of the Homeric ideal ... The question, 'Is [a man] *agathos*? ' is the same as the question, 'Is he courageous, clever, and kingly? ' And this is answered by answering the question, 'Does he, and has he, fought, plotted and ruled with success? ' " [69] Only gradually did the word *agathos* come to acquire a general sense of "morally good". A moral consciousness of a type recognisable to us is essentially a phenomenon of the fifth and fourth centuries B.C. In Pythagoreanism, good and bad are associated with Limit and Unlimited, or the One and the Many, rather than with light and darkness, as they are in the twin principles of Zoroastrianism, Ormazd and Ahriman, in spite of the other striking resemblances noted by the ancients themselves between the two doctrines.

Red is also widely used with symbolic meaning. In general, it seems to symbolise life and power, a meaning which no doubt stems from its association with *blood*. Red plays an important role in magical remedies: for fevers, Pliny the Elder mentions the use of "the dust in which a hawk has rolled himself, tied in a linen cloth by a red thread", or "the snout and ear-tips of a mouse, wrapped in red cloth"; [70] for headaches, "a plant that grows on the head of a statue, gathered with a piece taken from some garment and tied on with a red thread". [71] Sometimes blood itself is used: for the treatment of epilepsy, tortoises' blood is mentioned, along with pomegranate juice. [72] Epileptics also drink the blood of gladiators, Pliny says, "as if from living cups, though we shudder with horror when we see wild animals doing it here in the arena. But ... the patients think it most effectual to suck from a man himself warm, living blood, and putting their lips to the wound to drain the very life from him". [73] Red is also associated with fertility rites. [74] Menstrual blood, Pliny tells us, [75] was held to have beneficial effects in agriculture, although in general it works more for evil than for good.

In Theocritus' second *Idyll*, the symbolic meaning of red is less obvious: "Where are my bay leaves? Bring me them, Thestylis. And where are my magic stuffs? Wreathe the bowl with fine crimson wool that I may bind a spell upon my love, so hard to me. For eleven days now he has not visited me ...". [76] In Virgil's *Eclogue* VIII, in a similar context, three colours are mentioned: "I take three threads – three colours pick them out – and bind them round you first. Next, I walk round this altar with your effigy, three times. Odd numbers please the gods. Bring Daphnis from the town, my spells, bring Daphnis home". [77] (Similarly, in medical contexts, white and black appear beside red; for example, in Celsus' account of the treatment of epilepsy.) [78] Here, perhaps, all that is remembered is that colours have magical powers; what those powers are, and why they have them, is forgotten. Similarly with the *flammeum*, the flame-red veil worn by the bride: [79] According to one ancient commentator, it was red "because the bride must guard herself against the blush of shame". More plausibly, Varro is reported as explaining the use of red in burial rituals as a substitute for the cruel and expensive blood-sacrifices of an earlier period. [80]

Far simpler and more direct are the associations of the colour purple, at least in some of its uses. In Alcman's *Partheneion*, from the seventh century B.C., the chorus sings "for neither is abundance of purple enough for our protection, nor spangled snake of solid gold, nor Lydian cap, the pride of soft-eyed maidens ... It is Hagesichora for whom we pine". [81] The context of this fragmentary poem is of a competition between rival choirs: "mere finery and beauty is not enough; we need our leader Hagesichora". Lucretius writes bitterly of the emptiness of man's desires: "once men fought over skins; now it is purple and gold – such are the baubles that embitter human life with resentment and waste it with war. In this, I do not doubt, the greater blame rests with us. To the earthborn generation in their naked state the lack of skins meant real discomfort through cold; but it in no way harms us to go without robes of purple, brocaded with gold and gorgeously emblazoned...". [82] Pliny moralises too, although his tone is more literary and contrived: "moral corruption and luxury spring from no other source in greater abundance than from the genus shellfish ... It was not apparently enough that the sea should be stowed in our gullets; they had to be carried on the hands, in the ears, on the head and all over the body of men and women alike. What have our clothes to do with the sea...? We enter that element in a proper manner only when naked ... Is it always the rule that we get most satisfaction from luxuries which cost human lives to procure? " [83] Purple-dye was expensive, as Pliny testifies (and some varieties especially). As well as symbolising luxury, purple also represented a mark of distinction or office, as in the broad purple stripe of senators, the narrow stripe of the *equites*, and the purple-bordered *toga praetexta* of magistrates. The *praetexta* was also worn by free-born children, presumably if they could afford it. Pliny says that they wore it *pro maiestate pueritiae*, "as a mark of the dignity of boyhood", [84] no doubt arguing from its use by magistrates, and Quintilian makes a similar remark. [85] Wunderlich wishes to find a magical origin for all such uses, but this seems unnecessary and implausible. Purple is a mark of distinction simply because it is an expensive and distinctive colour.

Everything here is much as we would expect. Because of their simplicity, the general associations of black and white, and of purple, survive and are felt as strongly by each succeeding generation. But in the more specialised uses of colours, in medicine or in ritual, the form survives without the meaning. The gradual deadening of traditional form stands in sharp contrast with the continuous development and rejuvenation of the means of explicit description provided by language itself.

V

It is this development, overlaid by the peculiar habits of the Greek and Roman poetic tradition, which provides the focus of this paper; and in that process it is the earliest stage, that observable in the Homeric poems, which is of the greatest interest, since it betrays an attitude to the visual world which stands in marked contrast with our own. But that attitude is not, apparently, peculiar to early Greece. Recent research by two linguists in the United States [86] suggests that Homeric colour-usage falls into a pattern common to all societies at a certain stage of development. "Some languages have more basic [colour-] terms than others ..., but those terms which a language does have will have their foci at the same locations as other languages. Furthermore, if a language has, for instance, five basic color terms, these five will always have their foci at the same places ..." "Basic" is here roughly equivalent to my term "abstract" [87] : "an impoverished color vocabulary does not mean impoverished vision, and whatever a man's language may be, he can refine his reference to color by forming complex phrases or by citing particular colored objects. But, to be counted as a basic color term, a word must be a single lexical item (not a construction such as 'light blue', 'lemon-colored', or 'the color of the rust on my aunt's old Chevrolet'). It must not be merely a subdivision of a higher-order term (such as 'scarlet' or 'crimson', which are unquestionably varieties of 'red'); it must be applicable to more than a restricted range of objects (unlike 'blond', which is rarely used for anything except hair or wood) ... ". Then, importantly, "languages have been reported with no more than two basic color terms, and these always have their foci at black and white. It may help an English speaker to think of these terms as if they translate our own 'dark' and 'light', but when a Jalé of the New Guinea highlands is asked for the truest ['dark'] he will indicate the color we refer to as 'black', and when asked for the truest ['light'] he will point to white. (An English speaker would presumably indicate black and white as the foci of his own 'dark' and 'light'.) ... Languages with three basic colour terms always add the third one at the focus that we call 'red'. Most of the warm colors – yellows, oranges, and browns – may be included under red at this stage, but its focus is still a proper red". A language with four basic colour-terms will add yellow or green; one with five will add the one missed at the previous stage; one with six will add blue, one with seven brown. Four other English terms are considered basic: grey, pink, orange, and purple. [88]

Although claims are made about the relation between the number of "basic" colour-terms available in a language and the level of "cultural and technological complexity" of the society which uses it, Berlin and Kay's study is not, essentially, a study of the development of language, depending as it does on the evidence of existing languages in current use. Even so, the correlation between their reported results for four-, five-, and six-term languages and the apparent development of Greek in the fifth and fourth centuries is striking. But the scantiness and complexity of the evidence for that period probably makes such comparisons dangerous. For early Greek colour-usage, on the other hand, I have argued that we possess clear evidence in the *Iliad* and *Odyssey*. As we saw, Greek in the Homeric period possesses at most the three "basic" terms white, black and red. This was the first outstanding feature of Homeric usage; and the second, the importance of brightness and darkness, and in particular the ambiguity of *leukos* and *melas* between "white" and "bright", "black" and "dark", can now be seen, if Berlin and Kay are right, [89] as reflecting a general feature of "impoverished" colour-vocabularies of this kind. In this case, of course, the supposed correlation between the lack of a developed colour-terminology and a low level of culture and technology falls down, since in these respects Homeric society was on any analysis highly advanced. Nonetheless, the theory may in general be useful in so far as it may provide a firm basis for the distinction which I have demanded between what is merely accidental and what is conscious and artistic in the highly developed form of Homeric poetry. At the same time, it throws Homer's achievements into still sharper relief.

The changing nature of Greek colour-terminology is not merely a linguistic phenomenon, but embodies a transition between two types of sensitivity. Just as we adjust to a different moral framework when reading Homer, so we must adjust to a rather different kind of awareness of, and response to, the visual world, and not be disappointed when we fail to find those means of description which we are used to regarding as the essential marks of the poetic. Homer experienced the world not as essentially coloured, but as brilliant, gleaming, glowing, lustrous. His world is simpler, but for all that no less valid.

NOTES

1 W. E. Gladstone, *Studies on Homer and the Homeric Age*, Oxford 1858, vol.III, p. 458.

2 References in G. Reiter, *Die griechischen Bezeichnungen der Farben Weiss, Grau und Braun,* Innsbruck 1962, p. 9.

3 In this, of course, Gladstone was mistaken, as the discoveries of Minoan and Mycenaean culture were to show.

4 *Op. cit.*, pp. 487-8.

5 *Ibid.*, p. 459

6 *Ibid.*, p. 489

7 K. Müller-Boré, *Stilistische Untersuchungen zum Farbwort und zur Verwendung der Farbe in der älteren griechischen Poesie* (= *Klassisch-Philologische Studien* 3), Berlin 1922, pp. 43-4.

8 Some scholars (e.g. G. S. Kirk, in *The Songs of Homer,* Cambridge 1962) have argued for separate authors for the *Iliad* and the *Odyssey*; but in the present context, the point is unimportant.

9 This is, in essence, the view held by Müller-Boré ("*die epischen Farbenbezeichnungen sind der Niederschlag einer sich erst gestaltenden Sprache*", *op. cit.*, p. 14).

10 *Op. cit.*, pp. 484-5.

11 Placed by Kirk (*op. cit.*,) in the eighth century B.C.

12 The fundamental point, that the Homeric poems provide us with evidence for at least *some* period in the development of the Greek language, is accepted also by H. Gipper ("Purpur", *Glotta* XLII, 1964, p. 41). I do not, of course, deny that ordinary language may at least have begun to overtake epic usage; but there still existed a tight connection between them.

13 *Op. cit.*, p. 84.

14 X. 482-4.

15 *Op. cit.* (note 2), p. 26.

16 X. 437, 547.

17 Reiter, *ibid.*

18 XVI. 34-5.

19 See Gipper, *op. cit.* (note 12).

20 *Op. cit.*, p. 489.

21 See M. Ventris and J. Chadwick, *Documents in Mycenaean Greek*, Cambridge 1959, p. 107.

22 The material is taken from J. Chadwick and L. Baumbach, "The Mycenaean Greek Vocabulary", *Glotta* XLI, 1963.

23 *Iliad* XIX. 357-87.

24 *Odyssey* V. 55-74.

25 H. Diels and W. Kranz, *Die Fragmente der Vorsokratiker*, 6th ed., Berlin 1951-2, 31. A. 92 (Aetius).

26 Theophrastus, *De sensu et sensibilibus* 73ff.

27 67 c ff.

28 The word used here, *prasios*, is treated by Liddell-Scott-Jones as the same as Democritus' *prasinos*; and this is probably right. For the difficulties involved,

see Cornford's note on p. 278 of *Plato's Cosmology*, London 1937.

29 68 d (Cornford's translation).

30 *Op. cit.*, pp. 78 ff.

31 Cf. Mycenaean *polios* (above p. 339).

32 *Timaeus* 45 b ff. See also *Theaetetus* 156 a ff.

33 *Timaeus* 68 a (Cornford's translation is slightly modified here).

34 *De anima* 418 b 11.

35 439 b 6 ff. (Beare's Oxford translation, again slightly modified).

36 *Ibid.* 442 a 20 ff.

37 So Beare.

38 791 b 6 ff.

39 *Meteorologica* 374 b 35 ff.

40 Cornford's phrase (*op. cit.*, p. 277, n. 1).

41 *De sensu*, 440 b 20.

42 *Meteorologica* 372 a 5.

43 791 a 3-4.

44 *Meteorologica* 372 a 9-10, 375 a 7 ff.

45 See Bonitz, *Index Aristotelicus*, s. v. *kuanoeidēs.*

46 794 a 8-14.

47 IV. 1514.

48 E. g. Virgil, *Aeneid* III. 194, V. 10.

49 Müller-Boré, *op. cit.*, p. 96 (see also the review of Müller-Boré by H. Fraenkel, in *Deutsche Literaturzeitung*, N. F. 1, 1924, pp. 2368-9).

50 I. 832.

51 *De finibus* III. 2. 5.

52 *Noctes Atticae* II. 26. 5.

53 J. André, *Étude sur les termes de couleur dans la langue latine*, Paris 1949, p. 397.

54 See A. Ernout and A. Meillet, *Dictionnaire étymologique de la langue latine*, Paris 1951.

55 *Aeneid* III. 64.

56 *Iliad* XVII. 547.

57 Fr. 32 Diels-Kranz.

58 W. Schultz, *Das Farbenempfindungssystem der Hellenen*, Leipzig 1904, p. 114. Most of my basic material here is drawn from this source.

59 *Quaestiones naturales* I. 3. 12.

60 *Flauescens uel fuluus. Flauus, flauescens* is sometimes used of gold; *fuluus* is the standing epithet of lions. See André, *op. cit.*, pp. 128 ff.

61 XX. 11. 27-8.

62 *Op. cit.* (note 12), p. 65.

63 See e.g. G. E. R. Loyd, "Right and Left in Greek Philosophy", *Journal of Hellenic Studies* LXXXII, 1962.

64 *Odyssey* XXIV, 5-14 (Rieu's Penguin translation).

65 See G. Radke, *Die Bedeutung der weissen und der schwarzen Farbe in Kult und Brauch der Griechen und Römer*, Jena 1936, pp. 23 ff.; and W. K. C. Guthrie, *The Greeks and Their Gods*, London, 1950, pp. 221-2.

66 For references, see Radke, *op. cit.*

67 *Quaestiones Romanae* XXVI.

68 R. Bultmann, "*Zur Geschichte der Lichtsymbolik im Altertum*", *Philologus* XCVII, 1948.

69 A. MacIntyre, *A Short History of Ethics*, London 1967, p. 6.

70 *Historia naturalis* XXX 98-9 (this and many of the following references are taken from E. Wunderlich, *Die Bedeutung der roten Farbe im Kultus der Griechen und Römer* (= *Religionsgeschichtliche Versuche und Vorarbeiten* XX. 1), Giessen 1925).

71 XXIV. 170.

72 XXXII. 112.

73 XXVIII. 4.

74 See e.g. Horace *Satires* I. 8. 5.

75 XXVIII. 78.

76 Gow's translation, ll. 1-4.

77 Rieu's Penguin translation, ll. 73-6.

78 *De medicina* III. 23.

79 Also called *luteus* (e.g. by Pliny, XXI. 46), rendered by André, *op. cit.*, pp. 151-2, as "orange".

80 See Wunderlich, *op. cit.*, p. 53.

81 Page's translation, ll. 64-9.

82 V. 1423-8 (Latham's Penguin translation, slightly modified).

83 IX. 104-5.

84 IX. 127.

85 *Declamationes* CCCXL.

86 B. Berlin and P. Kay, *Basic Color Terms: Their Universality and Evolution*, Berkeley 1970. When this paper was first written, I had access only to the summary of their work cited below; and this remains sufficient for my present purposes.

87 Only roughly equivalent, because the definition of a "basic" term would, for instance, apparently exclude *prasinos* and *kuanous*, which on my account may

evolve at some stage into "abstract" terms (see pp. 38-9 above).

88 R. Burling, *Man's Many Voices*, New York 1970, pp. 47-8. (Very similar results, as Berlin and Kay themselves acknowledge, were reached by H. Magnus in Jena at the end of the last century.)

89 It should be added that their work has not been without its critics (for references see H. Zollinger, "Human Colour Vision as an Inter-disciplinary Research Problem", *Palette* 40, 1972); but even the sternest of these is prepared to allow it some value.

DOMINIQUE ZAHAN

WHITE RED AND BLACK:

COLOUR SYMBOLISM IN BLACK AFRICA

In Black Africa, as in other civilisations, especially ancient cultures, a distinction is made between three basic colours: white, red and black.

To understand this cultural phenomenon well it is necessary to forget, if only fleetingly, our own concept of colour based on the interpretation of the spectrum, which only at the beginning of the eighteenth century replaced the symbolism of earlier ages by a concept of shades that obeys the laws governing the distribution and number of light waves. Only by forgetting current Western cultural usage can we understand other traditions relating to light, traditions that are as worthy of interest as those we become accustomed to once we have received our first initiation into modern physics.

Before going into the heart of the matter, it might however, be useful to clarify three points which are essential for the discussion of the subject.

1. By saying that Africans distinguish three fundamental colours, we do not mean to imply that they are incapable of perceiving other colours. From the point of view of vision, their retinal and cortical cells undoubtedly function in the same manner as ours or those of any other human being. The statement is simply intended to mean: a) that to designate the different shades, which are sometimes highly varied, African languages use terms that refer to the

three above mentioned basic colours; b) that very specific emotional, social, religious, esthetic and moral values are attached to white, red and black.

2. In actual fact and in terms of their content, the three colours under discussion are much richer than the chromatic vocabulary of some populations suggests at first sight. For the Bambara of the Niger valley, for example, red includes: lemon yellow, café-au-lait brown, tender green and purple; – black: light blue, dark blue, dark green and grey; – white: bright white and pale white. In the same manner, we find that among the M'bay of Moïssala in the Republic of Tchad the following colours are classified as red: pink, light pink, mauve, yellowish green, bright green, yellow, orange and a warm brown; white includes: light grey, light green, light beige; and under black we find: grey, dark grey, very dark red, dark green, medium blue, dark blue, and dark brown. [1] Finally, the Thonga in South-East Africa associate black with dark blue; red with carmine or crimson and even yellow; the colour of algae is identified with sky-blue.[2] This means that the three colours we are concerned with involve in fact a whole range of luminosity, or a number of light gradations that are subject to modifications depending on the culture or the latitudes at which these people live on the African continent. The phenomenon is not confined to Africa. We know that for the Romans of antiquity *luteus* was both yellow and orange and that *purpureus* included at least the following colours: lilac purple, pink purple, carmine red, blackish red, reddish brown and dark brown. [3]

3. At the present state of affairs, Africa is the point of convergence of two cultural phenomena, which have tremendously enriched these peoples' sense of colour. On the one hand there is the development of traditional dyeing techniques. As we shall see further on, when we discuss one particular population, these techniques have their own history, and on the cultural level they have had their influence on the semantics of the various colours. On the other hand there has been the irruption of Western industrial dyes into the world of the Africans. These dyes impress their vision with the wealth and variety of colours that extend beyond nature. At the same time, this break-through of Western techniques also contributed to a sort of alienation of the black man from an interpretation of colours that he had inherited from his past. Until then, the African had been accustomed to understand the contrasts and oppositions of the two basic colours – white and black – in terms of lightness and darkness, of heaven and earth, in terms of what nature had to offer owing to the presence or the absence of light. As for red, he carried it in his veins, saw it in the blood of sacrificial victims and in the fire of his

hearth. Throughout Africa nature has always been the prime teacher of colour perception. When dying techniques were invented, the African did not try to look for colours outside of nature; instead, he took advantage of it, by imitating it. He settled on the two extremes, white and black as limits, and he placed red in the center, or at the "apex", as this colour possesses a superior function by comparison with the two others. For the African the three colours therefore form a sort of *continuum*, ranging from white to black, but passing through an aphelion where red is situated. As we shall see later, this is the very image of how the individual's life develops in society.

The Designation of Colours

The specific logic of language has always offered man a possibility of finding his way through the maze of facts and phenomena he encounters. Language is the most effective and the most marvellous human instrument for the organisation of the universe. In the field of colour, the designation of shades constituted a particular difficulty for the Africans: that of defining the category, to which this aspect of things and beings should be related. In the case of minerals, flora and fauna, such classifications are easier, since each object and each being possesses a number of aspects, which make it possible to associate them with one or the other individual possessing the same qualities. However, colour seems to be one of the rare aspects of reality, which from this point of view escapes the grasp of the mind. There is no doubt a great variety of coloured objects, but colour itself displays a remarkable poverty of content.

For the most part, the Africans do not have a generic name for colour. Wherever they use precise nominals for this purpose, these terms are always specifically determined (a type, which the linguists call dependent nominals). When talking about colour, the Bambara use the terms *nye* and *tyoko*, meaning eye, look, the visible aspect of things and the manner of being of these things. The M'bay use the word *bál* to this end. In neither case do we meet these terms in isolation.[4]

The variety of appellations for the different shades of colour is much vaster. For, in addition to having recourse to certain grammatical categories to name them directly, African languages use comparative constructions, thus obtaining indirect designations whose scope is almost unlimited, but which are not specifically confined to the expression of colours. One of the best studied cases from this point of view is that of the M'bay. [5] For the purpose of directly denominating the three colours we call white, red and black, as well as the other colours that come under these three categories, the M'bay use three intransitive verbs and several adverbs. The verbs indicate everything that is light (white), dark (black) and the things that are warm (red). [6] The adverbs are combined with one, two or three preceding verbs, no doubt in order to clarify the designation, by either enhancing or diminishing its quality. To define some shades, which are perceived in a manner that makes it impossible to classify them with one or the other basic colour, or which require clarification, the same population uses comparative locutions, such as: "to be like the plumage of the bulbul bird (*Irena puella*)" , in order to indicate a certain shade of blue; – "to be like the bush-buck's hair", in order to denote a shade of brown; – "to be like the egg of a fern-owl", to describe a shade of blue; – "to be like the stripes of a striated rat", to define a shade of yellow; – "to be like serpent's poison", to indicate a shade of green; – "to be like the water in which the *Cochlospermum tinctorium* plant has been soaked", to define a shade of yellow, orange and pink.

Apart from the fact that indirect denominations generally tend to belong to the realm of poetic language, it is also obvious that they are more difficult to grasp. One has to know in fact the element of comparison, in order to understand the nuance involved. In other words, it is absolutely essential to have a good knowledge of the culture that uses the nuance to understand what it means. A striking example of this kind is the expression *rilambyana*, used by the Djonga (a South-East African population) to denote the green of spring grass. Literally this locution means: "that which makes the dogs bark". [7] On the surface there is no possible link between the barking of dogs and the green colour of new-grown grass. Nonetheless, a relationship does exist between these two facts, if one realizes that in tropical regions the time of new-grass coincides with what is called the period of the spring-gap. Not only men, but also animals have difficulty in finding food during this season. The cereal supply of the previous year has been exhausted, whereas the corn in the fields has not ripened yet. The green colour of grass is therefore associated with the bark of hungry dogs.

Linguistic procedures of this kind are very widespread on the African continent, just as in all ancient civilisations. Even in our culture we use constructions to describe shades which it would be difficult to describe otherwise. Expressions like olive green, lie-de-vin red (purplish red), lemon yellow, straw yellow, carmine red, etc., are there to remind us – if necessary – that our concern with accurate colour designations also results in indirect constructions.

History and Techniques of Colour Preparations

Each one of the three basic colours has its own history. The stories describing their "invention" and technological development should not always be taken literally. For, frequently some miraculous elements or symbolical allusions are mixed into these tales, which probably relate the users' colour concepts, but not the true history of colours. It is also important to know that these stories refer to certain hues and not all the reds, whites and blacks that may be used in a given society. Each chromatic category consists in fact of various colours, which man may have occasion to use, depending on the circumstances and the symbolism attached to the hue and the substances from which it is made. The story that follows is concerned with the colour varieties most commonly used by the Bambara, a society that has been of particular interest to us.

According to the legend, an old woman, called Nyéfladyan, from the village of Siguidlo (near Konobugu) was the first to discover the cotton and the spinning techniques, from which the Bambara subsequently benefited for the purpose of making their clothes. [8] At the beginning, clothes were white and their brightness filled men with wonder, because they felt as if wrapped in light when dressed. The whiteness of cotton and the clothes people were able to make from it induced Nyéfladyan to look for a product, whereby she could imitate the colour. The old woman noticed the whitishness of certain soils on the banks of the Niger. Once this soil was mixed with water and then dried, it provided a white (*dyema*) quite similar to that of cotton fluff. She suggested to her fellow citizens that they use it for white-washing their huts. Later, it was discovered that the earth from paupers' graves could also be used to obtain white. However, the product obtained from these sites was used exclusively for whitewashing the homes of important persons, in particular the king's dwelling.

For a long time the Bambara only used the white extracted from the soil, according to the processing methods taught them by Nyéfladyan. The moment came, however, when they realised that calcinated river shells supplied a product that was vastly superior to kaolin. This was a decisive turning point in the history of white, since the new techniques made it possible to obtain a highly resistant dye, which, moreover, could be produced on a large scale. *Guala mugu* (literally, shell powder) is used for a great variety of purposes to this very day: for cotton spinning, whitewashing of houses, for ritual objects, etc., except for the dyeing of skins, because here shoemakers use other products, which have their own history.

The history of red (*blema*) is – as might be expected – closely related to forging and pottery techniques. The blacksmiths are in fact said to have been the first to "invent" a red dye in an attempt to imitate the colour of fire and that of the rainbow. They obtained the product by rubbing two stones, called *konolo* and *konolo ba*, against each other, and by pouring at the same time some water on the contact surface. The resulting red liquid was capable of dyeing objects and fabrics. Subsequently, other processes for obtaining a red dye were developed, but from plant extracts. Among the techniques most widely used to this day we find the crushing of kola nuts in water and the soaking of a certain variety of sorghum leaves, also in water.

Like the two preceding colours, black (*fima*) has its origin in the soil. The legend describing the discovery of the first dye in this colour range recounts how men thought of clothing themselves in dark garments to imitate the stormy skies during the rainy season. The farmer's clothes were bound to become muddy from working the land and thereby they grew darker. The idea of darkening his work clothes artificially merely indicated that man was prepared to follow in the path of nature. Bending over the soil, a peasant would harmonise with the mood of the rainy sky. In an effort to achieve this result, his attention was attracted by the blackish earth of certain ponds. In this mud he soaked white cloth, which darkened as time went on. Thus a black dye was found.

Later this dyeing technique was improved by the addition of *nere* (*Parkia biglobosa*) husks to the pond mud. Depending on the proportion in which they were added, the dye would darken to a greater or lesser extent. But the technique was only a rudimentary one; the black fabric did not acquire the lustre that man would have liked to give it,[9] like the marvellous and fascinating lustre of the cloud-covered sky. For materials this quality was obtained by adding *buwana*, the fruit of an acacia variety, to the black mud. With the discovery of dyeing techniques through soaking indigo leaves in water, black dyes came to be used at the handicraft industry level. According to legend, it was a Sarakolé woman who discovered this method. Even now, the Sarakolés are the master dyers in that part of Africa.

Colours and Clothes

Man might never have thought of using dyes if he had not invented clothing. Garments enabled him to differentiate himself from his fellowmen. They provided him with a social language, that is, a means of communication, for which colours have become the code. The Bambara, like other African populations, have developed a veritable theory of the naked and the clothed body. [10] The first is considered vile and lacking in speech, whereas the latter is worthy of consideration, since it belongs to a true man possessing speech.

A garment is considered to possess an effectiveness of its own, which may increase or decrease that of its owner. It is a reservoir of strength. At the same time it displays the energy (*nyama*) of the person wearing it.

Colours have the role of bringing out the " strength" or the "energy" (*nyama*) of the fabric as well as that of the individual and of protecting him against the dangers, emanating from the things and beings with which he comes in contact. The effectiveness of the colours depends on their combination in a cotton band, as well as on the place, where this band is applied on the garment.

An entirely white garment imbues its wearer with superiority and glamour. In general, it is worn by officiating priests and sacrificers when they are executing their functions. It guards them against the dangers lurking in certain forbidden places and some altars. A cotton band with small checks, formed by crossing the two white warp threads with two black woof threads (a so-called *buguni* band) is designed to protect the wearer from certain diseases. Men sew such bands on their white garments in the places that cover the most sensitive parts of the body: the shoulders and ribs (in front and in back), the chest and spinal column. To the same end, women sew cotton patches of this kind into their white loin-cloths. Sometimes the entire loin-cloth is made up of *buguni*.

Red garments always have been and continue to be extremely rare. In the past they were reserved for kings. This is still the practice among the Mossi in the Republic of Upper Volta. As chief of the executive and the armies, only the king was able to impose capital punishment and declare war, that is, to cause bloodshed. For this reason, he was the only man entitled to wear fabrics dyed in the colour of the liquid that carries life. However, arranged in stripes on a white garment, red is worn by blacksmiths and old men. In the case of blacksmiths, it is suitable because they manipulate fire in the art of forging; in the case of old men, because they are the carriers of that other "fire" – the supreme knowledge and wisdom.

Black clothes are compulsory for anyone in a state of sadness or in pain. It is also supposed to be worn by anyone who has come to the end of a very difficult job. However, it is chiefly worn by the Sarakolé, who are, according to tradition, the inventors of indigo dye methods, and by tanners. It is the prerogative of the latter by reason of their occupation. Since they work the skin wrapping the bodies of animals and because skin is assimilated to heaven, which envelops the earth, black clothing is considered perfectly suitable for tanners.

The wearing of yellow garments is reserved especially for hunters and boys, who have been recently circumcised. It should be recalled that yellow is part of the range of reds. For this reason, it is also associated with blood, as are the two categories of persons mentioned: the hunter sheds the blood of the animals he has killed, and the circumcised boy sheds his own blood.

Depending on the colour with which it is impregnated, a garment may therefore indicate a person's social status, his profession, his physical or moral status and in some cases even the human group to which he belongs. In addition, however, colours and materials acquire a certain effectiveness in the mind of the wearer, owing to the protection they offer against dangers and diseases. In the minds of Westerners, such beliefs would fall within the province of superstition or "magic". In actual fact, the situation is slightly different. The so-called *buguni* band is not believed to offer protection against diseases because it possesses itself such a quality but because it concretises a conjuncture, similar to that desired by the wearer in terms of the relationship between health and sickness. This piece of cotton is in fact woven in a manner designed to indicate that the white (warp threads) hold prisoner the black (woof threads), which means that peace and happiness prevent the unleashing of trouble and misfortune. Worn on the human body, the material becomes the harbinger of the expected relationship between health (represented by the white warp threads) and illness (represented by the black woof threads). In other words, colours reveal their full potential only if they are transposed to the realm of symbolism and meaning. However, their effectiveness results from nothing else than what man's mind put into them

Colour Symbolism

A number of locutions, found in most parts of Africa, enable us to generalise to a certain extent as to the symbolism of black and white, especially at the moral level. A good, affable and pleasant person, someone who is open and does not hide his intentions, will be considered to "have a white belly".

The belly, seat of most of the vital organs, in a way situates a person as a whole from the point of view of social relations.

More precisely, "to have a white belly" therefore means to conform to what society expects of its members, and society wants mutual understanding and peace.

White is above all the sign of harmony and joy. In terms of space, it is the colour associated with the south, since the colour of the atmosphere is more whitish during the period between the spring and the autumn equinoxes than at any other time of the year. As it is associated with social harmony and the south, white is also the colour of ancestors, who, according to the Bambara,dwell in the southern regions of the world, and with whom human beings must live in peace. This explains the presence of white in ancestor worship. The victims sacrificed to the deceased, who have been kind and charitable, must have a white coat, while other offerings consist of white millet flour dissolved in water, or crushed cola nuts, which are also white.

Moreover, white is also related to the home. When kaolin was discovered for the preparation of a white dye, men used it chiefly to whitewash their houses. At the same time, home is the first place, where peace should prevail. Especially its door, through which all living things must pass, is the very image of the harmony and peace that characterise a good society. It is therefore the appropriate place for receiving and expediting offerings to ancestors. These offerings are in fact poured outside on the two jambs of the doorway of the house.[11]

White also symbolises abundance and food; for, the time of the year it characterises is that of the harvest and plentiful food supplies, reaped after the toils of the rainy season. Like nature, which seems to rest between the two equinoxes, man also slows down his work, entertaining himself on the occasion of various feast days and consuming the riches he has acquired.

Black is the colour of the north, the rainy season, of vegetation and water. The northern parts of the world are associated with darkness. With the return of the sun to the northern hemisphere, clouds gather and the sky darkens. The rains come. The light loses in brightness by comparison with the preceding season. This is all the more true, as nature, slumbering until then, awakens. The new grass and corn begin to grow; the trees turn green once again. "The earth is cloaked in black", say the Bambara.

But with the change of season men exchange their quiet way of life for the arduous task of working the land. The land, work, whose outcome no-one can predict, since nobody can be quite certain about the timely onset of the rains, on which the crops depend. For all these reasons black also symbolises work and pain, uncertainty and doubt.

Black is not considered by man to be a mere abstraction that hardly affects him. In religious manifestations black is activated to become effective. All requests for the rains to come down from heaven to water the seeds in good time are supported by sacrificing victims in black coat. They are expected to bring fertility to the altar in the same manner as the rains are expected to cause the seeds to sprout. The farmer thus gives himself the benefit of his own hope. Far from being a sad and accursed colour, black is a powerful psychological factor, involved in patience and the ability to wait.

Red is the colour of the center or the "summit" of the world. It is associated with the zenith and that part of the year when, owing to its position at the apex, the sun "scorches" everything it touches. Red is characteristic of the very dry, hot season, when tempers rise easily and passions are stirred. Since it is linked to these states of mind, it is also related to justice, which is supposed to redress wrongs, to seek out and to punish evil-doers. As a result, red has come to be associated with the chief, who – like the sun in its zenith at the summit of the celestial vault – occupies the highest place in the social hierarchy. Red is also a symbol of war with its killings and bloodshed. The warrior is thought of as a man with red eyes.

In the field of sacrifice, red-coated victims are indispensible for all altars designed to make for the maintenance of the individual's, society's and the world's *nyama*. Now, *nyama* is precisely the sort of usually latent force that is found in all things as well as the bodies of all beings and that is lodged mainly in the blood. It is believed that blood obtained from red-coated victims is more effective and more active, since it would contain more *nyama* energy. Owing to the association of this colour with energy and strength, the beings possessing it inspire fear. Chiefs and warriors are feared because they may release the blood from the bodies of those who are at their mercy; so is the blacksmith, because he is the master of fire, of the red-hot metal he forges in his workshop, of weapons that shed blood and tools that "wound" the earth.

As we have just seen, the symbolism of red is chiefly focussed on activity and excitation. Of the three colours, red is the only one that harbours a sort of dynamism, filling people with both wonder and fear.

It goes without saying that the constraints imposed by the symbolism for the three colours under discussion are considerable. Nobody would think of contravening this tradition. For, to do so would be equivalent to rendering void the effectiveness of the act and the results that hinge on it. But for the purpose of sacrifice, it is not always possible to find a victim, whose colour meets the intentions of the sacrificer. For reasons of precision and to preserve the correspondencies, man may therefore feel induced to dye the coat of the victims available to him in the colour required for the rite. [12] This is not evidence of excessive formalism but of man's need to adjust things to each other, to establish valid correspondences, because ultimately this is how the religious act becomes effective.

In 1924, Léopold de Saussure published a very interesting article on: *L'Origine des noms de Mer rouge, Mer blanche et Mer noire* (The Origin of the Names for the Red Sea, the White Sea and the Black Sea), in which – having first demonstrated the influence of the Chinese on these nominations – he suggested a correlation between the problem involved in the names for these three seas and the fundamental character of the Sino-Iranian cosmology. The author claims, that the latter is based on the concept of "the pole, centre of the heavens, that is, on the concept of diurnal and therefore *equatorial* revolutions, since the dial of the diurnal revolutions is the celestial equator, which the Chinese of antiquity called 'the contour of heaven'." [13]

According to our present body of knowledge, the link established by some Africans between the three basic colours and the cardinal points indicates that in their cosmogonies they attribute a similar value to the celestial equator. For the black men, the space allocated to human beings in the universe consists of the portion located between the two tropics, that is, between the positive and the negative declination of the sun. The Bambara call the equator, which divides this space into two even halves, "the direct course taken by the sun in moving from east to west". In the sky it is marked by very specific planets and on earth by reference points on the eastern and western horizon. [14]

In fact, the three colours under discussion refer to this space. They are thus related to a view of the world, according to which the alternative movement of the sun between north and south is even more important than its daily movement from east to west. Not light as such is considered to give man the opportunity to distinguish between colours, but the effects it has on the ecological environment he lives in. The colour changes occurring in nature are brought about chiefly by the onset or the end of a season, in other words, by the double oscillation of the sun from one side of the equator to the other.

Colours and Elements

Earlier it was pointed out that the earth gave rise to the three colours. In this context, the earth is a concrete reality, the earth or soil that supplies human beings with food and carries them on its "back", as well as the earth that swallows them up, receiving the dead in its bowels.

However, the earth is also something else. Along with water, air and fire, it is one of the constitutive principles of the universe. These four elements have their place in African cosmogonies [15] and have provided some populations on the Black Continent with the roots of their language. [16] Each of these constitutive principles of the world has its own colour. Moreover, ultimately each one of them is made of colour and visual harmony.

Although, at the beginning of time, before anything existed, "night" was the primordial moment in creation, this does not mean, according to the Bambara and the Dogon, that this instant was devoid of any possibility to arouse perception. The "night" referred to here was, in the words of a *komo* (initiation society) chant, obscurity, but not an empty obsurity; it was "full" of a mixture of white, red and black. And this intimate association of the three shades involved colour, primordial elements and the spirit of divinity (*miri*). In becoming mingled, the elements acquired the consistency of the constitutive principles of beings and things, each principle having its own specific colour. Air is identified with white, earth and water with black, and fire with red. Thus, creation has not only its own make-up, consisting of four elements, but also a visible aspect, consisting of three colours. According to the beliefs of these populations, neither things nor beings in the world of creation are determined by one colour only. In addition to the four elements everything in this world is made up of colour mixtures, although one of the three is always dominant.

The relationship between the three colours and the four elements is a subject worthy of special investigation. It should be pointed out that additional research would be necessary to analyse the subtlety of African thought in this respect. For, Africa is the land of thaumaturges of matter and elements. Africans are maybe even greater manipulators of the elements than the Greeks, or at least they are their equals. One need only think, for example, of all the rituals designed to make rain, or those intended to dispel the winds, or the fire rites, – African thought and religion abound in such undertakings – to get an idea of the efforts made by the black man to master creation by controlling the elements underlying it.

Very eloquent in this respect are the rites for the domination of fire, that is, in fact those intended to gain control and mastery over the potential of red. There are two types: those that might be called solar rites and those called rites of lightning.

I studied the first variety among two populations, which are very different and far apart in space, in fact several thousand kilometers along a north-south axis. Geographically speaking, both populations live close to the fourteenth parallel, but the Mossi in the Republic of Upper Volta live at latitude 14N, whereas the Baronga live at latitude 14S.

Around the winter solstice, both populations celebrate a very important annual feast, which is also the festival of chieftaincy. In preparation of the ceremony all the paths leading to the royal palace are cleared of undergrowth and swept clean. This is called: "opening the road". Among the Mossi, the festival itself consists of wild cavalcades, mutual exchange of presents between the chief and his subjects (although it is mainly the chief, who receives gifts from his people, especially millet for his horses), rifle shooting organized by the blacksmiths who participate in large numbers, and finally in sacrifices offered on the family altar of the king's palace. Among the Baronga, the festival traditionally involves gifts of Kaffir tree fruit (*Sclerocarya caffra Sond.*) offered to the chiefs (they are intended for the preparation of the fermented festival drink), dances and chants glorifying the "old woman", that is, the sun, and finally, sacrifices made on the altar of the chieftaincy.

In either case this festival is designed to "act" on the sun and, as a result, on its red heat, which is expected to ripen the fruit and the corn. In both cases the chief and the sun are associated in the ritual of the ceremony. Basically, the festival has the objective of getting the sun to "come up again" from the south and to move north (for the Mossi) or to keep it over the southern tropic (for the Baronga) in order to ensure ripening of the cereals.

Rites concerned with lightning are legion. Among all African populations lightning is the fire that is most feared, the one that elicited institutionalized reactions from society. The place struck by this heavenly element calls for a special desacralisation which has to be accomplished by agents appointed for this purpose. Wherever lightning strikes, it leaves behind a "thunder-stone", which has to be picked up and deposited in special sanctuaries. On the other hand, those struck by lightning have to be buried apart and their funeral pottery are never deposited alongside with those of the other deceased. The fear aroused by lightning is actually due to the suddenness, with which this fire of heaven strikes. This is believed to bring about instantaneous confusion between heaven and earth, to an extent that the person, the object, or the place that is struck become like heaven, or is heaven itself. For this reason, in Uganda, for example, a woman struck by lightning, but who escaped death, used to become the property of the king, who also was considered to be heaven.

The control of lightning, its "domestication" as it were, calls for special precautions and rites, which some authors have described in great detail. [17] By analysing some of the anti-lightning "medicines", these studies enable us to understand the mechanism and the logic behind the African approach to the concoction of these preparations. It should be stressed once again, that this is neither sympathetic "magic", nor is it magic of avoidance. But it is simply an attempt to put things in order, to put them into categories, and to classify them, so as to enable man to guide things according to his own intentions, in harmony with their nature, and not according to the disorder, in which they are momentarily caught up. There is a whole philosophy behind these techniques. African thought attributes a certain order to things and to beings. This order is defined by their classification into categories in accordance with their nature and their affinities. If for one reason or another an element leaves the place allocated to it, disorder manifests itself; in this case it is up to human intelligence to lead the "troublemaker" back to its place, so that the world can function properly. This tells a lot about the power man attributes to himself, as well as the effectiveness of the means used. The question is, whether to re-establish order it is enough to present a disorderly element with specimens of its own variety or its antipode, while reciting formulae for the purpose of the tautology of the act. This is the whole problem of human intervention in creation, a form of intervention, where the word plays almost as important a role as the divine word at the beginning of the world.

However, the domestication of the celestial fire calls for further consideration. In African mythologies, this fire, which contains in itself the red colour with all its connotations, is frequently stolen from heaven by man. Often the deed is accomplished by human beings; sometimes man sends emissaries – insects or other animals – to carry out the theft. Many versions and shades of the Promethean myth exist on the Black Continent. What is interesting in the African myth and might even make it possible to arrive at a less historicist interpretation of the Greek story, is that it does not focus on the legal aspect of theft. The latter is not considered a transgression on the part of man, but an undertaking designed on the one hand to reveal what fire is, that is, manifestation and element of disclosure, and on the other to discover the thief, Prometheus himself. Prometheus could never have been unmasked, unless he had carried the luminous element. At the same time, fire would never have manifested itself to human beings, unless it had been taken from the hiding place that concealed it from their eyes. African Promethean myths (and perhaps even the Greek myth) are thus in fact only stories about ritual "thefts", intended to consolidate – and not to destroy – a certain kinship between the gods and men. This kind of kinship, is called joking relationship by cultural anthropologists and it is no doubt the most subtle form of kinship. The uterine nephew does not "steal" his maternal uncle to harm him, but to manifest himself and to consolidate the ties that bind him to his relative.

That this applies to at least a part of Africa is evidenced by the rites for the discovery of thieves and for the protection of seeds in the fields. Blackened wood, taken from a tree struck by lightning, is used for this purpose. Charcoal – vestiges of the manifestations of the celestial fire – is considered an effective weapon against attempts at stealing. Instead of manifesting itself or its "thief" the heavenly fire simply "denounces" the robber. The same ritual of unveiling the thief is accomplished by the Bantu populations of South-East Africa, who apply a certain mixture on the chameleon; as a result the chameleon turns white and finally dies. The colour is, of course, the same as that attributed to albinos, who are considered to have been struck by lightning in their mother's womb. The chameleon that has turned white is assimilated to a human being struck by lightning, and the fact that it is used to "discover" thieves is part of the same mental process as that involved in the tree burned by lightning. The effectiveness of the "white" chameleon may be even greater than that of charcoal from wood struck by lightning, because here we are dealing with "white" fire, that is, burning fire, whereas charcoal involves "black" fire, in other words, fire that has been extinguished. The relationship between lightning and the chameleon is based on the symmetries and dissymmetries existing between them: owing to the slowness of its movements, the animal is the antipode of lightning, whereas through the swiftness of its tongue in catching its prey (i.e., killing), it is considered to be the equal of the celestial fire when it kills those it strikes. This explains the presence and the importance of the chameleon in a great number of

African myths about the origin of death. The fact that for the purpose of unmasking thieves, the choice fell on an animal whose mimicry enables it to change colour is also significant for reasons other than the parallelism between it and lightning. Before becoming white, the chameleon goes through a series of successive colour changes. [18] In a very short space of time, it thus undergoes a similar evolution as that characterising the life of a human being who is considered white when he is received in the world of the deceased.

Owing to the relationship between colour and the elements it is possible to decypher one aspect of African culture, which has to be understood in its entirety with due respect for all the details. The advantage of the classic scholar has in this respect over the research scientist, who tries to understand living cultural traditions, resides in the fact that the first can have recourse to texts (even if they are only fragmentary), whereas the latter is obliged to move in the quicksand of facts, keeping his eyes open and oriented in several directions at a time – in other words, he has to be somewhat like the chameleon.

Colours and Personal Appearance

Among the many factors liable to amaze us when we try to grasp the world of colours one has always been a special puzzle for me. It seems to me that in all cultures, *homo sapiens* – and not *homo mecanicus* – has attached special interest to the colour of his skin when setting out – no doubt unconsciously – to construe his universe of colours. The white man has made his white skin his title of nobility; the place assigned by the Chinese to yellow was the center of the universe; the Blacks have attached to black a value of achievement and plenitude probably unknown elsewhere. Owing to the contrast between colours, their polarization always found – and still finds – its extension on the moral level. The white man has related whiteness to life and goodness; blackness to evil and death. The black man, on the other hand, has developed a system based on the same terms, but in the reverse: whiteness is for him related to death and the world beyond, whereas black is connected with life and fertility. What is behind these correlations? Why does the colour of people's skin seem to go hand in hand with their ideas of life and good, and why is it in contrast to their notions of death and evil?

I have no intentions of trying to solve these problems, if indeed there are any problems. I should simply like to make some suggestions regarding Africans.

There is a rather widespread concept in Black Africa, according to which human beings, before "coming" into this world, dwell in heaven, where they are white. For, heaven itself is white and all the beings dwellling there are also white. Therefore the whiter a child is at birth, the more splendid it is.[19] In other words, at that particular moment in a person's life, special importance is attached to the whiteness of his colour, which is endowed with exceptional qualities. To back up this statement, I wish to relate a Ronga tale, entitled "The Road to Heaven". It describes two young sisters, one of whom, having chosen the right colour, succeeds in bringing children into this world, whereas the other, having chosen the wrong colour, not only fails in her undertaking, but is even punished:

> "A young girl broke her pitcher while trying to draw water, and since she feared her mother's rebukes, 'she took her cord' in order to go to heaven. On the road an ant came to give her advice, and as the girl was pleasant and docile, she was wise enough to follow the ant's good advice. When she arrived in heaven she found a village. Her pleasant disposition won everyone's esteem and to show their friendship, the inhabitants offered her a child. Next day, they told her: 'We shall show you a beautiful house with many children.' When she had entered she saw one place that was red and another that was white. This was due to the clothes that covered the children. She was told to go and choose a child. Now, the young girl wanted to pick one from the red side. But the ant in her ear advised her to take one from the white side. She took a child; it was very beautiful!"[20]

The story is followed by a counterpart tale, according to which the younger sister also went to heaven, but she did not listen to the ant's advice, and when the people in the village sent her to pick a child, she chose from the red instead of the white side. She failed and returned to earth in a thousand pieces.

This predilection for white and light skin also becomes manifest in connection with young girls of marriageable age. The light-skinned girl is in fact considered to possess more charm than one whose skin is jet-black. The light-skinned girl "shows up" better. Her whiteness makes for light and youth.

According to the same concept, it is also claimed that a newborn baby is not only white but also a soft being during the time between his birth and his acceptance into the society. Furthermore, during this entire period, he is not considered a real person, and this may go so far that parents and society may do away with him at will for reasons that are peculiar to each social group. Having been done away with, these beings are considered to return automatically to the place they came from, that is, to heaven.

If a child dies a natural death during this period, its mother buries it secretly in a piece of pottery near a river. It is not mourned, because it belongs to the other world.

Many rites celebrated during early childhood have the objective of "hardening" this "soft" being. I shall confine myself to one of the most important ones. One week after the birth of a first-born Thonga child, a special ceremony is celebrated. The maternal grandmother daubs the young mother's hut with clay and then:

> "She returns to her own place, assembling all female relatives, of whom there may be as many as twelve or fifteen. They take along food, ochre and specially prepared fat. Two or three men accompany them. They enter the child's village, executing a special dance, called *khana*, and singing the following chant: 'I glorify my pot, which has produced *ngélébendjé*'." [21]

This term is untranslatable according to H. A. Junod, who explains, however, that:

> "they (the women) compare the child to an earthenware pot, which has been baked and then tested in accordance with custom by allowing it to drop on the ground. The pot does not break; for, it did not crack in the oven, it remained intact. This is what the qualifying adverb *ngélébendjé* means." [22]

Whiteness and softness thus define a human being's state during the first years of his life.

It should be recalled in this context that in many regions of France whenever a young girl got married before her older sister, the latter was seated on a hot stove to "cook". It was in fact believed that in this case the younger sister had "matured" (i.e., had been "cooked ") before the older one, who therefore needed "cooking" so as to make her capable of marrying. [23]

For the new man, the time that follows this initial period is that of "baked pottery" and red colour. It is marked by his apprenticeship devoted to learning about life and social practices. It is the time of his education and training. He undergoes initiation rites and is taught the essential principles of the society's intellectual, religious and moral life. Like the baked pottery that has been reddened by the fire in the oven, but has not yet been used for cooking, the individual is at that time of his life a sort of passive tool in the hands of his educators. He is then frequently compared to iron in the red-hot forge, where it is steeled under the influence of the heat that penetrates it. Red and solidity behoove the individual in the process of physical and social training, because they mark the transition from inception to plenitude. Red is, in fact, the intermediary colour between white (the white of the sky, as well as the white of the clay from which pottery is made) and black, whereas solidity indicates that the pottery and the human being are at the disposal of society. The idea that, during his formative years, man is available to society is easy to understand, but it is less so in the case of pottery. However, the rite called "rite of the new pottery", practised by the Bantu, will help us grasp this idea. Among these people, a new pottery is never used until a handful of maize grains have been cooked in it and subsequently thrown away. For, it is believed that, if a meal is served in a receptacle that has not undergone this ritual, those who would eat the food would be exposed to a rash, covering the arms, or even the entire body. Junod reports that the rite in question is called *kwangula*,[24] a term coming very close to the expression for rainbow, *kwangula tilo*, and which in transliteration means "that which wards off the danger of the sky". Rainbows are in fact known to appear after a rainfall, when the sky begins to clear. They mark the transition period between storm and good weather, between the period of danger (due to lightning) and that of calm.

Like new and red pottery, a young person is considered to be at the disposal of society; like pottery and like the sky, charged with the fire of lightning, such an individual would be a danger to society if he were entrusted with social tasks. On the other hand he can be asked to perform duties in conformity with his condition. Thus, the women who make pottery, for example, entrust small children with the job of lighting the fire for baking the pots.

Red, being typical for a young person who is still undergoing the process of education and training, appears, however, not only in connection with new pottery. During initiation ceremonies, young men wear bracelets made of red fibres around the joints of their arms and legs. Now, our limb joints are precisely those places in the body, which make it possible for us to walk and to work. The purpose of associating them with red is to classify them with all the phenomena representing activity. At times, the head, face, or the entire body of the initiate are painted ochre, as if to stress the participation of the whole human being in the movement and dynamism which he must acquire.[25]

When he has been molded into a man and achieved social maturity, the human being is associated with black, the colour of his skin. He is thus likened to the pottery that has undergone the above rite. Like the kitchen utensil, whose exterior blackens with use, man attributes increasing importance to the blackness of his skin and this very blackness gives him authority. The type of body care and the concern with skin during the entire period that follows an individual's admission to society reflects the value that is attributed to the part that envelops the body. Great emphasis is placed on the smoothness and brilliance of the skin. Its lustre and sheen are a sign of vigour and good health. Plant and animal fats are used to contribute to this exaltation of the skin and its black colour. Often people use the remains of gravy fat on their fingers to grease their thighs and legs. This is not done in a spirit of economy, to make sure that nothing is lost. It is part of a cosmetic treatment, intended to enhance the beauty of the skin and its colour.

The fact that man conceives of himself in different ways depending on the colour of his appearance is an aspect of human culture in general and of African culture in particular that can hardly be stressed enough. In this connection it should be pointed out that the importance the African attributes to his own skin is at least as great as his interest in animal hides. Cosmetics is related to the art of tanning and leather work, which is not practised in all human cultures. Judging from biblical texts, the Hebrews, for example, never practised this art. Even in the form of clothes, animal hides are mentioned only two or three times in the Bible, as far as I know, whereas most Africans know and practise the art of tanning. In some places, animal skins are even used for ritual purposes and therefore play a much more important role than ordinary clothes.

However, Africans do not really feel different when they alter the colour of their skin by various means. The three colours they associate with the course of their lives actually reflect a process based on the idea of maturing. Traditional African cosmetics is not intended to enhance the esthetic appearance of the individual, but to show up his inner richness and possibilities of radiance. The colours applied on the skin may be a way of expressing one's self and the African may therefore paint half of his face white or red, while leaving the other half its natural tint. Sometimes, he even accentuates the blackness of this half, darkening it by means of charcoal powder or other similar ingredients. [26] The two colours thus appear in symmetry on the vertically divided halves of the head. This division raises an extremely interesting problem.

The arrangement of the two colours to mark the opposition between the two halves of the head, is not the only case of this particular kind. Many myths and legends recount events reflecting the concept of man's symmetrical division into two halves along a vertical axis. As a result of division, the two opposing parts become "autonomous". A.J.N. Tremearne relates the following story about a woman who died in pregnancy and was buried near a dyers' pit:

> "During three subsequent months the dyers were molested by an unknown person who repeatedly spilt the dye, hid the dyeing poles, and generally made mischief. By day nothing was seen of him, but a watchman placed at night in a *chedia* tree close by reported next morning that he had seen a boy crawl out of a hole in a neighboring bank, play the same pranks with the dyers' property as before, and finally return to his hiding-place. When the place was dug open the body of the woman was found within with a live child beside her. Though dead, only one half of her body had corrupted. The other half from head to foot had remained fresh and undecayed, so that her body had been born and successfully weaned. As they gazed at this remarkable sight the woman's body dissolved into dust." [27]

Other tales describe strange beings, composed of two perpendicular halves, one derived from the left or right side of a human being, and the other from a whole animal. Sometimes these "monsters" appear simply as half-human, with one arm, one foot, one eye, as if the human being had been split from the head (along the metopic and sagittal sutures) to the pubic symphysis. The Zulus even talk about an entire tribe of such creatures. This is only meant to show how widespread the phenomenon is in Africa, although it is by no means peculiar to that continent.

As an isolated phenomenon it might not be very suggestive of anything, but we also know figures and fabulous monsters, half man, half animal, in other cultures. If we compare, for example the Centaurs, Silenes, Satyrs, Gorgons, Sirenes, Griffons, etc. of Greece with the African "monsters" described above, we find that their bodies are not divided vertically into two functional halves, but that the partition is a horizontal one. There is no symmetry. The problem acquires significance both in the case of Greece and in that of Africa, precisely because of this difference in approach.

The question then arises, why Greek civilisation (to mention only one), which left behind immortal esthetic works of art that gave us mathematics and geometry, ignored the symmetry of the human body in "creating" the Centaurs and the other "monsters"? And why did the African cultures, which apparently cannot be compared with that of Greece, insist on respecting that symmetry in creating their "monsters"? This is probably not the place to discuss the problem.[28] However, I did wish to point out that, through the ritual division of the human body into coloured halves, the Africans have enabled us to get a glimpse of their concept of mankind and its destiny.[29] Half white, half black, human beings are symmetrically divided into their feminine and masculine aspects. The white half corresponds to their femininity; the black half to their masculinity. Both are considered here in terms of generation and completion. The white half is the *genitrix* part, and the black half is the completion of virility. We recall that it was a woman, who invented white. This was no coincidence. As she generates the lineage, she is considered white like her progeny and white like heaven. In some Bantu languages the woman who gives birth to twins (that is, the woman who best fulfills the role of *genitrix*) is called by the same term as heaven itself, i.e., *tilo*.[30]

In some cases, African cultures conceive of the human being as neither red nor black, but in terms of one colour only, that is, white.

Consideration must be given to two types of arguments.

First of all, there is the case of the albinos, who never turn black owing to the lack of melanin in their skin tissues. For us the phenomenon can be explained physiologically and biologically, but the Africans attribute it to heaven. As we have heard earlier on, the Bantu of South-East Africa consider the albino to have been struck by lightning while still in his mother's womb. Elsewhere he is the heavenly child in the highest sense of the word. In fact, he is like heaven and remains so throughout his whole, often short life. For, in Black Africa, albinos used to be pre-eminently sacrificial victims. It was believed that their hair, mixed with seed grain, would offer the best guarantee for a good harvest. Their blood, poured over altars for crop sacrifices, was expected to do the same thing for man's food, since it would make sure that the life-giving rains would come in time. How could it be otherwise, since – through the sacrifice – heaven had been introduced into the earth?

The other argument is related to cases, where white as the ritual colour is applied on the head, the face, or even the entire human body. This practice has a mystical component. It is customary in many places in Africa: among the Nyakusa, the Ova-ambo of Angola, and the Kuanyama, among others. Obtained from kaolin, or by dissolving ashes in water, white becomes the colour of initiates who have reached the final stage of their initiation. In this case they are considered to have been newly born to life in heaven. Having first been human beings, they now become like gods, and they are white. The *korè*, the Bambara's supreme initiation institution, does not allow its adepts to wear anything but white, and the same thing applies to sacrificial victims. The *korè* claims that the individual is transposed by transfiguration from the human to the divine level. The adepts of this confraternity "are" no longer men but gods, and as such they ignore the difficulties of life and even the pains of death. They do not feel death as a separation, but as a union modelled on the pattern of marriage.

Human beings thus complete the cycle of their existence by passing through three colour stages. Just as they are white in appearance when they come to earth, they are white when they return to heaven, whence they came. However, they do not stay there, for their existence has no end. Their destiny is on earth and this is why they are constantly reintegrated into the life cycle by new acts of procreation on the part of women. White therefore takes the meaning of mystical life, or of union with God.

One should, however, not approach the expressions I used to describe the Africans' concept of life and religion from the standpoint of their Western interpretation. The mystical life and the union with God referred to here are only analogies of Theresian terminology, or that of St. John of the Cross. African mysticism does not try to induce people to isolate themselves or to shun the world. Quite on the contrary, their presence in life is required. The world is the very foundation and an essential aspect of this mysticism. There is no union with God, a Bambara would say, without the world we live in.

This approach helps the black man, who lives his religion according to these precepts, to free himself of all feelings of anguish. Anxiety is out of place here, because of the incessant movement, or reincarnations between heaven and earth, that is, the two poles, between which the destiny of man unfolds. The idea of eschatology is completely absent from this religion. It is as if man felt that he was indispensable to the world and that the world was also indispensable to him.

Translated from French by Ruth Horine.

NOTES

1 See J.-P. Caprile, *La dénomination des "couleurs": méthode d'enquête avec application à langue du Tchad, le m'bay de Moïssala*, p. 8 (unpublished).

2 See H.A. Junod, *Moeurs et coutumes des Bantous*, Payot, Paris, 1936, vol. II, p. 261

3 See J. André, "Sources et évolution du vocabulaire des couleurs en latin" in *Problèmes de la Couleur*, S.E.V.P.E.N., Paris, 1957, p. 334.

4 About the M'bay, see J.-P. Caprile, *op. cit.* (note 1), pp. 4 and 5.

5 J.-P. Caprile, *op. cit.* (note 1), pp. 3 to 6.

6 They have a specific verb (*ndàng*) to describe the multicoloured, variegated, mottled, or striped.

7 See H.A. Junod, *op. cit.* (note 2), p. 261.

8 It is alleged that this woman's spindle is still preserved in her birthplace.

9 The problem of lustre beset the human mind ever since coloured fabrics made their appearance. For the African it is linked to embellishment and adornment, the lustre of garments being the first "gem" of mankind.

10 The basic garment is the loincloth. Anybody who wears this piece of dress is thought of as a true man, though the remainder of the body may be naked.

11 It should be noticed in this context that the corpses of persons who have seriously disturbed the social order are never removed from the house through the door, but through an opening made in the wall.

12 E.E. Evans-Pritchard mentions that the Azande also have recourse to this practice during the initiation ceremony of future witch-doctors: "When, as frequently, light-coloured animals are tabooed during ritual action they must be 'blackened' before the person who has abstained from them may eat them." *Witchcraft, Oracles and Magic among the Azande*, Oxford, The Clarendon Press, 1963, p. 460 and pp. 220-21.

13 See *Le Globe, Organe de la Société de Géographie de Genève*, Payot, Genève, 1924, t. LXIII, pp. 23 to 36, (quote on p. 35, note 2).

14 See also, D. Zahan, "La Notion d'écliptique chez les Dogon et les Bambara" in *Africa*, vol . XXI, No. 1, Jan. 1951, pp. 13 to19.

15 See S. de Ganay, "Notes sur la théodicée bambara", *Revue de l'Histoire des Religions*, vol. CXXXV, No. 2-3, Paris, avril-juin 1949, pp. 187 to 213; D. Zahan, "Aperçu sur la pensée théogonique des Dogon, *Cahiers Internationaux de Sociologie*, Paris, avril-juin 1949, pp. 113 to 133.

16 See Mgr. Bazin, *Dictionaire Bambara-Français*, Paris, Larose, p. XXI.

17 See H.A. Junod, *op. cit.* (note 2), vol. II, pp. 268 to 270.

18 It changes "from green to orange and from orange to black", see H.A. Junod, *op. cit.* (note 2), vol. II, p. 306.

19 It should be recalled that during the first few hours after birth African babies do not have a very dark complexion.

20 See H.A. Junod, *Les chants et les contes des Ba-Ronga*, Georges Bridel & Cie, Lausanne, 1897, p. 237.

21 See H.A. Junod, *op, cit.* (note 2), vol. I, p. 49.

22 Idem. p. 50.

23 See A. van Gennep, *Manuel de Folklore Français*, A. et J. Picard et Cie, Paris, 1946, vol. I, 2, Du berceau à la tombe, pp. 632-33.

24 See H.A. Junod, *op. cit.* (note 2), vol. II, p. 106.

25 See a.o.: Hugh A. Stayt, *The Bavenda*, New impr., Frank Cass & Co., London, 1968, pp. 109, 112, 123, 135, 141; Edwin M. Loeb, *In Feudal Africa*, Indiana University Research Center in Anthropology, Folklore, and Linguistics, Bloomington, Mouton & Co, 1962, pp. 245 and 249; G. Parrinder, *La Religion en Afrique Occidentale*, Payot, Paris, 1950, p. 130; I. Schapera, *The Khoisan Peoples of South Africa*, 3rd Impression, Routledge & Kegan Paul, London 1960, p. 281.

26 I myself have witnessed such ritual practices among the populations of the Republic of Mali and the Republic of Upper Volta. A.J.N. Tremearne observed them in the northern region of Nigeria (*The Tailed Headhunters of Nigeria*, Seeley, Service & Co., London, 1912, pp. 112-13, 186, 192); Clement M. Doke in Northern Rhodesia (now Zambia) (*The Lambas of Northern Rhodesia*, George G. Harrap & Co., London, 1931, pp.186-7).

27 See A.J. N. Tremearne, *Hausa Superstitions and Customs*, Frank Cass & Co., London, 1970, pp. 90-1.

28 G. Dumézil has clearly shown that centaurs "(...) are not mere fantasies" since the earliest representations of these creatures are "(...) masks of monsters more or less clumsily made up of a human being and some accessories", whereas "(...) the horse centaur with four horse legs and a torso finishing in a human bust

with the head and arms of a man" did not develop until much later. See *Le Problème des Centaures, Etude de mythologie comparée indo-européenne*, Paul Geuthner, Paris, 1929, p. 167. In any event the question raised remains open, if not for the centaurs at least for the other "monsters".

29 In the following passage I limited myself on purpose to the symbolism of black and white, which is almost the same in a great number of African cultures. Nor is it possible to go into the details of the rites concerning the right-left symmetry of the human body. But I should mention that some purification ceremonies take into consideration the opposition of the vertically divided parts of the body. In many African populations the position of the corpse in the grave also respects this concept of symmetry. Moreover, left-handed persons, whose symmetry is considered contrary to that of normal persons, benefit from a special status during their lifetime, and after their death they are buried according to special rites.

30 See H.A. Junod, *op. cit.* (note 2), vol. II, pp. 387 to 393.

ERNST BENZ

COLOR IN CHRISTIAN VISIONARY EXPERIENCE

I must preface my lecture with the digression of a personal remark. For several months now, ever since the Eranos program for this year was announced, I have constantly had to justify to colleagues, friends, and acquaintances the fact that I am speaking about such a curious topic as color in Christian visions. The reason for this is that for many theologians theology has shrunk into a politically militant social ethic. Just before I came here I was visited by a former American student of mine, who is now the president of a college for social workers. When he heard my topic he was so astonished that he could only say, "Oh color, how funny!" He was unable to make any connection between color, theology, and social ethics.

For me the subject is in fact not as funny as it appears. Already in childhood the theme of color engaged me in the most lively way. Most of all this had to do with Lake Constance, my home. Of all the landscapes in Germany, Lake Constance has the strongest light intensity. Moreover, the variety of scenic form is unusual – the broad flatness of the lake; the pre-Alpine morainic landscape, very rich in its alternations; the Linzgau mountains; the Hegau volcanic cones; and above all, looking from the German side, the entire Alpine chain, extending from the Bavarian and

Austrian Alps over the Silvretta glaciers to the Säntis massif, and from there across the Glärnisch to the Bernese Alps. Thanks to this multiformity, as well as to cloud formations quite extraordinary in their polymorphism, the light has an unusually impressive creative effect, bringing out colors and iridescences in water, land, mountains, and clouds, ranging in nuance from that of the northern sea to that of the upper Italian lake. Already as a boy I mused over this peculiar, world-transfiguring effect of colors. But in addition to this there was above all the wonder of the rainbow, both simple and double, after thunderstorms. The appearance of the colorful arc of light, which overarched the entire lake and all earthly national boundaries, deepened one's awareness that involved there in that light and in that color was something supernatural, heavenly, glorifying. Inasmuch as we luckily had excellent religious instruction in school – which unfortunately seldom seems to be the case – with a certain self-evidentness I connected the rainbow over Lake Constance with the rainbow which God established for Noah after the flood, as a sign of the future preservation of mankind from similar catastrophes. So I felt completely at home in naively ascribing to the heavenly world the colors which served as an element in the transfiguration of the earthly world.

Thus, early in my subsequent church history studies I was fascinated by the colorful world of light in the visions reported by the prophets and seers of the Old and New Testaments and, after them, by the great visionaries of later Christian centuries.

Among the Christian visionaries – and here we shall be speaking only of them – the visionary world of the heavenly realm is full of colors. Characteristically, descriptions of colorful images are to be found very much earlier among the visionaries, who report their views of the heavenly sphere, than among the writers and poets of the ancient world. Thanks to the unusual intensity of the ecstatic experience, heavenly colors evidently engaged man earlier than did earthly colors; in this area the visionaries were centuries ahead of the art historians. The green of the heavenly meadow was always greener than that of earthly pastures, even in the description of the Alpine meadows in Haller's famous poem. In this regard the rainbow appears again and again as a juncture between heavenly and earthly iridescences. On the one hand, the great visionaries repeatedly come to speak of it in their visions and, on the other hand, it has also provided the most important stimulus towards optical science.

Visions in Color

As an illustrative example of a vision in color I would like to start with the introductory vision of the Johannine Apocalypse. John, the seer, tells of his stay on the island of Patmos "on account of the word of God and the testimony of Jesus." The visionary experience which fell to him there is a characteristic joining of vision and audition: the vision, as is frequently the case, announces itself by auditory means. John is carried away, or, as he says: "I was in the Spirit on the Lord's day." He hears behind him a mighty voice "like a trumpet." Through it the heavenly speaker reveals himself in a mysterious intimation: "I am the Alpha and the Omega." Then he dispenses a charge to the seer which he is to execute: "Write what you see in a book." He is to send this book to the seven churches in Asia mentioned by name. This auditory perception causes the seer to look around for the origin of the voice, and with that the description of the vision commences (1:12ff.). John describes his visionary experience as a seeing "in the Spirit," instead of with one's physical sight. As a rule the eyes are closed in the visionary ecstatic state; the physical capacity for sight through the eye is eliminated. The visionaries see, as they say, with their "inner eye." We know as little about how that is carried out in the brain as we do about the visual process in dreaming.

> I saw seven golden lampstands, and in the midst of the lampstands one like a son of man, clothed with a long robe and with a golden girdle round his breast; his head and his hair were white as white wool, white as snow; his eyes were like a flame of fire, his feet were like burnished bronze, refined as in a furnace, and his voice was like the sound of many waters; in his right hand he held seven stars, from his mouth issued a sharp two-edged sword, and his face was like the sun shining in full strength.

After this description of what he has beheld, the seer portrays the effect which the vision had upon him: "When I saw him, I fell at his feet as though dead." Then the vision goes on: "He laid his right hand upon me, saying, 'Fear not.' " Thus it is not only a picture-film running before the eyes of the seer; rather, he himself becomes drawn into the visionary act. The figure in the apparition lays its right hand upon the seer, who is now paralyzed from fright. It is the liturgical gesture of healing and transmission of power. Simultaneously the figure introduces himself more clearly than the first time: "I am the first and the last, and the living one; I died, and behold I am alive for evermore, and I have the keys of Death and Hades." It is thus the transfigured Son of Man himself who reveals himself to the seer, and who now renews and expands upon his charge to him: "Write what you see, what is and what is to take place hereafter." The vision is portrayed as a plastic, colorful and luminous appearance of the heavenly scene in three-dimensional space. One can clearly picture the image to himself and even sketch it – which has in fact often happened in the history of Christian art, as already, for example, in the medieval miniatures illustrating the Latin manuscripts of the Johannine Apocalypse. John sees seven golden lampstands and standing – or "walking about," as is stated later – in the midst of them the figure of the Son of Man, as it first appears in the vision of Daniel (7:13). With Daniel, to be sure, this figure is not described in detail as to color and garments. Here in John, on the other hand, a clearer picture is found.

Already in this first example several characteristic features emerge which are repeated in many later visions.

1) With regard to colors, designations of colors are at the same time designations of material and of quality. In the visions of heaven, colors are readily expressed through precious metals or gems with particular color characteristics. Already in its designation the color is given a distinct character as to quality and value. The vision of the heavenly city with its walls and gates of jewels (Rev. 21:10ff.) is an especially graphic example of this.

2) The preferential use of designations of quality and value for colors directs our attention, as members of an industrial age, to a fact of relevance to the theme of the conference as a whole: up until a few decades ago, there were no ready-made paints at all which one could buy. In the period prior to the industrial production of aniline dyes, the preparation of the paints themselves was still a professional secret of the painters and dyers. This professional secret also entailed, above all, a knowledge of the vegetable, animal, and mineral substances from which paints could be obtained, as well as knowledge of the times and places of their extraction and mixture. The connection between the production of paints and alchemy was not yet ruptured. Occasionally new colors were themselves the by-product of alchemical processes – as for instance Prussian blue, which was a by-product of the alchemical pursuits of Christian Edelmann at the Prussian royal court.

3) The heavenly colors display heightened qualities of light and luminosity – they glow like melted metal, they radiate, they shine, they have fluctuating phases of light intensity, which can increase to the point of

unbearableness.

4) We have already referred to the fact that the visionary himself participates in the visionary action.

5) Still another feature emerges from the visionary account. The visionary image does not appear just as a film on a visionary screen or stage. Rather, it expounds upon itself; the figure which is the subject of the vision and which introduces itself in the course of the vision interprets in a particular way its appearance, its actions, the details of what transpires in the visionary picture, and frequently at the same time the significance of the colors in the visionary image as well. Often the interpretation is restricted solely to the main point of the vision. Thus, in the instance at hand, out of all the many details about color and substance in the vision, only two things are explained: "As for the mystery of the seven stars which you saw in my right hand, and the seven golden lampstands, the seven stars are the angels of the seven churches and the seven lampstands are the seven churches." Both of these elements of the vision are important as regards the special charge to write down what is heard, and to send to the seven churches the letters dictated to the seer.

The details of this vision reoccur in the letters themselves. In dictating the latter to the angels of the seven churches, the Son of Man, whose figure John sees, successively portrays himself in terms of the same characteristics emphasized by the seer in his vision of him. In Rev. 2:1ff., the Son of Man says: "To the angel of the church in Ephesus write: 'The words of him who holds the seven stars in his right hand, who walks among the seven golden lampstands ...' " (2:1); "And to the angel of the church in Smyrna write: 'The words of the first and the last, who died and came to life ...' " (2:8); "And to the angel of the church in Pergamum write: 'The words of him who has the sharp two-edged sword' " (2:12); "And to the angel of the church in Thyatira write: 'The words of the Son of God, who has eyes like a flame of fire, and whose feet are like burnished bronze' " (2:18); "And to the angel of the church of Sardis write: 'The words of him who has the seven spirits of God and the seven stars' " (3:1). In this it becomes clear that the individual attributes of the Son of Man are each time related to the specific spiritual nature of the churches; they have a correlative character which discloses the spiritual state of the church in question.

In the Johannine Apocalypse, however, all of these spiritual correlations are not yet systematically worked out; rather, they roll forth in a stream of images, colors, lights, symbols, parables, and correspondences, which for their part are again interpreted through new images and parables. Still, a basic schema is already etched out: the color vision interprets itself; it is not, for instance, subsequently interpreted by the seer. The self-interpretation of the vision is its subject, and all the vision's elements – colors, fire, lights, substances – have a spiritual meaning appertaining to and fixed in them.

A similar structure of the vision in color is found in the same Johannine Apocalypse in the demonic counterpart to the appearance of the transfigured Son of Man, namely in the appearance of the woman upon the beast, the great harlot Babylon.

> Then one of the seven angels who had the seven bowls came and said to me, "Come, I will show you the judgment of the great harlot who is seated upon many waters ... " And he carried me away in the Spirit into a wilderness, and I saw a woman sitting on a scarlet beast which was full of blasphemous names, and it had seven heads and ten horns. The woman was arrayed in purple and scarlet, and bedecked with gold and jewels and pearls, holding in her hand a golden cup full of abominations and the impurities of her fornication; and on her forehead was written a name of mystery: "Babylon the great, mother of harlots and of earth's abominations." And I saw the woman, drunk with the blood of the saints and the blood of the martyrs of Jesus. (Rev. 17:1-6)

What is described here is, so to say, a vision within the vision. An angel promises to show the seer the great harlot and the judgment being passed upon her, and leads him "in the Spirit" into the wilderness. Then he sees there the woman upon the scarlet beast. Here too the vision is interpreted, and here too this is not done subsequently by the seer himself; instead the vision interprets itself. But in this case it happens not through the chief figure of the vision, the Son of Man, but rather through a heavenly interpreter, the selfsame angel who shows him the vision.

The interpretation is the angel's response to the wonderment of the seer, who does not understand the vision. That too is a classical feature of the visionary experience. Already in the prophet Daniel, for example, after the description of his vision of the realms of the Medes and the Persians, represented with the ram and the he-goat, it says: "When I, Daniel, had seen the vision, I sought to understand it; and behold, there stood before me one having the appearance of a man. And I heard a man's voice between the banks of the U'lai, and it called, 'Gabriel, make this man understand the vision.' " (Dan. 8:15) It is similar here in John: "When I saw her I marveled greatly. But the angel said to me, 'Why marvel? I will tell you the mystery of the woman, and of the beast ... that carries her.' " (Rev. 17: 6-7) Thereupon follows first the interpretation of the seven heads and ten horns of the beast, and then the interpretation of the woman: "The woman that you saw is the great city which has dominion over the kings of the earth" (Rev. 17:18), i.e. Rome. The interpretation of the colors and the jewels of the woman then follows in the 18th chapter, in connection with the announcement of the judgment upon Babylon:

> And the kings of the earth ... will say, "Alas! alas! thou great city, thou mighty city, Babylon! In one hour has thy judgment come." And the merchants of the earth weep and mourn for her since no one buys their cargo any more, cargo of gold, silver, jewels and pearls, fine linen, purple, silk and scarlet, all kinds of scented wood, all articles of ivory, all articles of costly wood, bronze, iron and marble, cinnamon, spice, incense, myrrh, frankincense, wine, oil, fine flour and wheat, cattle and sheep, horses and chariots, and slaves, that is, human souls. ... The merchants of these wares, who gained wealth from her, will stand far off, in fear of her torment, weeping and mourning aloud, "Alas, alas, for the great city that was clothed in fine linen, in purple and scarlet, bedecked with gold, with jewels, and with pearls! In one hour all this wealth has been laid waste." ... Then [spoke] a mighty angel, ... "All nations were deceived by thy sorcery, and in her was found the blood of prophets and of saints, and of all who have been slain on earth." (Rev. 18:9-24)

Scarlet is interpreted here in a double way, as an expression of splendor and lust as well as a sign of the blood shed by the saints, while purple is an allusion to the imperial purple of the capital city of the Imperium.

The fact that explanation of the colors is a part of the self-interpretation of the vision shows that the designations of color and quality have an objective meaning – at least in the opinion of the seer – and further that they constitute essential elements and characterizations of the spiritual corporeality of the heavenly world itself. It shows moreover that they are the heavenly prototypes of the earthly colors.

This self-interpretation of the vision, precisely with regard to its colors, remains characteristic of the history of Christian visions. As an illustration let us cite the visionary who has recorded probably the most striking descriptions of visions in color (and of whom we have already heard an example from Peter Dronke): Hildegard of Bingen (1098-1179). Precisely through the colorfulness of her visions she already inspired the contemporary recorders of her manuscripts to produce colored miniatures, which adhere exactly to the color details of her visions.

I have selected a vision especially delighting in color, the vision of the figure of the church, which indeed already appears in the Apocalypse as the woman, the Bride of the Lamb.[1]

> Thereupon I saw how a snow-white, crystal-clear brilliancy illuminated the woman from the crown of her head to her throat. Another reddish, shimmering light bathed her figure from the throat to the middle of her body. Down to her breast this light gleamed like the red of dawn. It descended in sparkling colors of purple and hyacinth. From there, where the auroral red glowed, the figure effused its glory up into the innermost realm of heaven. Then there appeared in the midst of this orbit of light a charming little maiden. Her head was uncovered, her hair dark, almost black. A red, crease-laden tunic descended to her feet. And I listened as a voice from heaven spoke: "This is the blossom of the heavenly Zion. Mother she will be, and yet a rose blossom and a lily of the valleys. O blossom, you shall be wed to the most mighty of kings and, when you are grown stronger, when your time has come, you shall be mother to the most exalted of children."
>
> And round about the maiden I saw an enormous multitude of people, brighter than the sun, wonderfully adorned with gold and gems. Several of them were veiled. A golden ring glittered on their dazzling white veils. In the form of a circle there appeared upon these, as if engraved, that image of the ineffable Trinity which was shown me in an earlier vision. Upon their foreheads the Lamb of God became visible, upon their necks a human figure, on their right ears a cherub, on the left ones an angel; and all these forms received a golden ray from that image of the glorious Trinity. Others had miters upon their heads. The august episcopal pallium adorned their shoulders. And once again there resounded a voice from on high: "These are the daughters of Zion. Among them are zither-playing and pleasing tones of every kind, never-ending sounds of exaltation and joy upon joy."
>
> Yet beneath that radiance, which glowed like the red of dawn, I saw ascending between heaven and earth the densest darkness, so dreadful that a human tongue is incapable of describing it. Once more I heard a voice from heaven: "If the Son of God had not suffered upon the cross, this darkness would make it utterly impossible for man to reach the heavenly light."
>
> But where the light glittered in colors of purple and hyacinth, the radiancy became fixed about the figure of the woman, so that she appeared as if girded with fire.
>
> In its lowermost portion, finally, the figure was incomplete. There a last brilliancy hovered as a veil, like a dazzling white cloud.
>
> Now suddenly the three-fold radiancy bathing the figure in light effused more broadly, and in it numerous steps and staircases became visible in the most

> splendid and appropriate succession. At this sight such trembling befell me that my strength disappeared. I sank to the ground and was unable to talk. Then there drew near a brightly shining radiance, which touched me as with a hand, and I thus regained my strength and speech.

Visionary color imagery is not perceived simply as a film unrolling before the eyes of the seer; rather, the seer participates in the image: the brightly shining radiance which Hildegard beholds is not an aesthetic idea but a power. The radiance "touches her as with a hand," and this touching has an empowering and enlivening effect. The interpretation which the image gives of itself ensues through the voice of a heavenly interpreter, who is a component of the vision itself.[2]

> Now I listened as a voice said from the radiance: "These are great secrets ..."
>
> "Now behold, therefore, how the snow-white, crystal-clear radiance bathes the woman in light from the crown of her head to her throat. This is the teaching of the apostles, which proclaimed the incarnation – radiant in dazzling whiteness – of him who, as the strong and brightly shining mirror of all the faithful, descended from heaven into the womb of the Virgin. This light shone round about the church, the inviolate bride of the Son of God, from her founding and initial construction on until that time when she had grown strong enough to partake of the solid food of life. The apostles adorned, so to speak, the head of the church with the light of their teaching, for through their preaching they laid the first foundation for its construction ...
>
> "Through the teaching of the apostles and their successors the young church grew up. She became capable of truly discerning the food of salvation and she made it completely her own. She therefore blossomed to full strength. This is indicated by the red light which glowed round about the figure from the throat down to the womb. It symbolizes the perfection of those souls who betake themselves into the utmost self-discipline in order to gain strength inwardly, because with ardent love they have tasted of the heavenly sweetness. ... Thus the radiancy glows like the red of dawn from the throat down to the breast: for this perfection, which was impelled by the savor of a wonderful food, is nourished by the sweet milk of the bodily beauty of virginal purity. From the breast down to the womb the light glitters in the colors of purple and hyacinth, since these souls, strengthened through such nourishment, are arming themselves for the self-discipline of deep inward purity ...
>
> "Therefore it is from where the red of dawn glows that the figure of the church also pours forth its glory up into the innermost realm of heaven; for every perfection whose blossom is the honor of virginal purity directs its strength not below towards the earthly, but rather above, and strives, wonderfully sure

of the aim, after that which is in heaven.

"In the midst of this orbit of light, which rises on high, there appears a charming little maiden. Her head is uncovered, her hair almost black. This is the most lucid virginal purity, untouched by all the ugliness of human greeds. Her head is uncovered, for she does not bend her spirit with the shackle of depravity. But in her children, so long as they are in this world, she is unable entirely to avoid the assaults of the darkness, although she manfully struggles against it. These sufferings are indicated by her dark, almost black hair.

"She is completely enwrapped in the red tunic of toilsome effort in virtuous works, and this tunic descends, crease-laden, down to her feet – that is, virginal purity perseveres in this struggle up to its very end of all-encompassing spiritual perfection, wholly garbed in the most manifold virtues in imitation of him who here is the fullness of all holiness.

"Her progeny stand about her in a luminous chorus, more radiant than the sun, wonderfully adorned with gold and gems. For their glory shines more brightly before God than does the sun upon the earth, since they spurn themselves and thereby manfully conquer death. Hence they also appear in the marvellous array of the highest wisdom, owing to the light-filled works which they humbly consummate for Christ's sake.

"Several of them are veiled, and upon the dazzling white veil there glitters a golden ring. This is meant to intimate that those who aspire to the adornment of virginal purity must ward off every detrimental fervor from their spirit and, in the glittering embellishment of discipline, strive after the dazzling brilliancy of innocence.

"In the form of a circle there appeared upon their veils, as if engraved, the image of the ineffable Trinity ....as a sign that, in the endeavor to acquire love and constantly to practice chastity, one must unflinchingly and resolutely seek the honor of the exalted and glorious Trinity. ... All of these figures receive a golden ray from the image of the glorious Trinity engraved upon the veil, since it is the Trinity which unceasingly works the most wondrous miracles of its profound wisdom in the faithful who strive after virtue and shun diabolical temptations ...

"Thus now you see a dreadful darkness ascending beneath the brilliance which glows like the red of dawn. It is so terrifying that a human tongue is incapable of describing it.

"This is the peril of sin, which has grown for man out of the guilt of the ancestral father, the black night of unbelief ...

"But that the radiancy encircling the church becomes fixed about its figure where

> the light glitters in colors of purple and hyacinth, so that it appears as if girded with fire, signifies the perfection of those souls who in burning love imitate the suffering of my Son and through their strict self-discipline come to grace the church in the highest way."

This is now interpreted in detail as regards the different statuses in the church, for which definite spiritual rules are set up.

Apostleship and the priesthood are the builders of the church, virginal purity and monasticism its finest adornment. But it is through the laity that the church attains the full complement of its members. It is, above all, marriage which constantly tenders the church new souls and through this continual growth leads it towards its ultimate consummation. "Thus a last brilliancy hovered obscuringly, like a dazzling white cloud, over that part of the church which is yet incomplete. Kings and dukes, princes and leaders with their subordinates, rich and poor, the entire people that devoutly observes the commandments of God in the world – they all contribute to the noble embellishment of the church."

"Suddenly the three-fold radiancy bathing the virgin church in light effuses more broadly, and in it numerous steps and staircases become visible in the most splendid and appropriate succession."

The priesthood, the status of perfection (virginal purity and the monastic orders), and the laity radiate the three-fold brilliance which enrobes the church with luminous beauty. The brilliance effuses more broadly – i.e., it manifests the vitality of the church, which again and again breaks forth in new offshoots and constitutes the fullness of virtues through which the church itself gains strength and at the same time leads its children on high to their heavenly home. " ' Thus in the midst of the brilliancy a row of steps and staircases also appears in the most splendid and appropriate succession. They symbolize the manifold gradations in the spiritual and worldly estates which consummate the beauty of the mystical body of Christ through their divinely ordained conjunction, and which prepare the way to heaven for the children of the church.' "

Whereas, in the realm of visions having as subjects scenes of the heavenly or spiritual world, colors appear which are always clearly distinct and are interpreted in a definite way, it is otherwise with the visions of God. The divine light is inaccessible to the human eye, even to the eye of the seer. Should the seer be deemed worthy of a manifestation of God at all, then it appears to him only in the veil of a fiery cloud or, if in color, in the form of the rainbow, the spectrum of all the colors. The rainbow appears already in the vision of God which fell to the prophet Ezekiel, which is described in the first chapter of the book of Ezekiel.

This vision takes a very complicated course. It begins (Ezek. 1:4): "As I looked, behold, a stormy wind came out of the north, and a great cloud, with brightness round about it, and fire flashing forth continually, and in the midst of the fire, as it were gleaming bronze." In this fiery cloud with its bright kernel of light there first appear heavenly figures (v. 5): "And from the midst of it came the likeness of four living creatures ... They had the form of men." These heavenly beings are then described in detail. With regard to their colors, "there was something that looked like burning coals of fire, like torches moving to and fro among the living creatures; and the fire was bright, and out of the fire went forth lightning" (v. 13). Next appear the heavenly wheels, which constitute the wheels of the throne of God: "The Spirit of the living creatures was in the wheels" (v. 20). It is only at this point that the appearance of the glory of the Lord Himself then emerges out of the preparatory manifestations of the animals and the wheels.

> And above the firmament over [the living creatures'] heads there was the likeness of a throne, in appearance like sapphire; and seated above the likeness of a throne was a likeness as it were of a human form. And upward from what had the appearance of his loins I saw as it were gleaming bronze, like the appearance of fire enclosed round about; and downward from what had the appearance of his loins I saw as it were the appearance of fire, and there was brightness round about him. Like the appearance of the bow that is in the cloud on the day of rain, so was the appearance of the brightness round about. Such was the appearance of the likeness of the glory of the Lord. And when I saw it, I fell upon my face, and I heard the voice of one speaking. (vv. 26-28)

There follows out of the brightness of the cloud the divine charge to the prophet.

Whereas here in Ezekiel's vision of God the luminous appearance of the glory of God is *compared* to a rainbow, in the vision of God in the Johannine Apocalypse the rainbow constitutes the manifestation of the Lord Himself. There the appearance of the Son of Man, described in the first three chapters, turns into an epiphany of God.

> After this I looked, and lo, in heaven an open door! And the first voice, which I had heard speaking to me like a trumpet [the voice of the Son of Man], said, "Come up hither, and I will show you what must take place after this." At once I was in the Spirit, and lo, a throne stood in heaven, with one seated on the

> throne! And he who sat there appeared like jasper and carnelian, and round the throne was a rainbow that looked like an emerald. Round the throne were twenty-four thrones, and seated on the thrones were twenty-four elders, clad in white garments, with golden crowns upon their heads. From the throne issue flashes of lightning, and voices and peals of thunder, and before the throne burn seven torches of fire, which are the seven spirits of God. (Rev. 4:1-5)

Here too the nucleus of the vision is an intangible figure: "with *one* seated on the throne" – but his figure is described with regard to the colorful brilliance which it radiates, and his colors are iridescent and fluid and play into one another like the colors of gems ("and round the throne was a rainbow that looked like an emerald").

The rainbow appears yet a third time in the manifestation of the angel of revelation, who brings down from heaven the little scroll that the seer is to consume. In the descent of the angel of revelation is repeated the very epiphany of God.

"Then I saw another mighty angel coming down from heaven, wrapped in a cloud, with a rainbow over his head, and his face was like the sun, and his legs like pillars of fire. He had a little scroll open in his hand. And he set his right foot on the sea, and his left foot on the land." (Rev. 10:1-2)

The mutual interpenetration of three colors is the characteristic mark of later visions of God, of which we have already met Hildegard of Bingen's vision of the Holy Trinity. This can be supplemented by a similar vision of the divine Trinity to be found in Saint Birgitta (1303-73), as occasioned by her looking upon the heavenly book as the representation of the divine word. The vision runs as follows:

> And immediately, in the selfsame instant, I beheld in the sky a house of wondrous beauty and size, and in the house there was a desk, upon which lay a book, and in front of the desk I saw two figures standing, namely an angel and a devil ...
>
> As I now attentively and with my entire inner cogitation gazed upon the desk, my understanding was insufficient to grasp it as it was; my soul was unable to comprehend its beauty, nor could my tongue give expression to the same! One looked upon it as one would a stream of rays from the sun, which had red, white, and shining golden colors. The golden color shone like the sun, the white color was like brightly gleaming snow, and the red color resembled a red rose. And each color was to be seen in the other, for when I looked at the golden color, I saw in it the white and the red colors, and when I looked at the white color, I saw in it both the other colors. It was similar when I viewed the red color. Thus each was seen in the other, and yet each was separate from the other, and in

> itself none was earlier or later, smaller or larger than the others; rather, in every respect and throughout they were seen as equal. And when I gazed upwards, I was unable to grasp the length and breadth of the desk, but when I gazed downwards, I was unable to take in the immensity of its depth, since viewing everything was inconceivable.
>
> Afterwards, however, I saw upon the desk a book, which glittered like the most gleaming gold and was opened. But its text was not written with ink; instead, every word in the book was alive and spoke of its own accord, as if someone said: "Do this or that!" and as if, as soon as the word was spoken, it also were done. No one read the text of the book; rather, everything contained in the work was seen upon the desk and in those colors.[3]

The vision proceeds in several clearly distinct stages. First the seer beholds in the sky a house of wondrous beauty and size, a heavenly palace, and in the house a desk upon which lies a book. This is disclosed to be the book of divine revelation, a representation of the divine word. The divine glory is revealed, which overlies the desk and the book. Three colors are in motion in this epiphany of the glory of God, which "appears as a stream of rays from the sun." But they are not divided into three different spheres; instead, each color is present in each and is visible in each, three in one and one in three. They reflect the mystery of the divine Trinity. Then in a third phase the desk re-appears in the brightness, but in a dimension of immensity, and upon it is the book itself, glittering in gleaming gold. The book commences to confirm its divine qualities in a wondrous way: it is not written with ink, but consists of words that are speaking.

Every word of the book is alive and speaks of its own accord; moreover, it not only speaks, its speaking is a creative action. As soon as a word is articulated, it is also already realized. The book, moreover, is not read in terms of a successive deciphering of letters; rather, the contents of the book reveal themselves and are radiated forth in the colors of the divine garment of light which encloses it. Here we have it quite unequivocally stated: the divine word reveals itself in colors. "Everything which the book of divine revelation contains and effects is seen in those colors."

The Theology of Color

Now not all visionaries were theologians, but among the theologians there is a line of visionaries who developed a theology of color out of their visions. This theology of color is the subject of our following considerations.

It is impossible even to intimate the history of the theology of color. It occupies a much larger place in the history of Western theology than is usually expressed in school presentations; it extends from the earliest inceptions of Christian theology among the apostolic fathers right into the beginnings of modern scientific optics and theories of color. Here we can only stress some characteristic turning-points in the history of the theology of color. In doing so, attention should above all be paid to those thinkers whose theology was itself inspired by their own visionary experiences, who thus did not just repeat handed down, extrinsic ideas, but instead formulated their theological views under the impact of their own religious experiences.

Dionysius the Areopagite

Here we ought first to speak of that enigmatic theologian, Dionysius the Areopagite, who since the era of his discovery in the West has influenced Western theology in the most vigorous way. His works were translated from the original Greek into Latin by the famous John Scotus Eriugena, in the commission of Charles the Bald. The mystical theologian who masks himself behind the name "Dionysius the Areopagite" is a Syrian mystic of the fifth century, writing in Greek, who is strongly molded by the Neoplatonic philosophical tradition.

It is the name – Dionysius the Areopagite – that has lent his works special eminence in the West, in connection with the authoritarian focus of Western medieval theology: Dionysius, council member of the Areopagus law court, is the follower of the apostle Paul, mentioned in the book of Acts, who was converted by Paul to the Christian faith (Acts 17:34). In the Middle Ages, theologians considered the writings of this Neoplatonic theologian to be those of an immediate follower of the apostle, who according to Eusebius was the first bishop of Athens. As regards their authoritative rank and ecclesiastical status, they figured directly next to the letters of the apostle Paul, and laid claim to containing apostolic teaching. Their esteem followed immediately upon that of the New Testament. This also explains the immense prestige evinced by these writings in the entire Western theological tradition up to Thomas Aquinas, but primarily as well in the German mysticism – inspired by Thomism – of a Meister Eckhart or a Tauler. It was only in the period of the Renaissance that the authenticity of the writings of the Areopagite was doubted by Laurentius Valla and other pioneers of historical criticism such as Erasmus.

The theology of color found in the Areopagite is directly connected with his theology of light.

> Calling, then, upon Jesus, the Light of the Father, the Real, the True, "Which lighteth every man that cometh into the world, by Whom we have access to the Father," the Origin of Light, let us raise our thought, according to our power, to the illuminations of the most sacred doctrines handed down by the Fathers, and also, as far as we may, let us contemplate the Hierarchies of the Celestial Intelligences revealed to us by them in symbols for our upliftment: and admitting through the spiritual and unwavering eyes of the mind the original and super-original Gift of Light of the Father Who is the Source of Divinity, which shows to us images of the all-blessed Hierarchies of the Angels in figurative symbols, let us through them again strive upwards towards Its Primal Ray. For this Light can never be deprived of Its own intrinsic unity, and although in goodness, as is fitting, It becomes a manyness and proceeds into manifestation for the upliftment and unification of those creatures which are governed by Its Providence, yet It abides eternally within Itself in changeless sameness, firmly established in Its own unity, and elevates to Itself, according to their capacity, those who turn towards It, as is meet, uniting them in accordance with Its own unity. For by that first Divine Ray we can be enlightened only in so far as It is hidden by all-various holy veils for our upliftment, and fittingly tempered to our natures by the Providence of the Father.[4]

God is the primeval light, the light beyond light, which is inaccessible, and which the Areopagite also characterizes as the divine darkness. Out of it goes forth the divine Logos, Jesus Christ the Son, as the initial light, which disperses the illumination of divine truth throughout the different levels of the creation. The Jewish prohibition of images is replaced with a theology of icons. Instead of, "You shall not make for yourself a graven image or any likeness," it is now affirmed that God is the first maker of images and icons, for He has figured Himself in His Son, the reflection of His glory and the likeness of His nature (Hebrews 1:3).

The saints are the images of Christ. Here, then, the Christian idea of the Logos, as well as that of the Incarnation, the descension of the divine Logos into the flesh, are fitted into the Neoplatonic schema of the emanation of the divine primeval light. The fundamental presupposition for this descension of the divine light is the hierarchical arrangement of the creation. The world above, the celestial hierarchy, is the world of the celestial spirits, who were created first. The earthly hierarchy is the church, the institution of salvation created by God. It is to lead back into the upper hierarchy the community of the elect of mankind on this earth, which was created after the revolt of the angels as a substitution for the rebels expelled from heaven to replenish the kingdom of God. Thus the first book of the Areòpagite treats the celestial hierarchy, the realm of the heavenly spirits, and the second book the ecclesiastical hierarchy, the realm of the church, through whose sacraments the initiates are led to the hierarchy above.

The basic idea of the theology of light is that no one can look upon the primeval divine light itself. God "dwells in unapproachable light, whom no man has ever seen or can see," Paul writes to his fellow-apostle Timothy (I Tim. 6:16), who characteristically also appears as the recipient of the dedicatory letter of the Areopagite at the beginning of his work on the celestial hierarchy. This idea is accordingly repeated regularly in both writings of the Areopagite. "For neither is it without danger to gaze upon the glorious rays of the sun with weak eyes."[5] The primeval divine light reveals itself only in that, corresponding to the powers of comprehension of the creatures of the lower spheres, it garbs itself in envelopments, symbols, analogies and images.

Here is also the locus of the colors. Colors are the veils of the divine primeval light in its descent and its radiation into the lower worlds. Moving downwards, the divine light differentiates itself into the individual colors on the various levels, in accordance with the assimilative capacity of those belonging to these levels. At the same time, however, the divine light works in an anagogical sense, in that it leads the initiates of the lower realms back again from one level to another into divine oneness. Returning the colors to the radiant whiteness of the light of the Logos corresponds to the differentiation of the divine light into the color spectrum.

This ascent and descent comes to pass, however, through an ordered hierarchy of teachers and a corresponding system of mysteries. Not just anyone, moreover, can enter into this process of participation in the celestial light; rather, it is for the consecrated initiate alone, the *thyasótes*, who belongs to the *thýasos* of those enlightened by the divine light. The purpose of this hierarchical structure is the initiate's greatest possible similitude to, and becoming one with, God.

> By taking Him as Leader in all holy wisdom, [the aim of Hierarchy is] to become like Him, so far as is permitted, by contemplating intently His most Divine Beauty. Also it moulds and perfects its participants ["participants:" in the Greek text *thyasótai*, i.e. participants in a *thýasos*] in the holy image of God like

> bright and spotless mirrors which receive the Ray of the Supreme Deity Which is the Source of Light; and being mystically filled with the Gift of Light, it pours it forth again abundantly, according to the Divine Law, upon those below itself.[6]

The designation of the participants as *thyasótai* is taken from the parlance of the ancient mysteries. So too, further transmission of the Christian mysteries is subject to the ancient rule of the esoteric mystery cults, which is expressed in a New Testament image: "Treasuring deep in the soul the holy Mysteries, preserve them in their unity from the unpurified multitude: for, as the Scriptures declare, it is not fitting to cast before swine that pure and beautifying and clear-shining glory of the intelligible pearls."[7] (cf. Matthew 7:6) Thus the divine light disseminates itself into ever more colorful pencils of radiation; it enlightens the members of the particular stages in the celestial hierarchy, and each one so enlightened passes the divine rays on to those of the next grade who are called to enlightenment.

> Those who are illuminated should be filled full with Divine Light, ascending to the contemplative state and power with the most pure eyes of the mind ... Those who illuminate, as possessing more luminous intelligence, duly receiving and again shedding forth the light, and joyously filled with holy brightness, should impart their own overflowing light to those worthy of it.[8]

In this connection the Areopagite marks a direct analogy between the physical laws of optics – and thereby also of the optics of colors – and the laws for the emanation of the divine light.

> Thus, according to the same law of the material order, the Fount of all order, visible and invisible, supernaturally shows forth the glory of Its own radiance in all-blessed outpourings of first manifestation to the highest beings, and through them those below them participate in the Divine Ray.[9]

Accordingly, in the work on the celestial hierarchy colors are initially spoken of in connection with the angels. For the realm of the angels is the highest and the first sphere of the Creation; in it the light falling from heaven first differentiated itself into a color spectrum. In the interpretation in *The Celestial Hierarchies* of Biblical passages that speak of the luminous attire of the angels we read:

> Their shining and fiery vesture [cf. Luke 24:4; Ezekiel 1:4, 13, 14, 27; Daniel 10:6] symbolizes, I think, the Divine Likeness under the image of fire, and their own enlightening power, because they abide in Heaven, where Light is: and also it shows that they impart wholly intelligible Light, and are enlightened

intellectually.[10]

And similarly in another passage:

> The Scriptures also liken the Celestial Beings to brass and electron, and many coloured jewels ["many coloured jewels:" cf. Ezekiel 28:13, Rev. 15:6]. Now electron [an alloy of gold and silver], resembling both gold and silver, is like gold in its resistance to corruption, unspent and undiminished, and its undimmed brightness; and is like silver in its shining and heavenly lustre. But the symbolism of brass ... must resemble that of fire or gold. Again, of the many coloured varieties of stones, the white represents that which is luminous, and the red corresponds to fire, yellow to gold, and green to youth and vigour. Thus corresponding to each figure you will find a mystical interpretation which relates these symbolical images to the things above.[11]

Correspondingly, the colors of the horses of the Apocalyptic riders in Revelation 6:2ff. are also given an anagogical, spiritual interpretation:

> The symbolism of horses represents obedience and tractability. The shining white horses denote clear truth and that which is perfectly assimilated to the Divine Light; the dark, that which is hidden and secret; the red, fiery might and energy; the dappled black and white, that power which traverses all and connects the extremes, providentially and with perfecting power uniting the highest to the lowest and the lowest to the highest.[12]

The spiritual interpretation of colors is correspondingly repeated at the level of the church. The earthly church is analogous to, and corresponds with, the heavenly church above. Its sacraments, symbols, and ceremonies matchingly reflect the orderings of the church above, and the colors of the church correspond to those of the angelic world. This is true not only of the colors of the liturgical vestments, but also of the colors used in church icon painting. In this connection the Areopagite himself employs the simile of the painter: the earthly copy or image has the function of reflecting and leading to the heavenly original.

> As in the case of sensible images, if the artist looks without distraction upon the archetypal form, not distracted by sight of anything else, or in any way divided in attention, he will duplicate, if I may so speak, the very person that is being sketched, whoever he may be, and will shew the reality in the likeness, and the archetype in the image, and each in each, save the difference of substance; thus, to copyists who love the beautiful in mind, the persistent and unflinching contemplation of the sweet-savoured and hidden beauty will confer the unerring and most Godlike appearance. ... After the Divine example ... they are Divine images of the most supremely Divine sweetness, which, having the truly sweet within itself, is not turned to the anomalously seeming of the multitude, moulding

> Its genuineness to the true images of Itself.[13]

Meister Eckhart, with his imaginal intuition, took this idea further in that he spoke of how the soul itself there becomes divinely colored (*gotfär*) where it touches God with its tip.

For the church, there holds the general principle of the descent of the divine light through the stages of the hierarchy:

> Naturally, then, the Head and Foundation of all good order, invisible and visible, causes the deifying rays to approach the more Godlike first, and through them, as being more transparent Minds, and more properly adapted for reception and transmission of Light, transmits light and manifestations to the subordinate, in proportions suitable to them.[14]

The light of the upper hierarchies is reflected in the enigmatic, colorful integument of the ceremonies of the church's mysteries.

> Let us, then, as I said, leave behind these things [the ceremonies], beautifully depicted upon the entrance of the innermost shrine [*adyton*], as being sufficient for those, who are yet incomplete for contemplation, and let us proceed from the effects to the causes; and then, Jesus lighting the way, we shall view our holy Synaxis, and the comely contemplation of things intelligible, which makes radiantly manifest the blessed beauty of the archetypes. But, oh, most Divine and holy initiation, uncovering the folds of the dark mysteries enveloping thee in symbols, be manifest to us in thy bright glory, and fill our intellectual visions with single and unconcealed light.[15]

This is especially true of the mystery of the Eucharist, which reflects and anticipates the central content of the divine revelation, the descent of the divine Logos into the flesh.

> So, too, the Divine initiation (sacrament) of the Synaxis, although it has a unique, and simple, and enfolded Source, is multiplied, out of love towards man, into the holy variety of the symbols, and travels through the whole range of the supremely Divine description; yet uniformly it is again collected from these, into its own proper Monady, and unifies those who are being reverently conducted towards it.[16]

The interpretation of the anagogical purport of the mysteries, however, is reserved solely for him who has already advanced to the spiritual meaning and is illuminated by the divine light, and who is capable of becoming a leader for the others upon the path of ascension to the primordial divine light:

> For, as in the case of the bright shining of the sun, the more delicate and luminous substances, being first filled with the brilliancy flowing into them, brightly impart their overflowing light to things after them; so it is not tolerable that one, who has not become altogether Godlike in his whole character, and proved to be in harmony with the Divine influence and judgment, should become Leader to others, in the altogether divine.[17] (cp. Acts 1:24)

Jakob Boehme

In the later development of the theology of color, Jakob Boehme (1575-1624) plays a special role. Not only did his natural theology influence the esoteric schools of his own time – those of the successors to Paracelsus, of the English Philadelphians, and the Dutch Boehmenists, to which belonged many physicians and scientific researchers – but he also had an effect upon the sphere of English science: Newton was very strongly influenced by Boehme in his cosmological views. Most of all, however, despite all the church persecution, in Germany itself the teachings of Jakob Boehme have seen ever new periods of renaissance. The first significant thinker who rediscovered him, and made him the basis of his theosophy, was Friedrich Christoph Oetinger (1702-82), the visionary founder of the theosophical direction of Swabian Pietism. After Oetinger came his philosophical students, above all Schelling, Hegel, and Franz von Baader. Thanks to translations of him by Saint Martin, Boehme also exerted a great influence upon French philosophy. Saint Martin characterized himself as a student of Boehme.[18]

Jakob Boehme's precepts on color are intimately connected with his teaching about the seven spirits of God – a Christian parallel to the Cabalistic doctrine of the *Sephiroth*, the emanations of God. Out of the innermost dark depths of his being, God presses towards self-revelation, towards the manifestation of his essence. This process takes place as a "disclosure of the wonders of God"; it is this process of which the colors are also a part. What makes Boehme different from the Cabala is the fact that, under the influence of the basic Christian notion of the Incarnation, he stresses more strongly the idea that corporeality is the goal of the self-revelation of God. This is already true of his teaching on the seven spirits. The final form of the seven spirits of God is "eternal nature," which realizes itself in the Creation.

> In the day and the hour when the creation was accomplished in mystery, and was set as a mirror of eternity in the wonders [of this time]. That took place on the sixth day, past noon. There [also in the end] the mystery with the

wonders is revealed and is known.[19]

The colors belong to the mystery of the divine nature, the mystery of the Incarnation of God; they emerge in the wake of this radiation of God, this path of His self-incarnation and self-imaging. Thus further on in the *Mysterium Pansophicum* we read:

> For the first revealer, viz. God, ordained not malignity to the government, but reason or wit, which was to reveal the wonders and be a guide of life. And here there meets us the great secret which has from eternity existed in mystery, viz. the Mystery with its colours, which are four. The fifth is not proper to the mysterium of Nature, but is of the Mysterium of God, and shines in the mysterium of Nature as a living light.
>
> And these are the colours wherein all things lie: blue, red, green and yellow. The fifth, white, belongs to God; and yet has also its lustre in Nature. It is the fifth essence, a pure unblemished child; as is to be seen in gold and silver, and in a white clear stone that resists fire.
>
> For fire is the proof or trial of all the colours, in which none subsists but white, the same being a reflection of God's Majesty. The black colour belongs not to the mystery [of the wonders of creation], but is the veil or the darkness wherein all things lie.[20]

Corresponding to these four basic colors, in which is revealed the mystery of Nature, are the four "tongues" – i.e., languages and alphabets, the foremost of which is the language of Nature as the fifth or the first tongue. This analogy needs to be grasped in its complete meaning: directly corresponding to the revelation of the mystery of Nature in the colors is the revelation in languages. Thus, immediately following upon the preceding quotation, Boehme writes:

> Further, we find here the tree of tongues or languages, with four alphabets. One signed with the characters of the Mystery, in which is found the language of Nature, which in all languages is the root. But in the birth of plurality (or of many languages) it is not known save by its own children, to whom the Mystery itself gives understanding; for it is a wonder of God. This alphabet of the language of Nature is hidden among them all in the black colour; for the black colour belongs not to the number of colours. The same is mystery and not understood, save by him who possesses the language of Nature, to whom it is revealed by God's Spirit.[21]

Hebrew, Greek, and Latin are then named as further languages, tongues, or alphabets. The text then continues:

> The fifth is God's Spirit, which is the revealer of all alphabets; and this alphabet can no man learn, unless it reveal itself in man's spirit.
>
> These alphabets take their origin from the colours of the great Mystery, and distribute themselves moreover into seventy-seven languages.[22]

The plurality of languages corresponds, therefore, to the rainbow's color spectrum, the "great Mystery."

Crucial here is the fact that the colors do not appear as "chimera" of the creation, but instead are connected with the self-revelation of God. They belong to the "source" (*Quaal*) of the essence of all beings, whereby Boehme, in a naive etymological interpretation, understands *Quaal* to be the corresponding German word for the Latin *qualitas* (quality).

> And thus we understand here the essence of all beings, and that it is a magical essence, as a will can create itself in the essential life, and so enter into a birth, and in the great Mystery, in the origin of fire, awaken a source which before was not manifest, but lay hidden in mystery like a gleam in the multiplicity of colours.[23]

The colors were hidden in the gleam – the gleam in that which is designated in the first passage above as the "Mysterium of God." The colors are still covered over with "the veil or the darkness wherein all things lie," but in the "mysterium of Nature" they issue forth, as does the gleam, which belongs to the "Mysterium of God" and "shines in the mysterium of Nature as a living light."

Thus it is understandable that the colors also appear in the table of the macrocosm, which is Table III of the *Tabulae Principiorum*. This table bears the following caption:

> In this Table is signified how the hidden, spiritual, eternal World (as the *Mysterium Magnum*) by the Motion of God's Word issued forth, and became visible, manifest, and material; [and how from the Properties creatures were created, in which one should understand the inner spiritual world to be hidden;] and how the inward Powers, through God's working, have comprehended and fashioned themselves; how Good and Bad in every thing is to be understood; and yet there was no Evil in *Mysterium Magnum*, but existed through the Sensibility and Assumption of Self-Desire. [Out of this Ground came forth all the creatures (of the visible world).] Here also is shewed what in the Working issued forth from every Property, and which [among the seven] have the Predominancy; according to which every thing is formed and governed.[24]

Now in the table a whole system of categories is drawn up, of which the colors are also a part. The different realms to which they appertain can be gleaned from the table – e.g., the constellations (the theory of colors as a component of astrology), the elements (the theory of colors as a component of alchemy), the temperaments (the theory of colors as a component of psychology), the realms of the animal and plant worlds, etc. In the lowermost corner of the right-hand row of the seventh quality, which corresponds to white, stands Sophia, whom Boehme described as the "body" or the "housing" of God, through which the corporeal manifestation of God takes place.

If we wish to pursue Boehme's theology of color still further here, we come upon a realm which is difficult to translate into our contemporary conceptual language and mode of thought. Boehme lives in a world of knowledge which is determined by quaking visions and flashing intuitions, whose trains of thought move within a world of images, analogies, correspondences, and symbols. The background to this is incomprehensible for us – today, indeed, in an age of predominantly conceptual thinking focussed upon information, it is still less comprehensible than for those belonging to earlier periods of thought. In Boehme's language of imagery, pictorial elements of alchemy and astrology are joined with the entire world of images of the Old and New Testaments in a mystical-allegorical interpretation, whereby traditional features are blended with Boehme's own intuitive insights. The unravelling of all the threads of this linguistic fabric is extraordinarily difficult. Even if it were successful, a mere heap of threads would perhaps remain, but the design of the fabric would be destroyed. In the first part of his work, *Of the Incarnation of Jesus Christ*, Boehme writes in Chapter II, "Manifestation of the Deity by the Creation of Angels and Men from Divine Essence":

> Seeing then there has thus been a mystery from eternity, we are now to consider its manifestation. We can speak of eternity only as of a spirit, for the whole has been spirit only; and yet from eternity has generated itself into substance by desire and longing. We can in no wise say that in eternity there has not been substance, for no fire exists without substance. So also there is no gentleness without the production of substance. For the gentleness produces water, and the fire swallows this up and transforms it in itself, one part into heavens and firmament, and the other part into sulphur, wherein the fire-spirit with its wheel of essences makes a mercury, then awakens Vulcan (that is, strikes fire), by which the third spirit or air is generated. In the middle is found the noble tincture, as a lustre with colours, and has its rise originally from the wisdom of God. Every colour remains with its essence in the gentleness of the water-

fountain, black excepted, which has its origin from the sour fierceness.[25]

Accordingly, in Jakob Boehme's description of God's revelation, the colors initially appear in the sphere of the creatures created first, namely the angels. The will of God for self-revelation presses towards a bodily representation of His fullness in a realm of spiritual-corporeal figures, the realm of the angels, the founding of which constitutes the first act of the creation. The angels compose the realm of free spirits, which are created after the image of God. Their corporeality-in-the-spirit is determined by the combined action of the seven spirits of God, which characterize God's hidden life. In the angels too the seventh figure, the seventh spirit, brings the first six to corporeality.

> When the Deity moved itself to the creating of angels, then in *every* circle, wherein each angel was incorporated or compacted together, there the Deity, with its *whole substance* and being, was *incorporated* or compacted together, ... and became a body, and yet the Deity continued in its *seat*, as before.
> Every angel is created in the *seventh* qualifying or fountain spirit, which is Nature, out of which his body is compacted or incorporated together, and his body is given him for a propriety ...
> For the body is the incorporated or compacted spirit of nature, and encompasseth or encloseth the other six spirits; these generate themselves *in the body*, just as it is in the *Deity*.[26]

This general determination of the angels' corporeality-in-the-spirit, however, by no means implies identity and uniformity as regards their being, their form, or their appearance. Rather, they all bear the character of personality. In all of them the divine primordial image finds individual expression in a personal structuring of their spiritual-corporeal nature. At numerous points in his work Boehme provides a detailed picture of the angelic realm and its different personalities and communities. In the *Aurora* – Boehme's earliest writing (1612), after a "glimpse into the being of all beings" had been revealed to him – we already find a first image outlined which is striking in that distinctions between the individual angels are described according to the different colors of their spirituality. There we read:

> Here thou must know that the angels are *not* all of one quality, neither are they equal or alike to one another in power and might: Indeed *every* angel hath the power of all the seven qualifying or fountain spirits, but in every one there is somewhat of one quality more predominant and strong than another, and according to that quality is he also glorified.
> For such as the *Salitter* was in every place, at the time of creation, such also was

> the angel that came forth; and according to *that* quality which is strongest in an angel, he is also named and glorified.
> As [in] the *flowers* in the meadows, every one receiveth its colour from its quality, and is named also according to its quality, so are the holy angels also:
> Some are strongest in the *astringent* quality, and those are of a brownish light, and are nearest of quality to the cold.
> So when the light of the Son of God shineth on them, then they are like a brownish or *purple* flash of lightning, very bright and clear in their quality.
> Some are of the quality of the *water*, and those are light, like the holy heaven; and when the light shineth on them, then they look like to a *crystalline* sea.
> Some are strongest in the *bitter* quality, and they are like a green precious stone, which sparkleth like a flash of lightning; and when the light shineth on them, then they shine and appear as a *greenish red*, as if a carbuncle did shine forth from it, or as if the life had its original there.
> Some are of the quality of *heat*, and they are the lightest and brightest of all, *yellowish* and reddish; and when the light shineth on them, they look like the flash or lightning of the Son of God.
> Some are strongest in the quality of *love*, and those are a glance of the heavenly joyfulness, very light and *bright*; and when the light shineth on them, they look like *light blue*, of a pleasant gloss, glance or lustre.
> Some are strongest in the quality of the *tone* or sound, and those are light or bright also; and when the light shineth on them, they *look* like the *rising* of the flash of lightning, as if something would lift itself aloft there.
> Some are of the quality of the *total* or whole nature, as a general mixture; and when the light shineth on them, they look like the holy *heaven*, which is formed out of all the spirits of God. ...
> Only in the colours and *strength* of power is there a difference, but *no* difference at all in the perfection; for every one hath in him the power of all the spirits of God; therefore when the light of the Son of God shineth on them, then each angel's quality sheweth itself by the *colour*. ...
> For as the Deity presenteth itself *infinitely* in its rising up, so there are unsearchable *varieties* of colour and form among the angels: I can shew thee no *right* similitude of it in this world, unless it be in a *blossoming* field of flowers in *May*, which yet is but a *dead* and earthly type.[27]

Thus colors belong to the primordial forms of the divine being and represent definite primordial qualities. They appear in connection with the self-revelation of God in the mystery of nature, in which the cover of darkness is taken away by the divine radiance. The colors possess a certain revelatory character, which is of the greatest significance in the interpretation of the nature of earthly and heavenly things. Boehme always pays special heed to this revelatory character in his interpretation of the "signature" of things. Thus, in the passage just quoted, by way of analogy in interpreting the colorfulness of the angels, he points to the meaning of the flowers' colors in springtime meadows as a "signature" of their being. The colors descend from heaven, they are refracted in the different realms of the creation. Our earthly colors are but pale reflections, "dead and earthly types" of the rainbow of the heavenly colors, which settles round about the throne of God and in which blazes forth his glory. On the other hand, on all levels of being and life – even the lowest – the colors of things reveal ever again the selfsame primordial powers which have taken part in the creation of the corporeality of the creature concerned.

Swedenborg

The theology of color then underwent a significant further evolution with Emanuel Swedenborg (1688-1772). Swedenborg's development was unique in that he went from scientist to visionary. His visionary gift broke through relatively late, when he was fifty-seven years of age (1745), and after the impossibility of arriving at a total view of the universe on his accustomed path of analytical experimental science had become clear to him through a number of unnerving experiences. Swedenborg's visions likewise describe the heavenly world as a colorful one. His visions are so graphic that they have inspired great artists to reproduce them in color pictures. The drawings of William Blake (1757-1827), who himself displayed a visionary giftedness, are partially inspired through Swedenborg's visions. If Swedenborg must be mentioned here, it is not only because he had visions, but also because – as a visionary with a decidedly systematic scientific education – he outlined a theology of vision in which color has great significance. One finds this theology of color most clearly expressed in his great work, *Arcana Coelestia – The Heavenly Arcana*,[28] which presents a typological, allegorical interpretation of the book of Genesis. It is in this respect comparable to the *Mysterium Magnum* of Jakob Boehme. Swedenborg's theology of color is above all to be found in his interpretation of Genesis 13, located in the chapter concerning the light in which the angels live and their paradises and abodes. Here he first of all develops his notion of correspondences: all the images and forms of the lower stages of being are images and correspondences of the higher stages of being. The images and forms of the earthly world consist of prototypes and correspondences of the spiritual [*geistig*] world, and its images are in turn prototypes and correspondences of the heavenly world. The visionary, whose inward eye is opened, sees that which the ordinary man does not see with his physical eye, namely the things of the spiritual world, and he recognizes the correlational character of the things of this world.

Swedenborg knows himself to be endowed by God with the special gift of grace of being able to understand and attest to the correlational character and spiritual meaning of everything earthly; he sees the significance of the things of the spiritual world in being prototypes and correspondences of the earthly things. Thus he writes in the aforementioned work:

> Par. 1619. When man's interior sight is opened, which is the sight of his spirit, the things in the other life appear, which cannot possibly be made visible to the sight of the body [i.e., as visionary he sees with the opened inward eye of his spirit the things of the other life, the things of the spiritual world, which the ordinary man with his ordinary eyes cannot see]. The visions of the prophets were nothing else [i.e., Swedenborg identifies the gift bestowed upon him – the opening of the inner eye – with the gift of grace imparted to the prophets: to him, as to them, it is granted to behold the things of the other world]. In heaven, as has been said, there are continual representations of the Lord and His kingdom; and there are things that are significative; and this to such an extent that nothing exists before the sight of the angels that is not representative and significative [i.e., that does not contain a prototype, a sign (signature) of the heavenly world]. Thence come the representatives and significatives in the Word; for the Word is from the Lord through heaven.
>
> Par. 1620. The things presented to view in the world of spirits and in heaven [i.e., visible to the eyes of the spirit] are more than can be told. In this place, as the light is treated of, it is proper to tell of the things that are immediately from the light: such as the atmospheres, the paradisal and rainbow scenes, the palaces and dwellings, which are there so bright and living before the outer sight of spirits and angels, and are at the same time perceived so fully by every sense, that they say that these are real, and those in the world comparatively not real.
>
> Par. 1621. As regards the atmospheres in which the blessed live, which are of the light because from that light, they are numberless, and are of beauty and pleasantness so great that they cannot be described. There are diamond-like atmospheres, which glitter in all their least parts, as if they were composed of diamond spherules. There are atmospheres resembling the sparkling of all the precious stones. There are atmospheres as of great pearls translucent from their centers, and shining with the brightest colors. There are atmospheres that flame as from gold, also from silver, and also from diamond-like gold and silver. There are atmospheres of flowers of variegated hue that are in forms most minute and scarcely discernible; such, in endless variety, fill the heaven of infants. ... There are other kinds besides, for the varieties are innumerable, and are also unspeakable.
>
> Par. 1622. As regards the paradisal scenes, they are amazing. Paradisal gardens are presented to view of immense extent, consisting of trees of every kind, and of beauty and pleasantness so great as to surpass every idea

> of thought; and these gardens are presented with such life before the external sight that those who are there not only see them, but perceive every particular much more vividly than the sight of the eye perceives such things on earth. [I.e., the intensity of perception with spiritual sight is much greater and sharper than is the case with the physical eye.]

Swedenborg then appeals again to his own visionary experiences:

> That I might not be in doubt respecting this, I was brought to the region where those are who live a paradisal life, and I saw it; it is in front of and a little above the corner of the right eye. Each and all things there appear in their most beautiful spring-time and flower, with a magnificence and variety that are amazing; and they are living, each and all, because they are representatives; for there is nothing that does not represent and signify something celestial and spiritual. Thus they not only affect the sight with pleasantness, but also the mind with happiness.

Swedenborg then cites the testimony of several deceased people with whom he had had opportunity to speak:

> Certain souls, new-comers from the world – who, from principles received while they lived, doubted the possibility of such things existing in the other life, where there is no wood and stone – being taken up thither and speaking thence with me, said in their amazement that it was beyond words, and that they could in no way represent the unutterableness of what they saw by any idea, and that joys and delights shone forth from every single thing, and this with successive varieties. The souls that are being introduced into heaven are for the most part carried first of all to the paradisal regions. But the angels look upon these things with different eyes; the paradises do not delight them, but the representatives; thus the celestial and spiritual things from which these come.
>
> Par. 1623. As regards the rainbow scenes, there is as it were a rainbow heaven, where the whole atmosphere throughout appears to be made up of minute rainbows. Those who belong to the province of the interior eye are there, at the right in front, a little way up. There the whole atmosphere, or aura, is made up of such flashes of light, irradiated thus, as it were, in all its origins. Around is the encompassing form of an immense rainbow, most beautiful, composed of similar smaller ones that are the beauteous images of the larger. Every color is thus made up of innumerable rays, so that myriads enter into the constitution of one general perceptible ray; and this is as it were a modification of the origins of the light from the celestial and spiritual things that produce it; and which at the same time present before the sight the representative idea. The varieties and varyings of the rainbows are innumerable; some of them I have been permitted to see; and that some idea may be conceived of their variety, and that it may be seen of what innumerable rays one visible ray consists, one or two of the varieties may be described.

There now follow two examples of the rainbows beheld by him:

> Par. 1624. I saw the form of a certain large rainbow, in order that from it I might know what they are in their smallest forms. The light was the brightest white, encompassed with a sort of border or circumference, in the center of which there was a dimness as it were terrene, and around this it was intensely lucid, which intense lucidity was varied and intersected by another lucidity with golden points, like little stars; besides variegations induced by means of flowers of variegated hue, that entered into the intense lucidity. The colors of the flowers did not flow forth from a white, but from a flaming light. All these things were representative of things celestial and spiritual. All the colors seen in the other life represent what is celestial and spiritual; colors from flaming light, the things that are of love and of the affection of good; and colors from shining white light, those which are of faith and of the affection of truth. From these origins come all the colors in the other life; and for this reason they are so refulgent that the colors in this world cannot be compared to them. There are also colors that have never been seen in this world.

Thus the celestial colors are radiations, prefigurations, reproductions, representations of heavenly and spiritual things – ultimately of the divine essence, the true and the good itself. For the souls ascending into the upper realms there are infinite progressions in the vision of the heavenly colors, corresponding to the infinite progression in the knowledge of the heavenly representations. This is the basis as well for the statement: "There are also colors that have never been seen in this world."

The second example cited by Swedenborg is no less impressive:

> Par. 1625. A rainbow form was also seen in the midst of which there was a green space, as of herbage; and there was perceived the semblance of a sun which was itself unseen, at one side, illuminating it, and pouring in a light of such shining whiteness as cannot be described. At the outer border or circumference, there were the most charming variations of color, on a plane of pearly light. From these and other things it has been shown what are the forms of the rainbows in their minutest parts, and that there are indefinite variations, and this in accordance with the charity, and the derivative faith, of him to whom the representations are made, and who is as a rainbow to those to whom he is presented in his comeliness and in his glory.

Just as in the Johannine Revelation the vision of the "mother above," the heavenly city, appears alongside the vision of the "Ancient of Days" upon the throne surrounded by the rainbow, so too in Swedenborg the vision of the color realm of the cities of the heavenly world appears alongside the vision of the color realm of the rainbow.

> Par. 1626. Besides these paradisal scenes [of the rainbows], cities are also presented to view, with magnificent palaces, contiguous to one another, resplendent in their coloring, beyond all the art of the architect. Nor is this to be wondered at; cities of similar appearance were seen also by the prophets, when their interior sight was opened, and this so clearly that nothing in the world could be more distinct. This was the new Jerusalem seen by John, which is also described by him.

In Swedenborg's text there now follows the description of the heavenly Jerusalem with its walls and gates of many-colored gems (Revelation 21:10, 12, 18-20). He then continues:

> Similar things, beyond number, are seen by angels and angelic spirits in clear day; and wonderful to say, they are perceived with all fullness of sense. These things cannot be credited by one who has extinguished spiritual ideas by the terms and definitions of human philosophy, and by reasonings; and yet they are most true. That they are true might have been apprehended from the fact that they have been seen so frequently by the saints.

The charismatic visions of the saints are cited here as proof for the veracity of Swedenborg's visions!

But colors characterize not only the heavenly sphere – the realm of the angels, the gardens and cities of the paradisal fields – but also the true spiritual self of man, which after death enters into the spiritual kingdom. This is articulated by Swedenborg in his interpretation of the sixteenth verse of the ninth chapter of Genesis, where he speaks of the rainbow that God sets in the sky after the deliverance of Noah and his family from the flood. In his interpretation of God's establishment of the rainbow as a covenant sign, Swedenborg expresses the idea that the inner man possesses a colorful aura which, at death, becomes visible in the spiritual world.

> Par. 1053. "And the bow shall be in the cloud." That this signifies man's state, is evident from what has been said and shown above concerning the bow in the cloud, namely, that a man or a soul in the other life is known among angels from his sphere, and that this sphere, whenever it pleases the Lord, is represented by colors, like those of the rainbow, in variety according to the state of each person relatively to faith in the Lord, thus relatively to the goods and truths of faith. In the other life colors are presented to view which from their brightness and resplendence immeasurably surpass the beauty of the colors seen on earth; and each color represents something celestial and spiritual. These colors are from the light of heaven, and from the variegation of spiritual light, as said before. For angels live in light so great

> that the light of the world is nothing in comparison. The light of heaven in which angels live, in comparison with the light of the world, is as the noonday light of the sun in comparison with candlelight, which is extinguished and becomes a nullity on the rising of the sun. In heaven there are both celestial light and spiritual light. Celestial light – to speak comparatively – is like the light of the sun, and spiritual light is like the light of the moon, but with every difference according to the state of the angel who receives the light. It is the same with the colors, because they are from the light.

"Each color represents something celestial and spiritual. These colors are from the light of heaven, and from the variegation of spiritual light." Thus with the light of heaven the colors descend through the different gradational realms of the celestial and spiritual world down to the earthly world. Each descent means a depotentiation of the original radiating power and pureness of the colors; nevertheless, however, a correspondence in spiritual meaning continues to exist between the colors of the individual gradational realms. The lower points towards the higher, and conversely the higher recognizes the essence of the lower in its sublimer light. Thus, when a man enters into the spiritual realm after his death, his eternal being is recognized by the angels in the particular colorfulness of his sphere, which represents his spiritual self, his true being. It is to be discerned in all the variations of his color spectrum, which differ according to the state of each person as concerns both his faith in the Lord and what is good and true, the ethical and spiritual contents of his faith. Our true self appears in personal colors in heaven in accordance with the iridescence of our virtue and our discernment.

Friedrich Christoph Oetinger

In Friedrich Christoph Oetinger (1702-1782), the founder of Christian theosophy and the most significant speculative mind of Swabian Pietism, we have the most impressive formulation of a theology of color. In a unique way he combined a visionary gift, deep spiritual insight, and comprehensive Biblical and theological knowledge with an unusual familiarity with physics and alchemy. He had personal contact and corresponded not only with great visionaries of his time, such as Swedenborg, and with spiritual leaders of church renewal, such as Count Zinzendorf, but also with the great physicians and scientists of the era. There is special significance to the fact that Oetinger deemed colors an aspect of theology worthy of his attention, since it was he who influenced in the strongest way the great philosophers of Idealism, such as Hegel and Schelling, who came into contact with the intellectual tradition of Oetinger during their theological studies at the Tübingen *Stift*. Oetinger likewise inspired the most significant thinker of Catholic Romanticism in Munich, Franz von Baader. In his most important theological work, the *Biblisch-emblematisches Wörterbuch* of 1776, the Prelate of Herrenberg devoted a separate article to color.[29] At the time this book acquired its special meaning in the history of ideas by virtue of the fact that it was directed against the *Wörterbuch des Neuen Testmanents zur Erklärung der Christlichen Lehre* (1772) of the Enlightenment-minded provost of Berlin, Wilhelm Abraham Teller (1734-1804). The latter presented in this work an interpretation of Biblical concepts in the spirit of the rationalistic theology of the Enlightenment, and thereby propagated a rationalistic understanding of Scripture in the entire realm of German-speaking Protestantism. Over against this, Oetinger stressed the Biblical realism of his teacher, Johann Albrecht Bengel (1687-1752), and promulgated an eschatological and at the same time mystical understanding of the Holy Scriptures, in opposition to Teller's rationalism. In this *Biblisch-emblematisches Wörterbuch* there are articles about just such concepts. The rationalistic Enlightenment theology of Berlin could make nothing of them and thus passed them by. Among these articles was one by Oetinger on "color," which runs as follows:

> Color, *chroa, chrus, chroma*. It does not occur in the New Testament, yet in holy revelation everything is full of colors, and such things are of the essence and not merely chimera. This Newton has proved. Such is a part of natural philosophy, but since colors – red and white, as well as those of the rainbow – are intrinsic to the throne of God and to Him who sits upon it, certainly one must conclude that essential colors are also present in the majesty and glory of God. In their pure, welling forth motion the upper waters are the origin of the colors as well as of the principal substance of everything; but the glory of God, which bears all colors within itself, irradiates the latter. The mother above, Jerusalem, which is on high, is the spiritual epitome. Coming forth from her everything becomes corporeal; the new Jerusalem also comes to us in bodily form out of the upper waters and fires. The color white bears all colors within itself; red is their final goal. The color black has another origin. Of this one may read in *Aula Lucis*, p. 17, 26. 27. Now just as we see images of the eternal power of God, which is always at work, in all the plants, flowers, trees and vegetation, inasmuch as florescence involves such a wondrous play of colors, for which we can offer no reason, so there arises in man a longing, such as in the disciples of Jesus:

> "Lord, show us the Father," as Abraham, Isaac and Jacob have seen Him in concrete forms. But *Jesus* so showed himself only once upon the mountain, and afterwards he referred his disciples once and for all to the faculty of hearing, not seeing. And Jesus wonders at the fact that the disciples have been with him for so long without understanding that Jesus in the flesh is the greatest revelation of God, devoid of any magnificent form. He says to them: "He who has seen me has seen the Father." He thus pointed them towards the Spirit – not towards something visible, but rather towards something involving an inner elucidation of words and a discrimination between everyday thoughts we have and thoughts we note through the Spirit of God. Regarding this, one may read the "Catechism of Wisdom" in *Historisch-Moralischer Vorrath*; and do not torment yourself to see the Spirit of God. On page 727 one may read the query: "What kind of thoughts ought man to consider impressions of God?"[30]

The essential points of view of the older theology of color, as found expressed in Jakob Boehme as well as in Swedenborg, are incomparably summarized – while related to a basic conception – in this article. To begin with, it is clear from the outset that Oetinger is appealing to the colorful visionary experiences of the Holy Scriptures: the colors of the prophets' different visions of God, above all that of Ezekiel (1:7ff.), as well as the vision of God in the Johannine Apocalypse (4:2ff.). In both instances the rainbow is spoken of as the image of the appearance of the glory of the Lord. "In holy revelation everything is full of colors." He likewise explicitly refers to the vision of Jerusalem on high, with its walls of colored jewels, which comes down out of heaven from God (Rev. 21: 10ff.). The water above is there, the stream of the living water, clear as crystal, which flows from the throne of God and the Lamb (Rev. 22:1) and runs through the middle of the streets of the heavenly Jerusalem. On both sides of it stands the tree of life. On the basis of these testimonies of visionaries about the colors of the upper world, Oetinger declares that the salient colors in the self-revelation of God are "not merely chimera, but are of the essence"; they belong to the essence of the self-manifestation of God.

How is this possible? Is this idea of regarding colors as essential things to be attributed to the majesty and glory of God not a diminution and distortion of the pure spirituality of God? The answer to this question is found in the basic notion of the theosophical tradition, which can be traced throughout the entire history of Christian mysticism: corporeality is not foreign to the divine essence but rather belongs to the consummate nature of God. God is the *ens manifestativum sui*, the being who presses towards self-revelation, towards self-realization, towards self-representation, and this self-revelation presses towards corporealization. Oetinger's theology of color is an essential component of his theology of corporeality. Corporeality is "the end of the paths of God." "The mother above, Jerusalem, which is on high, is the spiritual epitome. Coming forth from her everything becomes corporeal." Here is intimated in Oetinger the old teaching of the heavenly *Sophia*, which is already fully developed in Boehme. The heavenly *Sophia*, the heavenly bride of God, the heavenly Jerusalem are the body of God; in her the will of God for self-revelation finds its initial form. She is the first step towards corporealization, the inception of the path of God, whose end is corporeality.

This self-revelation of God through the mother above, coming forth from whom everything becomes corporeal, reaches into the earthly creation. The earthly colors are "an image of the eternal power of God, which is always at work." The "essential colors which are present in the glory of God" are reflected in the plants, flowers, trees and vegetation, "inasmuch as florescence involves such a wondrous play of colors, for which we can offer no reason." As Oetinger says at the outset, the theory of colors is a part of natural philosophy, and for this he refers to Newton's theory of colors, with which he is acquainted. But the colors occurring among the creatures, the wonderful play of colors in blossoms, in plants, flowers, trees and vegetation – these are the "image of the eternal power of God," which is pressing towards self-revelation, towards incarnation.

This self-reflection of God in the creation therefore also awakens in man the longing desire to look upon the primordial image of him who is reflected in the colorful profusion of the creatures; it awakens the avid desire and yearning for the *visio beata*, the view of the Father in his glory, the desire which prompted Philip to ask of Jesus: "Lord, show us the Father" (John 14:8). The aim of the desire is to behold God "in concrete forms," as was granted to Abraham, Isaac and Jacob. According to the account in Genesis, Abraham, Isaac and Jacob each had a vision of God. The Lord appeared to Abraham when he was 99 years old (Gen. 18:1). The appearance of the Lord before Isaac is reported in Genesis 26:2, 24, and his appearance before Jacob in Bethel in Genesis 28:13ff.

Decisive, however, is Oetinger's concluding idea: the period of God's self-manifestation "in concrete forms" has entered into its final phase with His becoming present in Jesus Christ. Jesus Christ himself is the corporeal representation of God, albeit at first in the form of the suffering servant of God and not yet in the form of glory. During his earthly life Jesus appeared to his disciples in the form of glory only once – by way of exception, so to speak – upon the mountain of the transfiguration. Matthew 17:1ff. states: "And after six days Jesus took with him Peter and James and John his brother, and led them up a high mountain apart. And he was transfigured before them, and his face shone like the sun, and his garments became white as light." This appearance ends with an epiphany of God, whereby the disciples are overshadowed by a bright cloud from which the voice of God says: "This is my beloved Son, with whom I am well pleased; listen to him." Oetinger understands this scene of Jesus' transfiguration upon the mountain as the transition from the epiphany of God in "concrete forms" to His new mode of self-revelation in the word – the transition from looking to hearing.

> Jesus so showed himself [i.e., in a transfigured and glorious state] only once upon the mountain, and afterwards he referred his disciples once and for all to the faculty of *hearing*, not seeing. And Jesus wonders at the fact that the disciples have been with him for so long without understanding that Jesus in the flesh is the greatest revelation of God, devoid of any magnificent form. He says to them: "He who has seen me has seen the Father." He thus pointed them towards the Spirit – not towards something visible, but rather towards something involving an inner elucidation of words and a discrimination between everyday thoughts we have and thoughts we note through the Spirit of God.

"Everyday thoughts we have" are our thoughts on the world, viewed as it appears to us in the foreground. The thoughts which "we note through the Spirit of God" are those with which we see through the appearances to the essence of things; with them we perceive how things are images of the eternal power of God, reflections of the majesty and glory of God – how they are "of the essence" and not merely "chimera."

Goethe

The effects of this theology of color – which in Oetinger too has its origin in the vision of color – can be followed right into German classical and Romantic philosophy. The last representative of the tradition of Neoplatonic and Cabalistic mysticism, with its theosophical and spiritualistic esoteric teachings, was Goethe. In him, to be sure, this tradition no longer appears in a didactic form, but rather poetically transformed and as the expression of a new feeling for nature and the world. But Goethe's poetry acquires its special depth and fascination just because of the way in which the old ideas of color mysticism flicker through. This occurs in terms not of a scholarly, literary reminiscence, but rather of a spiritually experienced and personally thought through embodiment, a heritage transformed in Goethe's possession. This is shown at the conclusion of an interpretation of the opening scene of the second part of *Faust*, of which S. Sambursky already had occasion to speak in connection with the presentation of Goethe's theory of colors. Faust is portrayed in a high mountain valley, dozing off in early twilight in an alpine meadow before a rock face, over which plunges a waterfall. Faust's words seem to be the expression of a modern, purely aesthetic feeling for nature: a glorification of the beauty of nature at the instant in which the morning sun is rising.

> The throb of life returns, with pulses beating
> Soft to ethereal dawn ...
> But nature's deepest heart in light rejoices;
> Now burgeon, freshly quivering, frond and bough,
> Sprung from the fragrant depth where they lay dreaming;
> On flower and blade hang trembling pearls, and now
> Each color stands out clear, in glad device,
> And all the region is my Paradise.[31]

And yet, that it is here a question of more than an aesthetic experience of nature, is shown not only by the words of the hymn of dawn itself, but also by the preceding song of the spirits and the hymn of Ariel, the prince of the spirits. The breaking through of a transcendent experience is evident in the use of language which is still directly related to the mysticism of light and color of Jakob Boehme and Emanuel Swedenborg.

In the song of the spirits and the hymn of Ariel the sunrise is described as an appearance of God, an epiphany of the eternal light. What Faust, awakening from a gentle slumber, experiences as the silent declination of the first light of the heavens into the depths of the valley, is perceived by Ariel as the mighty din of the approaching epiphany of the light. The stage directions at the beginning of the scene prior to the hymn of Ariel run: "A great tumult heralds the approach of the sun." That is directly reminiscent of the appearance of God to Moses upon Mt. Sinai, which is preceded by a prolonged clamor (Exodus 19:16ff.). The slumbering Faust does not hear this "great tumult" of the approaching sun, but spirit prince Ariel does indeed:

> Hark! The Hours, with furious winging,
> Bear to spirit-ears the ringing
> Rumour of the new day-springing. ...
> Light spreads tumult through the air.
> Loud are trump and timbrel sounded,
> Eyes are dazed and ears astounded,
> Sounds unheard of none may bear.[32]

Ariel, prince of the spirits, admonishes the spirits to hide until the frightful epiphany of the sun god is past – just as the Lord warns Moses, who asked that he be allowed to look upon His glory: "You cannot see my face; for man shall not see me and live" (Exodus 33:20; cf. Gen. 32:30; Isa. 6:5; I Tim. 6:16). So too the Lord then exhorts Moses, having made his request, to step into the cleft of a rock and to hide while He passes by.

> Glide away to petalled bell,
> Deep in quietness to dwell.
> Deep in foliage, 'neath the rock,
> Lest deafness comes from that dread shock.[33]

Thus the sunrise is here poetically proclaimed to be the act of the divine epiphany. The divine light blinds, the divine tumult deafens. But this language of the epiphany of God – the language of the metaphysics of light of Plotinus, the Areopagite, and Meister Eckhart – also resounds in yet other words of the hymn of Faust.

"Sounds unheard of none may bear" reminds one of Paul's account of his vision in II Corinthians 12:1ff. Speaking of himself in the third person, he reports how he was carried off into Paradise and there heard words that are ineffable. What exceeds human powers of comprehension cannot be expressed in the human language of images or concepts or in intelligible words. But the image whereby "nature's deepest heart in light rejoices," as well as that of the "fragrant depth where [frond and bough] lay dreaming," are likewise taken from the language of visionary mysticism. The prophet Ezekiel describes his vision of God (chapter 43) in such a way that it almost seems the prototype for the dawn vision in the opening scene of the second part of *Faust*.

"Afterward he brought me to the gate, the gate facing east. And behold, the glory of the God of Israel came from the east; and the sound of his coming was like the sound of many waters; and the earth shone with his glory." (Ezek. 43:1-2) Paul tells of the vision of light which suddenly came upon him before Damascus (Acts 22:6ff.), and mentions that he "could not see because of the brightness of that light" (v.11). In II Corinthians 4:6, he speaks of "the light of the knowledge of the glory of God."

Last but not least, however, the final image also refers back to the mystic tradition – namely, that the light transforms into a paradise the depths it illuminates. The epiphany of God at dawn is the repetition of the dawn of creation. The divine light that appears creates the world anew, it restores the paradisal inviolateness of the divine creation; it is the anticipation of the end-time.

Faust's hymn then continues, with him turned towards the morning sun appearing over the mountain ridge.

> Look up on high! – The giant peaks that stand
> In joy of light above the mountain-brow,
> Are heralds of the solemn hour at hand,
> That brings the blessing down upon our land.[34]

What we hear there sounds like the language of the Christian liturgy of the Eucharist. "Look up on high" corresponds to the liturgical call, "Let us lift up our hearts!" (*sursum corda*), which the priest addresses to the faithful at the beginning of the Eucharist, and to which the faithful respond, "We lift them up unto the Lord." It is the *epistrophe* of Plotinus, the turning of the gaze towards the divine Logos. The term, "the solemn hour," also betrays the influence of liturgical language, no less than does the expression, "in joy of light." Here in this liturgical language it is not the worldly sun, the planet sun, which is meant , but rather the "eternal light," of which the Christmas hymn says: "Here enters the eternal light, that makes the world once more bright." It is the "eternal light" first enjoyed by the "giant peaks," which only later "brings the blessing down upon our land" – and this too is a liturgical expression, which in the liturgy signifies the descension of God into the flesh, the incarnation of God in his Son Jesus Christ. But it is already prefigured in the emanation doctrine of Neoplatonic mysticism, namely in the concept of the "turning downwards" of the divine light, to which corresponds its counter-movement, the *epanastrophe* – the turning back again towards its origin.

Faust, however, is not able to endure this facing of the epiphany of the divine light. He experiences in himself what Moses and Elijah had also experienced – that it is impossible to look upon the countenance of the Eternal. The hymn of Faust continues:

> The dazzling sun strides forth, and fills the air.
> I turn, from greater power than eyes can bear.[35]

Paul expresses this experience in the following words: the Lord "alone has immortality and dwells in unapproachable light, whom no man has ever seen or can see" (I Tim. 6:16). Whereas with the spirit prince Ariel the emphasis is upon the sensation of hearing ("Eyes are dazed and ears astounded, sounds unheard of none may bear"), Faust is completely attuned to visual perception. He is "blinded" by the sight of the eternal light, as was Paul before Damascus by the sight of the Lord's appearance; he is "pierced by the pain of his eyes" (as the text literally reads in German), and he finds himself compelled to "turn" away from the appearance of the light.

This agonizing experience is the occasion for Faust to make a general observation:

> And thus it is, when hope with earnest striving
> Has toiled in aims as high as man may dare,
> Fulfillment's open gates give promise fair,
> But from those everlasting depths comes driving,
> A fiery blast that takes us unaware:
> We thought to light life's torch, but now, depriving
> Our highest hope, a sea of fire surrounds us.[36]

Once again everything is permeated with reminders of Biblical and mystical language. "Hope with earnest striving, that toils in aims as high as man may dare," is reminiscent of the *summum desiderium* of Augustine. "Faith is the assurance of things hoped for" (Hebrews 11:1). "Hope with earnest striving" ("das sehnende Hoffen") is a familiar expression in the poetry of Tersteegen and many other pietistic hymn writers. The open doors of the gates of fulfillment allude to the open gates of the heavenly Jerusalem (Rev. 21:25), of which the church hymn sings: "Jerusalem, Thou city built on high, would that I were in Thee!" The "everlasting depths," however, connects directly with the idea of the eternal ground, and the whole terminology which developed out of this idea: *Urgrund*, primordial ground, and *Ungrund*, abyss. The latter terminology was coined by Meister Eckhart, the great creator of the language of German mysticism, and was then introduced into the conceptual language of philosophy by the thinkers of German Idealism – Hegel, Schelling, Franz von Baader – as a direct and further development of the language of the old German mysticism.

But it is the symbolism of fire that belongs to the oldest strata of description of the epiphany of God. Isaiah says: "Who among us can dwell with the devouring fire? " (33:14) Moses beholds how "the Lord descended upon [Mount Sinai] in fire" (Exod. 19:18). Leviticus 9:24 speaks of how "fire came forth from before the Lord." In Deuteronomy Moses describes the Lord as "a devouring fire" (4:24), a phrase which recurs in Hebrews 12:29. In Deuteronomy too, Moses thus speaks to the people: "Out of heaven he let you hear his voice, that he might discipline you; and on earth he let you see his great fire, and you heard his words out of the midst of the fire" (4:36). The "sea of fire" reminds one of the "sea of glass mingled with fire," which belongs to the heavenly Jerusalem (Rev. 15:2). The classical images of the terror of the prophets before the consuming and scorching presence of God, the eternal light, can be heard in the words of Faust.

And now the decisive turn in the poem. Paul remains blind for several days after the blazing forth of the divine light, but Faust retains the strength to resist being overwhelmed by the eternal light. He bends his gaze away from the paining sight of the "fiery blast" of the breaking light, and looks again towards the earth. Here there is expressed a new feeling for life and for nature, which with open eyes turns resolutely towards the creation.

> And so I turn, the sun upon my shoulders,
> To watch the water-fall, with heart elate,
> The cataract pouring, crashing from the boulders,
> Split and rejoined a thousand times in spate;
> The thundrous water seethes in fleecy spume,
> Lifted on high in many a flying plume,
> Above the spray-drenched air. And then how splendid
> To see the rainbow rising from this rage,
> Now clear, now dimmed, in cool sweet vapour blended.
> So strive the figures on our mortal stage.
> This ponder well, the mystery closer seeing;
> In mirrored hues we have our life and being.[37]

What Faust is describing here is the view of "life" in the reflection of the eternal light. Color appears here for the second time. It was suggested for the first time in the description of how the light of the heavens proceeds to slip down into the low-lying levels. There we read: "Each color stands out clear, in glad device." No individual color is spoken of, but rather a play of colors with its reflection in the morning dew – "on flower and blade hang trembling pearls." Here, however, after the dawn of the eternal light, we find the fully developed iridescence of the rainbow in the scattering spume of the waterfall which plunges over the rocks, "the waterfall ... crashing from the boulders." The rainbow appears here as the epitome of the entire color spectrum, with a specific ordering of the primary colors and their glistening, gentle shadings. It is the same rainbow that we already learned of as an essential element of the vision of God in the Old and New Testaments. Here too, colors are a part of the self-revelation, the self-manifestation of God, who makes Himself evident in His creation in the variegated manifoldness of His radiations. The whole spectrum of their efflorescence is the reflection of the divine self-revelation, the irradiation of the eternal light into the flowing, streaming, careering lapse of time. In this way the real mystery of color makes its appearance, which Goethe has expressed in the matchless phrase, "the fluctuating duration of the colorful arc" ("des bunten Bogens Wechseldauer"). It is the eternal light, which reveals its presence in the flux of earthly event. The notion of "fluctuating duration" seeks to retain the characteristic temporal-eternal aspect of the Incarnation. The eternal light is always present, but it is present in the fluctuating play of the colors, which, now clearly delineated, now in running hues, emerge in the arc, which reflects the figure of the eternal light. So it is clearly evident that it is not a question here of an aesthetic description of nature, a gifted interpretation of the iridescence of the waterfall, but that instead this vision is still sustained by the realization thus formulated by Oetinger: "In holy revelation everything is full of colors, and such things are of the essence and not merely chimera." It is the irradiation of the eternal light into the downward rush of thousands of torrents in which the "fluctuating duration of the colorful arc" bursts forth.

Traditional mystical language extends right into the final lines. For Faust speaks of how human striving is mirrored in this fluctuating duration of the colorful arc – the endeavor to grasp the eternal light itself in its reflection, to grasp in its vicissitude duration, and to find rest in its restlessness. It is the endeavor which Augustine, following his Neoplatonic basic ideas, defined as follows: "Cor nostrum inquietum est donec requiescat in te." What the idea that "in mirrored hues we have our life and being" precisely does not mean is that life is made manifest to us only in its colorful appearance, in its transient, dispersive froth. It signifies instead that we "have" life – i.e., partake of it – in the representation, the manifestation, the revelation of the eternal light, that we can share in the presence of the eternal light in the fluctuation of its duration, in the rushing current of time.

The colorful reflection is that form of the revelation of the eternal light in which we can participate in its essence. This mode of representation is the likeness of human striving, which cannot yet partake of the *visio beata* of the eternal light in the here and now, but which aspires to this goal and without it would be incapable of recognizing the goal's anticipation in the revelation of the eternal light present in the fluctuating duration of the colorful arc.

If one keeps in mind both Oetinger's vision in his article on color and Faust's hymn at the beginning of the second part of Goethe's *Faust*, then I cannot help marking a striking analogy between the two. Oetinger's ideas appear to be similar to the heavenly primordial image in the vision of Faust. For Oetinger, "the upper waters in their pure, welling forth motion are the origin of the colors as well as of the principal substance of everything." So too, for Goethe, the waterfall that froths and scatters over the boulders is also the origin of the colors and of the principal substance of everything. For both men the rainbow appears to be the epitome of the colors – with Oetinger it is the epiphany of the divine glory, with Goethe it is the epiphany of the "eternal light." Oetinger says: "But the glory of God, which [in the welling forth motion of the upper waters] bears all colors within itself, irradiates the latter." In Faust's hymn it is the eternal light which, shining forth above the giant mountain peaks, makes the "fluctuating duration of the colorful arc" emerge in the rushing waterfall. In Oetinger we find that, as a result of this manifestation of the divine glory, "a longing arises in man" to ascend from the "image of the eternal power of God" to a beholding of the glory. Goethe has Faust speak of how "hope with earnest striving has toiled in aims as high as man may dare," and how the rainbow, the appearance of the eternal light in the "fluctuating duration of the colorful arc," reflects the human striving that yearns to ascend from beholding the likeness to beholding the original.

Hence it would be wrong to play the two visions – the heavenly and the earthly – off against one another. It cannot even exactly be said which of the two really stands closer to the earthly, the corporeal. Oetinger refers emphatically to the fact that the theory of colors is properly "a part of natural philosophy," and appeals to Newton. He stresses too that the self-manifestation of God in the colors reaches into nature, that in all the plants, flowers, trees and vegetation we see "images of the eternal power of God, which is always at work, ... inasmuch as florescence involves such a wondrous play of colors, for which we can offer no reason." At first sight, Faust's hymn seems merely to describe a nature scene, but his language, in all its images and concepts, opens up the transcendent background of the natural process. Through numerous intimations one recognizes that he too knows that what seemingly is described merely as a natural process is in reality and in essence an image of the "eternal light," and that "the eternal power of God, which is always at work," manifests itself in the "fluctuating duration of the colorful arc." Oetinger's theology of corporeality and his conception of the *physica sacra*, with its theory of colors, are still thoroughly present in Faust's hymn.

Again, in the second part of *Faust*, Goethe has Mephistopheles render a purely aesthetic interpretation of the selfsame mountainous scenery with its waterfall. This seems to me to confirm the fact that an interpretation of Goethe's verse in light of the color theology of the older mysticism comes closer to the original meaning of this poem than does a purely aesthetic exposition. In Act IV of the second part of *Faust* there is a scene which, like the beginning of Act I, takes place in a high mountain area. Here Mephistopheles appears as an aesthete of nature, who, presentient of the development of a secularized 20th century, regards the natural alpine setting as an aesthetic stage for erotic holiday adventures and wants to construct bungalows there (in that respect likewise anticipating modern developments):

Mephistopheles:

Then would I build in style, with conscious grace,
A pleasure-palace in a pleasant place ...
With velvet lawns, clipped verdant walls,
Paths true to line, trim shadows, waterfalls
From rock to rock cascading, well designed,
And fountain-play of every kind,
The centre soaring to majestic height,
The sides in squirting miniature delight.
To house the fairest women then I'd make
Small cozy villas, for seclusion's sake.
And there I'd spend the hours unfettered, free,
In the most charming social privacy.
Women, I say: to give the fair their due
I always have preferred a plural view.

Faust:

Sardanapalus: vice that's old – and new![38]

"Sardanapalus: vice that's old – and new!" This is Faust's response to the philosophy of Mephistopheles, who here takes the part of the aesthetic playboy and contents himself with frolicking around in a semblance of life. At the same time Faust's answer is a confirmation of the fact that we may understand both Faust's hymn to the epiphany of the eternal light and his vision of the color spectrum in the spraying spume of the waterfall against the background of the primeval theology of color. The latter has never forgotten that colors are "of the essence" and not merely "chimera," and that – to conclude with Meister Eckhart – there is a power in the soul which leads man beyond himself and which brings it about that the soul there becomes "divinely colored" where with its tip it touches the divine ground. Perhaps it is one of the tasks of Eranos – which is being surrounded and built over with intimately comfortable cottages in the form of luxurious bungalows – to make this insight heard again today, and perhaps even to make it again of value.

Translated from German by Jay Stoner.

NOTES

1 Hildegard von Bingen, *Wisse die Wege, Scivias*, übertragen und bearbeitet von Maura Böckeler (Berlin: 1928), Buch II, Visio 5, pp. 151ff. Dritte Auflage: (Salzburg: 1955) Buch II, Visio 5, pp. 175ff. (translation mine – TR.)

2 *Ibid.*, pp. 154ff. Dritte Auflage: pp. 176ff.

3 *Leben und Offenbarungen der heiligen Birgitta von Schweden*, neu bearbeitet, übersetzt und herausgegeben von L. Claus (Regensburg: 1888, zweite Auflage), in *Sammlung der vorzüglichsten mystischen Schriften aller katholischen Völker*, Bd. XII, III, Buch VIII, c. XLVII, pp. 368ff. (translation mine – TR.)

4 Dionysius the Areopagite, *The Celestial Hierarchies* (London: The Shrine of Wisdom, 1935), pp. 9-10.

5 Dionysius the Areopagite, *The Ecclesiastical Hierarchy*, in *The Works of Dionysius the Areopagite*, translated by John Parker (London: James Parker and Co., 1899), Part II, p. 75.

6 *The Celestial Hierarchies, op. cit.*, p. 17.

7 *Ibid.*, p. 16.

8 *Ibid.*, pp. 18-19.

9 *Ibid.*, p. 43.

10 *Ibid.*, p. 51.

11 *Ibid.*, pp. 52-53.

12 *Ibid.*, p. 53.

13 *The Ecclesiastical Hierarchy*, *op. cit.*, pp. 111-112.

14 *Ibid.*, p. 127.

15 *Ibid.*, p. 92.

16 *Ibid.*, p. 93.

17 *Ibid.*, pp. 108-109.

18 For more detail, see Ernst Benz, *Les Sources Mystiques de la Philosophie Romantique* (Paris: Vrin, 1968).

19 Jacob Boehme, *Mysterium Pansophicum, or a Fundamental Statement Concerning the Earthly and Heavenly Mystery*, in Jacob Boehme, *Six Theosophic Points* (Ann Arbor Paperbacks, The University of Michigan Press, 1958), pp. 151-152.

20 *Ibid.*, pp. 153-154.

21 *Ibid.*, p. 154.

22 *Ibid.*, p. 155.

23 *Ibid.*, p. 148.

24 *Four Tables of Divine Revelation,* in *The Works of Jacob Behmen* (London: M. Richardson, Joseph Richardson, G. Robinson, MDCCLXXII), Vol. III, p. 15. Bracketed portions of this quotation were omitted in this edition and inserted by the present translator.

25 Jacob Boehme, *Of the Incarnation of Jesus Christ*, translated by John Rolleston Earle (London: Constable and Co., Ltd., 1934), p. 12.

26 Jacob Boehme, *The Aurora*, edited by C. J. Barker and D. S. Hehner and translated by John Sparrow (London: John M. Watkins, 1914), pp. 412-413, 316.

27 *Ibid.*, pp. 269-272.

28 Emanuel Swedenborg, *Arcana Coelestia – The Heavenly Arcana*, edited by John Faulkner Potts (New York: Swedenborg Foundation, Inc., 1949), Vol. I.

29 A reprint has appeared in the *Emblematisches Cabinet*, published by Prof. Tschizewskij and myself: F. Chr. Oetinger, *Biblisch-emblematisches Wörterbuch* (Hildesheim: Georg Olms, 1969).

30 F. Chr. Oetinger, *Historisch-moralischer Vorrath*, hrsg. von G. Közle (Stuttgart: 1872), pp. 389f.

31 J. W. Goethe, *Faust – Part Two,* translated by Philip Wayne (Penguin Books, Ltd.: 1959), p. 25.

32 *Ibid.*

33 *Ibid.*

34 *Ibid.*, p. 26.

35 *Ibid.*

36 *Ibid.*

37 *Ibid.*

38 *Ibid.*, p. 219.

RENÉ HUYGHE

COLOR AND THE EXPRESSION OF INTERIOR TIME IN WESTERN ART

In speaking of art there is a traditional division: the division between forms and colors. Although this division appears to be facile and academic, it is in reality extremely profound: it not only distinguishes two aspects of the art object, but corresponds to a fundamental psychological difference between them. For form concerns space exclusively and so calls only upon our experience of space, whereas color calls simultaneously upon our experience of space – being spread on canvas – and also, psychologically, our experience of time.

When I say our "experience of time" I should specify that properly speaking, duration is meant. Bergson made this fundamental distinction between time and duration. Here it gains full meaning. Color is obviously fixed and does not move, it seems to be situated exclusively in space and to have nothing to do with time; yet it stirs up emotional forces in us which can be perceived only in time that has been lived through, in inner duration; consequently it is through inner duration that time is concerned with color.

That is why many great artists, as we shall see, have in recent years felt an analogy between color and music. Although painting was formerly neatly defined as a plastic art, one concerned with forms and the conditioning of forms in space, for several centuries now a great many painters have had unspoken misgivings about this; they have told themselves that because of color the art of painting was not solely concerned with form, was not properly speaking a plastic art like sculpture or architecture, but had analogies with music. Indeed, although music is performed in time and painting is not, one whole part of painting – which is color – does work upon us by occupying a succession of moments spaced out in time, ranging from the initial sensation, to the nervous excitation, to the emotions that follow the affective states. These are progressively realized moments; they unfold and thus occupy inner duration.

That is why color brings a wholly new kind of value to painting. I want to show how color at first played a limited role in art because the centuries of antiquity were unaware of this potentiality, but how, as an awareness of it evolved, color came to be used in a new way, instinctively to begin with and then even relying on theories for support. Actually this corresponds to the evolution that we find in all other fields, and I do not want to dwell too long upon it since I have often pointed it out in my books: man understands spatial phenomena first. Here again I will refer to Bergson, the man who has best posed this problem of inner duration. Intelligence, he showed, is a mental function initially applied to the conduct of life, hence to action, made to encounter the world that we call real: the world of space and matter. Intelligence gets ideas from there by analogy. Thus, when it attempts to express changing phenomena it does so with laws and ideas that again express fixity and form. In Greece the words "image" and "idea" had the same root, *eidos*, the view, the vision of form. We construct the moving world of our sensations by fixating them in definite forms which are ideas expressible in words, and these words in their turn are immutably defined in dictionaries. The fact remains, however, that beyond this we develop a whole internal life which we would often be unable to trace back to simple lucid ideas. The unconscious, in particular, belongs exclusively to inner duration, since by definition it ceases to exist when translated into *ideas*. That is why Jung, seeing much further than Freud, called attention to the continuing development – this fulfillment of our unconscious potentialities in the course of duration – that occurs in the "process of individuation". He perceived clearly that the unconscious acts in duration and can be understood only by observing the mutations it undergoes and brings about in the course of duration; that it exists in a process, an evolution. On the contrary, an idea does not evolve, for then it would no longer fit its definition, it would become another idea: the idea is defined and fixed, just as form is. But though forms are defined, colors are not.

Thus a first connection may already be seen which leads to a sort of "entente" between color and our sensibilities, whereas form is what interests the intellect, the intelligence, ideas. Here we encounter two distinct planes in the range of human experience.

Men make practical use of their intelligence and, since by definition this is turned toward spatial phenomena, they have been very slow to apprehend the phenomena of inner duration. Thus theories of color entered extremely late into the history of painting. I would like to demonstrate that.

Ordinarily we talk about color vaguely without analyzing it further. Yet chronologically color has been used pictorially in three ways which clearly show the increasing ascendancy of the symbiosis between color and the inner life.

In antiquity color was at first disdained, it was reduced to subaltern uses precisely because it was in essence an affective phenomenon, and the whole intellectual effort at that time was directed toward ideas to such a point that Plato's theory of Ideas supplied the foundation for all occidental thought. Unsatisfied with reducing everything perceptible to the idea that we have of it, he went on to attach our ideas to a more essential and unitary form, the Idea – the matrix idea.

Along the same line it is easy to cite testimony from antique authors who show a curious disdain for color in art, consigning it to an inferior order of "phenomena". Pliny tells us that "with no more than four colors Apelles and others executed immortal works". Comparing these with the art of his time, he said: "Today, with India sending us the silt of its rivers, the bodies of its dragons and elephants, no one creates masterpieces anymore." Thus the painting of antiquity was evolving toward a softer, more refined coloration, and Pliny was shocked. Vitruveus, being an architect, was even more shocked, and he too condemned it: "Today men appreciate only one thing, brilliant color. The painters' science no longer matters." As though color were not the supreme science in painting! Lucien provides more testimony of the same sort. He judges a work esteemed for its color as "a spectacle produced for barbarian eyes: barbarians love what is worthy less than what is rich". Thus in antiquity color was condemned as secondary. This does not mean it was unused, only that it was considered subordinate.

Architecture certainly was painted, but to emphasize its parts, its members, that is, its forms, and furthermore the shades used were plain and simple.

Beyond this, studies have been made from a purely physiological point of view which seem to show that color perception has evolved in the course of time. Relying on testimony obtained from texts and works of art, we can conclude that mankind's perception of color has increased in the cold colors, that is, toward the blue and violet end of the spectrum. Nevertheless I would object, by noting that there are mauve shades in the paintings of antiquity, to some authors who affirm that blue, as a frequently used color, does not appear in medieval manuscripts until the VIIIth century and that violet is not found until the XIVth century. One must never be too strict in such matters, and I am inclined to believe there are exceptions to their chronology. But even expressed as it is, it indicates a great deal, and experiments that have been made to extend color perception confirm it. The eye can readily be taught to see further into the infrared end of the spectrum but it is resistant at the ultraviolet end. Why? Doubtless because the eye has long benefitted from a structure that is much better developed to see the red end than the violet, where it is still quite inexpert. Doubtless it will be up to our descendants to increase their perceptions in this area.

I am limiting myself to repeating the statements of specialists. There is no question that the old texts lead in the same direction. Studies have been made on the place of colors in the speech of antiquity – particularly in the Latin language. For example, J. André has remarked that it actually seems that the ancients did not perceive violet, and in fact violet – the color of the flower – was often assimilated to black. This kind of color-blindness is particularly noticeable in Virgil, where black is given as the color of violets; similarly, the hyacinth is considered to be *nigra*, black, in the ancient texts. Thus the philologists verify what the physiologists have suggested: that vision has evolved and increased in the colder zones of the spectrum.

Other testimony confirms this relative penury of perception in the ancients. For example: the rainbow is said to be red in Greek texts. Today it would not occur to us to say the rainbow was red. Sometimes it was more subtly described as "trichrome". Then the three colors of the rainbow were given as crimson (royal purple), *chloros*, a yellow green, and red: so blue and violet were not perceived, nor indigo, as we see them in modern times.

There are therefore a whole series of indications showing that antiquity was more reticent about color than we are: being more intellectual, it was not yet very open to anything touching upon the perception of duration, and also the field of color vision was then less richly physiological.

We can trace the evolution of the role granted to color into modern times. At first it was used only as an adjunct of form. In Renaissance painting the colored areas still coincided exactly with the contours of a form or object. Thus color was localized and associated with form. As an example let us take a painting by Raphael, a great classical artist of the Renaissance, the *Couronnement de la Vierge (Crowning of the Virgin)* at the Vatican. Immediately it is apparent that the color is one with the form and serves it. Objects have one definite color from end to end in accordance with a concept quite the reverse of the Impressionist concept which will deny form entirely and no longer see anything but transitions and vibrations of color. Here the role of color is completely different. The artist composes with colors just as he composes with forms; that is, he makes them into a harmonic whole. If there is a green mass on the right, it will be balanced by a red mass on the left; but on the upper level, the red mass will be on the right and the echo of green on the left. As a result, the composition, conceived in horizontal bands (which always entails a risk of broken unity), is corrected by the color which follows the movement of the diagonals. Raphael avoids the danger of allowing his forms to separate into two distinct zones by a compensatory architectural use of color.

That concept of color lasted for a very long time; Delacroix was still opposing it in Ingres. Ingres continued to think of color as a simple supplementary ornament to objects, a "barbaric jewel", as Lucien would have said, whereas a man like Delacroix knew very well that color was not just a complement of form but played an autonomous role of its own. Being backward in this way, Ingres was quite different from Delacroix who had evolved a lot further. The celebrated Winckelmann[1] who dominated art theory in Napoleon's time and inspired the classicism of that period stated: "Color contributes to beauty, but it does not constitute beauty, only throws it into relief." He even added: "It serves to give value to forms." Impossible to go further! The neo-classicist master, Balzac, was well aware of relying on an immutable concept when, in speaking of David in *Une double famille*, he evoked "the correctness of design and the love of antique forms which in a way made his painting into colored sculpture". Balzac assessed the contrast between David and the Romantics, especially Delacroix .... It was that David had stopped at the old teachings while Delacroix was at the end of an evolution traceable back, as we shall see, to the beginning of the XVIth century.

When we compare a classical XVIth century colorist, such as Raphael, to a great colorist of the next century, like Velasquez, we meet entirely different understandings of form and its relation to color. Velasquez has passed from the discontinuous to the continuous. Discontinuity is the essential characteristic of space, which is always susceptible to being cut up and portioned out. The essential characteristic of time and duration, particularly duration in the psychic sense, is that it excludes any break, any interruption. You cannot stop your inner time from unrolling; you cannot cut it off; it is a continuous flow which can only modulate, or interrupt itself. Then it ceases to exist. The same difference is found between a crystallized solid and a fluid. In the *Infanta Margerite* at the Prado, Velasquez disassociates the color from the form; he sees the color as a component of the ambience. From a conception of color that was still architectural, he has passed on to one that is musical: the entire picture has turned into a harmony of silver and red. Simultaneously the red has been modulated, it has evolved. And speaking of evolution implies successive readings in time. A red predominates everywhere; at first it is very deep in the curtain at the right, then becomes lighter in the colored bands on the clothing, and finally, thanks to the light, changes into rose. This is the same color diversifying and renewing itself through successive transformations. The spiral concludes with a red in the center which concentrates it, while simultaneously harmonizing with the gray throughout. Furthermore the color has psychological prolongations. One of the beauties of the color in this picture by Velasquez comes from the red's being joined to the idea of vegetable life, to a flower. Red is there in the hand, and repeated in the pompons; whereas the gray evokes a metal, silver. So the play of harmony is established not only between the two colors but between their meanings: on the one hand a precious mineral or metallic substance, on the other, one that is living and floral. Thus a totally different concept of color is revealed, of its role and its compass.

Commentaries? Hypotheses? We always have to countercheck with texts to see if what we think we are seeing can be verified historically and is not a substitution of our own ideas for those of the past. However Paillot de Montabert, another great doctor of academic classical painting at the beginning of the XIXth century, recognized this different conception of color reflected in the works of the Romantics. He realized that: "There is a kind of coloring that is bright with a happy combination of shades, but it is entirely different from another kind, which by conforming with the subject creates a sad, somber, or pathetic harmony. In this case, what is beautiful coloring is no longer brilliant and sparkling, it is rather the coloring that suits the mood of the picture. Yet, at the same time, it should almost present a pleasing harmony to the eye [one would almost think he was analyzing Velasquez's painting]; likewise, the character of the color scheme should be morally and perfectly attuned [note the musical terms] to the subject in such a way as to dispose the soul of the person regarding it to a similar harmony." So here a new interpretation of color is being unveiled.

This constitutes a third step, bringing us to the stage where color becomes associated with inner duration and modifies its course by creating emotions, that is, what we call psychic states – and the word "states" is most unsuitable here, for the psyche has no states, it is never static. We misuse our spatial intelligence again when we try to cut the soul into psychic states. The soul's life has only modulations of sensibility.

That Paillot de Montabert,[2] who was academically-minded, should have accepted such new and audacious views in a classicist was due to the fact that the theory had been proposed first by the great Poussin in the XVIIth century. It was thanks also to an intuitive comparison with music. We will come back to that later. Let us just note here that it makes us agree to a kind of coloring which is no longer plastic coloring or even the coloring of harmonious relationships, but expressive coloring. It closely resembles a piece of music that attempts to express an inner state of feeling and impose it on the hearer. Music, like color, has a beauty born of its structure and tonal relationships, like those we find primarily in Bach, and another beauty derived from its power of emotional expression which induces a certain state of feeling in us, such as we experience when listening to Chopin. The evolution of sound from Bach to Chopin is the same that we find in the field of chromatics when we pass from our earlier examples to Goya.

Take the *Scène de Sorcellerie* (*Witchcraft Scene*) in the Lazarro Galdiano Museum at Madrid. We sense that Goya wishes to induce in us a state of mysterious oppression and anxiety. To begin with the colors are no longer localized or confined to the forms. They participate in an environment, an atmosphere, a continuum that shifts from one intensity to another. Goya is no longer choosing his tones for harmonic value but for emotional value. So here he chooses cold, nocturnal, sinister tones. And why is it that color-schemes have *meaning* like this?

Goethe's theory is much more profound than Newton's because it is not just physical, but also explains psychological effects by emphasizing the role that color plays in the drama of light and shadow, for we do experience it as a drama. Thus it is only fair that some specialists are now rehabilitating Goethe's theory, which has been unjustly underestimated. No doubt Newton saw what was there, but in a limited field. Goethe opened a field that was much greater. To tell the truth the two theories are not irreconcilable. They just don't have the same object. Newton's theory is limited to the world of space and Goethe's implies inner duration. Consequently there is no contradiction between them; they are situated on different planes.

It is tempting to go more deeply into this problem and ask how color, ordinarily no more than a tint applied to a surface, can acquire such dynamic emotional value as to set the inner life in motion and give it direction. Here, of course, we must not underestimate the basic role played by physiology. For my own part, although I do not feel as some positivists do that I can reduce everything to an exclusively materialistic explanation, neither do I believe, like some exclusive spiritualists, that the role of the physical must be eliminated. The richness of human nature is the way it embodies matter and spirit and assures the passage from one to the other; that is its merit and it should never renounce either of these terms of knowledge. Spiritual conclusions are strengthened, not hindered, when they are based on concrete physical study that nothing forbids us, quite the contrary, to transcend later. Thus our ultimate line of thought will be all the surer if we begin with a physiological study.

Obviously the nervous system is engaged in color perception, since the eye was originally nothing but an extension of the brain. Thus the retina, like the rest of the system, transmits and translates external stimuli to the cerebral organs. The sensitive cells are situated behind the retina, and in order to reach them the light traverses several layers of neurons and their axons. The excitation, therefore, begins at the retina, which is endowed with specially adapted organs, the cones and rods, approximately six million of the former and twenty-nine million of the latter. But the rods are insensible to color: they perceive only light and see best in semi-darkness. And what takes place? We know from modern theory that light consists not only of waves but of photons, and that each photon corresponds to one quantum.

Every quantum of light – that is, each photon – acts on the retina by decomposing one molecule of the visual purple. That molecule then changes to visual yellow, but with rest and darkness it is restored and prepared to react again by returning to the visual purple, which is composed of proteins and vitamin A. (That is why the old wives were right when they said that eating carrots was good for the eyes, and also why British fliers were required to eat carrots to improve their vision before making night flights.) As for the cones: it is they that perceive color.

What a difference! The rods perceive a *quantum*, that is a quantity: the cones perceive a *qualis*, a quality. Obviously some people will say that differences of color correspond with different wave-lengths, which are measurable and therefore quantitative. This simplification is no more than a conjuring trick, as the most learned men have been first to realize. Illustrious contemporary physicists, Oppenheimer in particular, have clearly confirmed the stand that the psychologists took long ago against the simplistic position of narrow-minded scientists. They point out that to explain color by the length of light-waves is to consider only what is anterior to the sensation of color itself: it in no way explains the specific nature of the sensation we experience. A blind man could never know what colors are even though he was familiar with the physical theory about them and knew the exact wave-length of each one. To state the wave-length of a color is to specify a causal phenomenon that has taken place earlier but cannot be confused with the sensation that constitutes the color.

So our distinction holds valid; to perceive color through the cones is to perceive a qualitative reality, whereas to register light through the rods is to record a quantity, to allot an appreciable number of quanta, that is photons, to the force of the sensation; it is a return to intensity as a measurement.

So far we have only gotten to the phenomena affecting the retina, that is, to the point of departure. The retina is no more than an intermediary between the phenomenon and the sensation; beyond that the cerebral world becomes involved and everything in the cerebral world concerns its totality. The physicists of former times did not understand this either, and they localized things and took them to pieces, believing that the whole was equal to the sum of the parts they were enumerating, just as a heap of bricks is equal to the total number of pieces composing it. But at the turn of the century gestalt theory demonstrated authoritatively that the psyche as a whole is not equal to the sum of its parts, as would be true in the physical world. A sensation cannot be isolated like a stone in a mosaic. Sensations do not add up like numbers; they give rise to psychological phenomena. A sensation whose origin was isolatable to begin with ends up as a sentiment, an affective condition; it has become associated with memory. No use attempting to trace this affective condition back to a simple association of neurons! From the moment the sensation comes into consciousness it is connected in time with what no longer exists except in memory – a tremendous step since from there on we enter the domain of duration. The sensation of color does not just affect our psychology at the time when it occurs, it connects with all of our experience in time. When I see blue, I cannot avoid thinking of the sky right away, because I have experienced blue sky daily. Thus every new perception of blue immediately becomes integrated into our duration, takes its meaning from the matrix of experience we have acquired in duration, and the feelings we have lived through in duration.

Now to follow these steps: it is certain that before they expand into the total psyche, colors act purely physiologically, and up to a point are independent of visual perception. Concerning this subject my eminent colleague at the Collège de France, Professor J. Benoît,[3] has made some curious experiments. He noticed that red was particularly able to provoke sexual excitation in many animals, in ducks, for example. When subjected to red rays, a reproductive reaction is excited in these birds even outside of their usual mating season. Going further, he enucleated some ducks and with a prism projected red light onto the optic nerve; although they were now blind the result remained the same. So it was not the perception of red that was provoking rutting in them by association but quite definitely the repercussion of the red wave-lengths on the nervous wave-lengths. In this way Benoît proved that colors are able to act on us outside of the optical system.

A great man who died recently, Jules Romains – then still using his family name, Farigoule – put forward a theory of paraoptical vision; he believed that we are able to see by a sort of internal eye, the pineal eye. Saying such a thing was a proof of his juvenal and unscientific audacity in a field with which he was insufficiently acquainted; yet instinctively he had started with the right idea. Professor Benoît found that orange and red radiations are very active and able to penetrate with their great wave-lengths through the skin and even the cranium as far as the hypothalamic region of the brain. That was why he obtained hypophysial-sexual reflexes in ducks, when plunging the blinded birds into a red-colored circumambiance.

Considering this it is curious, is it not, that the first color to be used by men with a spiritual meaning associated with life was red. In prehistoric times the bones of the dead were coated with red. This was thought to promote a continuity of vitality and promote posthumous rebirth.

If color exercises a direct effect on the organism, on its vital tone, should we not try to use it medically and create a color therapy? Some learned men, like Dr. Ponza in Italy, have indeed asked why, if each color has a wave-length of its own that affects our nervous system, it is not possible to use them to act on the physiology and psychology of the individual. Dr. Ponza experimented with rooms of just one color and applied the same color to the window panes, so that even the light was tinted. He verified the fact that colors do have definite effects on us, as I will explain, but he made an even more striking observation; the blind were affected too. When a blind person was put in a red room he obviously did not perceive the color, but he was nonetheless affected by it. And if he was moved from a red room to a green one he underwent the same physiological changes as a person with normal eyesight. Color really works like a bath. Red increases the muscular tone, the blood pressure, the breathing rhythm. It is at once a physical and a mental stimulant, to such a degree that putting red glasses on an athlete produces the effect of drugging him. Having learned this, one of the nations in the Tour de France gave glasses to their team. But they had not foreseen the effects: the red color turned out to be so active that prolonged use of it brought on psychic disorders.

Green, on the other hand, lowers the blood pressure but dilates the capillaries. In psychotherapy it has been used against insomnia and fatigue; the weary are, so to speak, advised to lay themselves down in green pastures (*se mettre au vert*). And reciprocally bulls are excited by red. Since they seem to be color-blind, this is a bit awkward to explain. But perhaps it is a new confirmation of the strong effect that color has on the organism, even when not registered by the eye.

As for blue, it is the most depressing color because it lowers the blood pressure, and simultaneously reduces the pulse rate and the rhythm of breathing; it is quieting and calming, sometimes too much so. There is an expression of this in American slang: "I am blue", meaning despondent or mournful. Thus the popular wisdom that knows so much through experience that has become instinctive, knows very well that blue is depressing and sad. I remember hearing Alexander Fleming say, "We don't believe enough old wives' tales. You know, they say I invented penicillin ... but it was the old wives who found it. Their advice was, 'When you have a wound and don't want it to get infected, spread a dusty spider web taken from a granary over it.' The pseudo-scientists cried out, 'What imbecility! What lack of hygiene! On a wound, imagine that! You'll infect it!' " But Fleming added, "Not at all, that's just where the penicillin mold is found." Thus we see that direct intuitive knowledge often precedes scientific knowledge.

More precise experiments have been made at the hospital of St. Louis in Paris in attempts to treat skin diseases with incandescent green and red lamps. However, the results may not prove anything absolutely, since it may have been simply the heat of the lamps that produced efficacious reactions. A much more interesting experiment was tried in New York around around 1950. A poultry raiser had some very aggressive hens, but peace reigned in the hen house after he put green glasses on them. The United States has made use of that discovery. Similarly, in color therapy, when red has been used on anemic children an increase has been noted in the number of red corpuscles; also, in horticulture red has been used to accelerate the growth of plants; on the other hand, a greenhouse with blue windows retards their growth.

Thus colors have biological effects that far surpass anything we can imagine. This is easily explainable: red is richest in heat rays, violet in electro-chemical rays; blue, on the contrary, has neither heat nor electro-chemical rays and therefore lacks the potential dynamism of the others.

But we cannot stop with this physiological aspect. It is inseparable from the psychological aspect. And here too the intuitions of the popular psyche can be verified experimentally.

Some experiments are classic: take the case of the product packed in dark containers that seemed so heavy to dock-workers that they complained. Someone then thought of painting the same containers light green. The dockers were completely satisfied and, for once, a strike was averted in England. Similarly we can turn to a current fact of life that we all know about: the international language used by plumbers, the language of color that they employ in lavatories when they paint one faucet red and another blue. Everyone knows right away that the red faucet will give hot water, the blue one cold. They never learned it, just know it instinctively. But sometimes the plumbers lose their own instinctive knowledge and attach the hot water to the blue and the cold to the red. – It seems they have become too intellectual!

These psycho-physical reactions have led to an instinctive symbolism. In

American factories when an object is obsolete, unusable, they paint it blue. What a profound and irrational intuition that is of the depressive, annihilating character of blue! Let me tell you an experience of my own: before the war I managed a review called *L'Amour de L'Art* (*Love of Art*): on its cover was the title and a big square of color. The sales of the different issues varied greatly. Was this because of the contents, the subjects treated? Not at all. The reaction of the public varied with the attractiveness of the color of the square. When it was yellow the sales increased, they declined when it was blue. Fluctuations like this are not reasoned out; the action of colors on the nervous system provokes psychological attractions and repulsions by reanimating obscure memories of past experiences. That is why Felix Deutsch said: "The affective excitations which manifest themselves in the blood pressure and the pulse rate are produced by thought associations."

The sensation of a specific color brings with it associations of past experiences which, in their turn, bring on affective changes in the blood pressure and the pulse. Deutsch said furthermore: "The superficial associations touch upon more profound memories, and that explains our emotions before colors." This is an expert's explanation of the effects that we have noted.

Goethe's theory explained these psychic repercussions. He pointed out the varying contrasts of light and shade in colors and distinguished the colors that tended toward the light, warm colors, which could be called positive (as in electricity) from the negative colors, cold colors, that are tempered with shadow. With red at one extreme and blue at the other, he placed green in the middle, marking the great divide between the colors in this struggle of light with shadow. Goethe's theory enables us to understand how blue, although the color of heaven, can have a depressing effect. Blue, as we know it in the sky, was for him a veil of light across a background of darkness, of shadows. You can see for yourself when you go to a high altitude how the blue darkens toward black as the layer of luminous air thins out.

Lüscher has worked out a psychological character test founded on choices of color alone. Having prepared some squares of color, he shows them to the subject. Then, according to the subject's preferences and the associations that they presuppose, Lüscher places him in a certain character classification. In passing let me say that this deduction is not simple since colors – as is further proved by their symbolism – can bring about reactions opposite to those that are expected. For if the effect of a color is exerted too long, a sort of organic defense sets in and the effect is reversed. By a similar mechanism there comes a moment, after a man has laughed a great deal, when exhaustion sets in and he experiences a compensatory inclination to melancholy. In the same way, when an organism is menaced with invasion by some harmful element, it secretes antibodies; this is the great universal rhythm of life, whether psychic or physiological.

With almost no other exception, colors act in definite ways on the nervous system, and then on our sensibilities. Men gain experiences of colors that are at first unconscious but little by little, through repetition, they come to attention, they become conscious. That is when color symbolism comes into being. Very early in antiquity, and earlier in Egypt, men thought that certain colors associated with definite affects had symbolic significance. Thus colors take on meanings. This can be seen in the coat-of-arms which probably originated in the East, where men are less rational and more open to such additions. Doubtless the Crusaders assured the transmission of this tradition. From the coat-of-arms, color symbolism must have passed on to stained glass, and then to painting. But it is sufficient just to turn back to the heraldic treatises. Vulson de la Columbière explains in his *Traité des couleurs des Armoiries* (*Treatise on Armorial Colors*) and also in 1644 in his *Science*[4] that: "the gules, or reds, in armorial bearings denote ardent love of God and neighbor, valiance but also fury and cruelty." There we have the effect of red; it augments the vitality, reenforcing both the warm side and the quarrelsome, hence temper, murder, and carnage – in modern terms we would call it aggressiveness.

Although the intuitive symbolism of colors was illustrated in this way in the Middle Ages, it always has existed: in antiquity, for example, each god was designated by a color. Mars, the god of war and bravery, was connected with red and orange; Venus, the goddess of reproduction, with a light green, the color of growing life; Jupiter, with heavenly blue and royal purple. Similarly, in Africa the god of the Ewe, and likewise his priests, is blue and white, evoking the idea of purity. And blue, as the image of limpid clarity, also appertained to the Virgin in the Byzantine symbolism that the crusaders brought back in the Middle Ages.

Admittedly variations occur between one culture and another, just as between individuals. In this intuitive symbolism there are no strict rules, and unlike physics, where laws are absolute because matter does nothing but repeat itself, psychology can only describe what happens most of the time. Modern materialism does not understand this difference: that the human psyche grows in diverse ways from a common basis. Yet the instinctive language of color is sufficiently constant for historians to take note of its range. Thus a great specialist in medieval history, like Huizinga, was able to show that in the XVth century, a violent and somber period, blue and green disappeared. And these are the two colors in symbolism that bespeak love, since blue stands for sweetness and constancy, while green, the color of Venus, is associated with the ardor of love. Huizinga noted that both of these went out of use after the flowering of the Courts of Love in the XIIIth century, when the Middle Ages entered a phase of convulsion and drama. On the other hand, the use of black in clothing spread in the XVth century, a period of mourning and trial, and only violet and crimson, both denoting tragic feeling, were acceptable with it.

What is true of the soul of a period is also true of the individual artist's soul. He seeks a range of colors equivalent to the tenor of his feelings. As long as twenty-five years ago I pointed out that the most personal painters, and therefore the greatest, show a preference for certain color-schemes and become attached to the aspects of nature that exhibit them.

Think of Botticelli's *Naissance de Vénus* (*Birth of Venus*). He employs the colors of the aurora, a rose, a light green, which are at the same time the colors of spring, also of youth. We feel the secret cohesion of this gamut. Botticelli's is the poetry of morning, renewal, adolescence.

Rubens, on the contrary, uses predominantly red. He is a fleshy man: red is the color of blood, it is elating, sensual, vital. His light is the light of noon, of summer. Everything works together in Rubens to bring us to the peak of natural intensity. Botticelli's women are always young and slender; Rubens' call to mind the plump, expansive women of Flanders.

In the XVIIIth century we find the same elements in Fragonard, but they are slightly less heavy. He was a vitally sensuous man too, was he not? The colors he loved incarnate the sparkle and splendor of high noon.

A man like Watteau was very different! He was immature but at the same time exhausted, run down by illness; he died young. Youthful aspirations were united in him with the melancholy of a man undermined by tuberculosis. In his *Bal champêtre* (*Rustic Dance*), there is a glamor connected with the youthfulness of the songs and dances that amounts almost to possession, but mixed with it are surroundings of such deep and muted verdure as to already suggest the sunset. And later Watteau would go on to plunge the freshness of shining satins into twilight autumnal landscapes; he loved evening when the day's vitality abates, and autumn when the year's vitality goes to sleep.

The same revealing, melancholy harmony can be found in another painter who was also moving and poetic, a sort of Chopin in English portraiture – since Chopin belongs in this family too. I am thinking of Gainesborough. He lived longer and so retained the glamor of youth only when his models permitted; but with him all is bathed in the poetry of twilight: witness the *Portrait of Mrs. Graham*. Everything is enveloped and embraced by shadow; the woman's freshness is, as it were, smothered by the surrounding melancholy which, to return to a line of Baudelaire's, passes "like Weber's stifled sighs."

A quotation from St. Thomas Aquinas, the psychology of which is astonishing, throws light on the mysterious way that the artist's intentions agree with his ways of expressing himself: "Ideas are abstracted from sensible things. Therefore the soul must draw all its knowledge from the sensible, even its knowledge of the intelligible."

But how have artists (who have at the primitive level, like children, depicted principally their own *ideas* of *things*), managed to gain command of their intuitions about those sensible forces and put them at the disposition of magical expression? How, returning to St. Thomas, did they find their way back to the "sensible"? By a slow evolution, which we must follow if we want to understand how the sense of color and its powers of suggestion have been remade.

Here we must make place for a man whose genius is never sufficiently explored, who always has fresh surprises in reserve: for Leonardo da Vinci. No one did more than he to de-intellectualize art and bring back direct experience, greatly to the benefit of color, which was now no longer devoted to the better definition of forms, as it had been, but to furthering the emanation of suggestion. His chiaroscuro opened a new era in painting, illustrated principally by the Venetian School. To accomplish this he had to overthrow the occidental tradition that made art an essentially plastic organization of space, and bring the realities of time to it, the revelations of inner duration. A cardinal aspect that has been too long neglected.

Indeed, contrary to what some people have written, Leonardo da Vinci was not a Platonist. Living close to the University of Padua, he was Aristotelian and followed in the wake of the XIVth and XVth century writers. We know what his library contained, it has been studied. If a rapport has been found by Fred Berence between Leonardo's esthetics and those of the Platonists, it is because he could not entirely escape the ideas in which his period – the Renaissance – was steeped. But his thought went the other way. His fundamental conviction, which made him one of the creators of the modern epoch in all areas, was that we should not start from ideas, but from experience. In that there is an echo of St. Thomas Aquinas. Thus he was led to break with the abstract dogmatism that had come down from Plato to the Renaissance. And when he was attacked for this, he answered: "I am a man *senza lettere,* an unlettered man. I am not a humanist." Impossible to show more resistance to the preference of the period. We must not forget that Leonardo was a bastard. Perhaps that aroused an aggressive attitude in him toward current ideas. He believed and proclaimed that all our concepts should be founded on what we directly perceive. He wrote: "The things of the mind that do not come through the senses are useless and bring us no truth." (Manuscrit B, Institut de France)

Basing himself thus on experience, Leonardo must necessarily have realized that psychic reality is made of duration, and that transcribing the ideas developed by Humanism and the Greco-Latin culture was an obstacle to the true awareness of duration. That is why in a phrase that is essential, although it has been too often neglected, he enjoined himself: "Write about the nature of time, so distinct from that of geometry." (Ms. of the British Museum) Such an investigation already foretells the end of the XIXth century. He understood that time divided into measures – the only notion that his contemporaries had of it – is an abstract idea, that its real nature is contrary to the cut-up nature of geometry, in short, to the nature of form, and has nothing to do with the discontinuous dial of a clock, distinctly marking such and such an hour and minute. Time is a continuum, and it cannot be thought of in any other way. It has to be felt, to be lived.

Leonardo concerned himself persistently with what flows in a continuity, hence with fluids; he was the first man in the Renaissance with this preoccupation. Ever since the XVth century, since the time of Paolo Uccello and Piero della Francesca, art had been devoted to the cult of form and the proportion between forms, or to the composition of forms. The *section d'or* (golden section) had reigned. This certainty interested Leonardo too, to the point that he illustrated a treatise Luca Paccioli had written on the subject; but he brought an entirely different spirit to it because, attracted by a law of continuing growth, what he found was a problem relating to time, and no longer to fixed proportions. It could be said that in setting himself against Plato, Leonardo returned to the pre-Socratic thought of Heraclitus – another tremendous genius – who left us the formula *panta rei*, "everything flows". This was already an expression, was it not, of what most characterizes the fluid continuum? Banishing the rationalists' references to elements being cut apart or put together, he referred to a fluid undergoing continuous modulations. Obviously Leonardo preferred to use a fluid for a visible and intellectual model, rather than a sectionable solid. Indeed a preoccupation with liquids had always pursued him not only in art, but also in his drawings and writings, and in his engineering works. He was one of the great hydraulic engineers of the Renaissance; it was to him that they turned, for example, to make a study of how the Po should be regulated. He specialized in fluids, in water.

In a drawing made in 1513, and now at Windsor, he represented himself, more or less, in the figure of an old man with a great beard that evokes the look of an oriental sage, or magus, which he took on in his later years, and he shows himself meditating, meditating before water. Thus he demonstrated his interest in fluid forms, forms that are continuous by contrast with the discontinuity of crystalline forms. In my last book, *Formes et Forces*,[5] this is one of the points that I emphasize particularly, because it is possible to conceive of a geometry that would be a natural science, in addition to the abstract geometry that we have derived from postulates by successive deductions. Beyond abstract geometry there is room for a geometry that would be somehow phenomenological, based on observations of nature; because nature has laws too, and they are no longer the laws by which the figures dear to geometers and theorists are constructed. Leonardo noted this curious fact.

Thus when he looked at water and analyzed the forms it took, he could not avoid remarking the analogy between the movement of water and the undulations in flowing hair – that is, of flexible forms. He made a drawing showing this comparison and annotated it with comments drawing attention to the rapport between the forms taken by running water and those assumed by the undulating waves of a woman's hair. And indeed this family of forms does depend on sinusoidal lines rather than the straight ones that are the rule in crystals.

You see how far his thought exceeded the limits of his time, and how it was founded on observation. By means of it he became a learned man at the same time as a painter; even more, he ushered in the development of modern science by putting experimentation ahead of principles.

Experimental science, *scientia experimentalis*, is not at all the invention of the Renaissance, that century of rational enlightenment, but rather of the Middle Ages, which we would like to point to as an epoch of darkness! Actually the term *scientia experimentalis* was invented in the XIIIth century by the greatest of the Oxford Franciscans, Roger Bacon. – How many simplistic ideas need reviewing! – And Leonardo, as his library shows, relied upon these thinkers.

Leonardo's study of fluid forms affected his art, and new approaches were opened through him that would eventually modify the entire meaning and scope of color. Let us follow this process step by step. It began with the discovery of new resources in wash or tinting. Before Leonardo, tinting had been used like color, simply for modeling, that is, for strengthening forms. It was actually used mostly along border lines where the contours were marked with a pen. The role of tinting, like that of hatching, was therefore to better define distinct volumes.

But Leonardo opened the way that led to Rembrandt; he used color tinting to obtain variations of intensity without form. He used it in a drawing (now in the British Museum) to give the impression of motion. In the smoke rising from the altar, and simultaneously in the flight of a figure of Fortune (to which he gave floating hair) he achieved an effect of continuity by using the liquid technique of water tinting and variations of it.

All of Leonardo's art and his use of light and shadow can be explained in this way. For what is his chiaroscuro other than a technique for abolishing the continuity of forms, for plunging them back into a continuum of shadow, into an atmosphere? In that way he destroyed and denied form, upon which art had rested from Greek times, down to Raphael and Michelangelo. He was much more revolutionary than we usually think. Like Heraclitus, he seized upon the *panta rei*, "the flowing of all things", as a key to open the passage from fluidity to psyche in terms of the Continuum, and then of inner duration. "The water that you touch in the river is the end of the wave that has gone, the beginning of the one to come. The present is like that." This is Heraclitus' description of liquid continuity, but it also describes psychic life. As with the water, each moment of our existence is simultaneously and uninterruptedly the end of the past and the beginning of the future. The present is the continuous, indefinable, unseverable link between past and future.

Leonardo came to the threshold that divides the physical from the psychological when he painted the *Bataille d'Anghiari* (*Battle of Anghiari*);

there he tackled the psychic continuum from the angle of the facial expressions used to exteriorize it. At first, like everyone else, he believed that it would be enough to ascertain the expressions typifying definite states – anger, gentleness, fear, for example – and he studied them as though they were masks covering our faces with predetermined muscular contractions. But soon he felt that he could never reach real psychology in that way, since psychic life is continuous and not divisible into separate moments characterized by typical, definable expressions. What disappears in the expressions is the imprecise psychic presence that keeps the soul at a constant level. For Leonardo the mark of that is the indefinable smile, the the ungraspable, "liquid" transition between a more serious and a more laughing state. The smile affirms less, it is fugitive and passing. People sometimes ask: "But what was it that Leonardo really wanted to express in the *Mona Lisa*? And that is just it: he did not want to express anything resembling a definite character trait; he wanted to bring out the actual presence of inner duration. That is what makes *La Joconde* one of the greatest masterpieces mankind has created.

Leonardo was not to carry the evolution of his ideas into the realm of color. For his discovery to bear full fruit Leonardo would have to encounter Venice, where he stayed for a while at the beginning of the XVIth century.

Like himself, the Venetians were anti-rationalists and anti-Platonists. The University of Padua was the University of Venice, and it opposed the Platonism of Florence. Impatient of intellectual tutelage, Padua had confirmed its neo-Aristotelianism. And at that moment Leonardo brought to the Venetians an art that was a revolution to them, exactly what they needed to free them from the grip of Florentine and Roman forms: its nature conformed to theirs. Yet Leonardo remained monochrome, whereas Venice to the contrary, through its Byzantine heritage, its contacts with the Orient, was a city that had always been receptive to color. Soon a productive conjunction would take place between Leonardo's consciousness of duration, affirmed by his chiaroscuro alone, and the Venetians' natural feeling for color. This conjunction was realized by Giorgione, a man who died too young but nonetheless found time to become one of the great connecting links in art history.

To measure how much Giorgione owed to the influence of Leonardo we need only to take as an example one of his paintings made prior to their meeting: the *Vièrge de Castelfranco* (*Virgin of Castelfranco*). As you know, Leonardo da Vinci lived from 1452 to 1519, and Giorgione's life spanned the years between 1477/78 and 1510; born after Leonardo, Giorgione died before him. Contact between them was established around 1505. In an earlier work such as this, Giorgione, like the Florentines, constructed his picture as a pyramid, that is, as a balanced symmetrical form. He liked to make straight lines, planes, and the angles connecting them dominate, as in crystals; in particular, he brought out points of equilibrium, marking the verticals and horizontals with connecting diagonals. This symmetrical structure was certainly learned from classical art. But at the end of his life, after he had undergone the influence of Leonardo, he gave evidence in the unfinished works, sometimes completed by his friend Titian and sometimes by Sebastiano del Piombo, of an entirely new conception. The famous *Concert champêtre* (*Rural Concert*) at the Louvre is an example.

This picture is no longer a composition of forms. One can no longer find a pyramid in it, or anything architectural. Its unity, as chiaroscuro teaches, comes from the ambiance: the enveloping continuity, aerial and atmospheric, counts more than bodies or objects arbitrarily isolated from the milieu they are situated in. To speak of ambiance is to speak of fluidity and continuity, as opposed to the discontinuity of formal definition. Leonardo had achieved this already with light and shade. What could Giorgione add? The Venetian color sense, to which his friend Titian would contribute a more lasting affirmation. And from that would come Velasquez. Thus was accomplished the great revolution that opened up modern painting. In painting, music would take the place of form and architecture, for if Venice was the city of color, it was also the city of music, with Gabrielli, Corelli, Monteverdi, Vivaldi, and many other illustrious names. This remarkable school of music-painting synthesized the Europe of that time: great men from Flanders came there to join it, and even became chapel masters at San Marco; at the same time great Dutchmen, like Sweelinck, and Germans like Schein and Schnitz, who sojourned in the city of the doges, were penetrated by the Venetian music. An extraordinary musical center came into being in this meeting place of the elite, for Venice, at the outlet of the Brenner Pan, was the site of all exchanges with the German world. Finally it was, above all, Venice that brought to its apogee the music of the violin, which is so far removed from the interrupted sounds hammered out on the keyboard. Because the bow draws a continuous modulation from the strings, the violin is the instrument that accords best with inner duration, is best able to follow its nuances. The same would be true of the color in Venetian paintings.

Such a union existed in Venice between painters and musicians that we have concrete evidence of it. The musicians were friends of the painters. And the painters constantly alluded in their works to the art of sound; from Bellini onward the angels were always musicians. The orchestra in Veronese's *Noce de Cana* (*Marriage at Cana*) was composed of the principal artists of the time; Veronese figures in it himself, together with Gassano, Titian, and Palladio.

Reciprocally the musicians interested themselves in painting although this is less well-known. Corelli made a collection of engravings and paintings, did he not? And his two students, Geminiani and Locatelli! Geminiani became an art dealer, like Vermeer (painters of that time often made part of their living selling art). As for Locatelli, he collected a great hoard of books, drawings, and engravings; his catalogue consisted of not less than forty-six pages. Would it be possible to better demonstrate the close association of painting and music in Venice?

Leonardo's chiaroscuro and the musical atmosphere worked together to renew pictorial vision and prepare a new conception of color. Later Delacroix, the master who best assimilated the contributions that Venice made to art, thanks to Leonardo and Giorgione, expressed this very well when he said: "We see a sort of connection among the objects that present themselves to our view, produced by the atmosphere surrounding them, and by all the various reflections that somehow make each object participate in a sort of general harmony."

So, how far have we come? Designs made up of forms tend to isolate their volumes, to constitute them separately. In such designs the primordial element is the contour which simultaneously encompasses both the volumes and the colors. But cutting through things in this way is distasteful to painters of inner duration. What they attempt is to merge the forms, and not render them motionless prisoners of their definitions; they try to fuse the forms into a total modulated unity. In well-chosen words, Baudelaire, who was an admiring disciple of Delacroix, spoke of "a unity of impression and totality of effect".

Unquestionably this is what Giorgione introduced into painting through color for the first time. You can see it for yourself in his *Concert Champêtre* (*Rural Concert*): His art rests entirely upon "participation". Its mainsprings are love, the relations of things, music, an enveloping ambiance of sound waves, and, finally, scenery, to which Michelangelo took exception because scenery presents a wholeness inside which all parts are absorbed. Until then

Italian artists had known only distinct forms, and color had contributed to their separation. Atmosphere was unknown; a luminous void replaced it. Giorgione compelled its re-cognition: through the love and music he invoked, the scenery, and above all, his harmonious color schemes, he made a tonal wholeness prevail. But it was the revolution of thought introduced by Leonardo that prepared him.

What Giorgione established his friend Titian extended. Here I want to speak of one of Titian's last works, which I saw as a revelation a very long time ago. It belonged then to the van Beuningen collection at Rotterdam but has gone since to the Musée Boymans. The principle subject is a young child, accompanied by an enormous dog. The repeated presence of animals in Venetian painting is also revealing. The animal, like the child, knows nothing of intellectual constructs made by the logical assembling of distinct ideas, of "*formes mentales*". Both bathe in the affective kind of communication that music with its subtleties tends to set up. And in this late picture all the techniques that are used are directed toward creating an ambiance.

Painting had changed camps. It had abandoned the classical, traditional way of seeing things as being segmented by forms, colors, and symmetry, and had substituted an ambiant, unified vision; a vision in which color played an essential part, at once melodic and orchestral. In fact everything in it leads us back to musical definitions, the melodic role being filled by the chiaroscuro which is modulated, and the orchestral role by the simultaneous association of colors and their actions, converging so as to exert a global effect upon the spectator.

Veronese, who was particularly fond of creating harmonious and often unfamiliar accords between colors, sometimes contacted in this way the all-powerful evocativeness of color, as in his *Calvaire* (*Calvary*) in the Louvre, for example. Christ is dead upon the cross, and the drama is expressed in the shades of red, representing the passions, blood, and death, and in the yellow veil of the Virgin, a strident, contrasting cry of pain. This rises literally like a wail into the space between the reds and against the darkened sky described in the Gospels. Here colors are no longer used only to gain an atmosphere of totality, but, by their combination and even their conflict, to obtain a dramatic effect.

Then came Tintoretto who, conforming to the logical relationships of color, light, and darkness that Goethe advocated, obtained his principal effects through the opposition of brilliance and shadow. In his *Christ et*

Pilate (*Christ and Pilate*) the Procurator, at the heart of the whole atmosphere, incarnates a world indifferent to essentials and abandoned to concrete power, and gives off a murky red light; but Jesus rises to confront him, holding his light up like the yellow veil of pain of Veronese's Virgin. His elongation is a prelude to the mystical elongations of El Greco, who, as we know, was strongly influenced by the old Venetian master.

Here we are irresistably forced to think of Plotinus who, we must remember, revealed openings to Westerners that we usually have to seek in the East, the East that he was curious about even then. For Plotinus wrote: "Matter is shadows; colors are lights of a kind; they testify to the approach of the invisible soul."

What Plotinus had stated in the third century was suddenly rediscovered in the sixteenth century by Venetian painting, by Tintoretto and his follower, El Greco, who would settle later in that less material, less fleshy land, which is Spain. Light for Plotinus was *nous*, spirit. Did he not confide to his readers: "Thou art, all of thee is, invisible light, absolutely light alone." A wonderful phrase that goes as far as it is possible to go.

In his *Christ sur les eaux* (*Christ on the Waters*), Tintoretto develops this play of lights and colors and combines it with the creation of more dynamic forms. Once again the light of Christ is contrasted with the shadows of matter. As psychoanalysis has taught us since then, the sea incarnates obscure and indeterminate elements that men are thrown into, that they are shaken and threatened by. Christ standing vertically here is a rising light to calm the waters.

El Greco pushed on, climbing still further onward. He transposed the Venetian teaching into a more mystical setting. In his *Prière au Jardin des Oliviers* (*Prayer in the Garden of Olives*), for example, the forms themselves no longer exist except to suggest unleashed powers. This sleeping disciple seems to have been thrown into the heart of a vortex. Another whirlwind appears to be stirring up the rocks. But everything takes place between the lunar clarity, expressive of the despair of the Christ during that night of moral agony, and the divine light, carried by the angel which descends upon Jesus. Between them arises the terrible dialogue of doubt, of solitary abandonment by men, and of clarity coming from God: "My Father!" In a picture such as this El Greco attained the summit of combining light and color, not only playing on the feelings but touching also on something much more profound, the relation between matter and spirit, perhaps.

Form is bound to matter, and furthermore all formal civilizations are predisposed to intellectualism, since the idea is also a form: these are therefore never great mystical civilizations; such was the case with Greece, and the case with Rome. On the other hand, when the mystical ideas implanted by Byzantine culture, whose art translated divinity into scintillations of light, came into the West following the Crusades, stained glass windows appeared there. Let us make no mistake about the meaning of this glass and its colors. A medieval theologian said: "Look well at the color of the stained glass windows. They are transpierced by the light which is the image of God, just as was the inviolate Virgin when the Holy Spirit entered her." From this we can estimate the full significance of color and light in the art of stained glass. For medieval man it was the image of the highest spirituality.

Such spirituality is unintelligible in our epoch, since we have miserably gone back to the substructure, to materialism. This is expressed in Monod's book, *Le Hasard et la nécessité, essai sur la philosophie naturelle de la biologie moderne*,[6] which as a biologist I admire, but which attempts to reduce reality to the *necessities* of matter and its laws, and to the effect of *chance* upon the development of life in its earliest stages. The ground floor and the mezzanine absorb Monod to such a point that the splendid edifice rising above these sub-basements is concealed. Yet one need only lift one's head to see it, and take the stairs and go up there. Obviously, however, if one limits oneself to the horizontal view at ground level, one can admit of nothing but matter obeying its necessary repetitions, and the effects of chance on the physiological, primordial aspect of life. But what a lot is left out! Over and beyond this, the advent of consciousness remains to be discovered, then the appearance of intelligence, then spirit; all stages that have been added to life, one after another, as I tried to show in *Formes et Forces*. Color, too, at first bound to the forms of solid bodies, develops so as to command first the obscure resources of unconsciousness, life-connected sensibility, then the symbolism of affectivity and of thought, and becomes increasingly more lucid; now it has achieved the supernatural access to spirituality that harmony of color and light provides.

Grünewald, more than anyone else, I think, was the great precursor who mastered this. He gave us the most troubling images. For example, take a detail of the wonderful altar-piece at Isenheim, such as the materialization of the angel. The angel penetrates into our visible world, but Grünewald does not paint him as a concrete being: he sees him as a light that condenses and becomes color. And though the angel appears almost dissolved, he emerges from that fusion, that nucleus of light, and radiates color. The Christ in the *Resurrection* goes through these changes in reverse. He is a corpse, matter gone back to its molecular reality, but he is to become divine again, and for that he changes from a sensible form into light, already he is disappearing before our eyes. We have come here to the highest spirituality in painting, and this requires a somewhat different reading than is generally accorded to it. This we can verify by approaching the most highly spiritual painter that I know, who is Rembrandt.

Rembrandt understood instinctively, entirely without intellectualizing, what Goethe would explain later, that colors are born of the play between light and shadow. He guessed that the highest evolution would come through a use of color so absorbed, so as to leave room for nothing but the drama of light and darkness, and he intuited that which Goethe would later comment upon: that for light, colors resemble activities or sufferings. And what can narrow-minded physicists with their eyes glued to telescopes make of that? But Goethe was a seer and he conceived by thought what the painters had discovered by intuition: that for light, colors do resemble activities and pains, and that in darkening they suffer. In light there are two active forces warring: brightness and darkness. Yesterday Henry Corbin showed us how conscious oriental thought was of this. In listening to him I thought of a reflection noted by Goethe: "There is not just an absence of light: the darkness, the shadows, are not absence of light but realities in themselves." Is this not the same thing that Henry Corbin pointed out in Iranian thought? Thus, over and beyond the divisions that too many historians cling to and take pleasure in, beyond the partitions wrought by the spirit of discontinuity applied to history, great symbioses exist, which faithful to the spirit of life bring into communion things that we believe to be distinct.

One of these universally perceived truths is pointed out by Gladys Mayer in her book *Colour and the Human Soul*:[7] "Color leads the artist to the experience of a non-sensible world." Right there the great step has been taken. Light is the only part of the real world which is at once immaterial and visible, and that is why light carries such meaning for men. It is the visibility of the ineffable. Therefore it is always spontaneously connected with God; in many religions the holy personages radiate a light of their own. Rembrandt, in some pictures, strongly marks the distinction between physical light – that of fire, for example – and other spiritual light that is the emanation of divinity; he contrasts them. In a work of his youth, such as *Siméon dans le Temple* (*Simon in the Temple*), executed around

1631, and therefore very early, he already allows the dialogue between light and shadow to overtop the colors.

What of his absolutely superior works like *St. Paul*, painted around 1657, and which now belongs to the Widener collection in the National Gallery in Washington? This is a real masterpiece, but is little known in Europe, I don't know why. We shall never understand Rembrandt until we realize that he left the world of forms and replaced the representation of the visible, which was concrete, by the expression of intensity. Thus it may be said that he passed from the discontinuity of forms to the continuity of variations in intensity. And variations in the intensity of light furnished him with something equivalent to and, as it were, emblematic of, variations of intensity in the inner life.

In composing this picture he no longer arranged it architecturally, he combined the points of intensity, which are areas of spirituality: the head that thinks, the hand that will write at the dictation of the head, and the book – the Gospel. Here are three points that are areas of thought, and from them clarity will dawn in an atmosphere inherited from Da Vinci and Giorgione.

A coherent theory of the role and power of color was also developed for the first time in the XVIIth century; completely lucid, it was based on an analogy with music. The man who formulated it was the painter Poussin.[8] He had observed that music really depended on the distinction of modes and that equivalents could be found in the realm of color. The seven modes of antique music are seven tones, each one of which determines the starting point for eight notes, the span of the octave. Poussin mentioned the Doric, the Phrygian, the Lydian, the Hypolydian, the Ionic, and also the Hypodorian and the Hypophrygian. These are the seven modes of music in antiquity. In the same way that music in a major key is notable for its joy and brilliance and music in a minor key seems melancholy, so the modes make it possible to put the hearer into the state of sensibility desired.

Poussin transposed this idea into painting. Take *L'Empire de Flore* (*The Empire of Flora*) in Dresden, for example. What Poussin had to express was the welling up of creativity, the birth and splendor of flowers. So he put the springtime light and the color of flowers together with the joy of young life. Here, remote as he was from Botticelli, Poussin went back to the palette that suited Botticelli's nature so well.

But Poussin was not just a poet expressing his own nature like Botticelli; he knew how to express different states of the human soul; he had only to change his tonal quality. When he painted *Le Mise en Tombeau* (*The Placement in the Tomb*), he felt it as if he were an inspired, and at the same time knowledgeable musician. The light gives way to shadows; the colors are dramatic tonalities: blue, the color of depression; red, the color of blood and cruelty. And with this red and blue symphony against a night sky he communicates to us a state of psychic oppression suitable to the subject.

But at certain times death, when it is not the death of God, may be no more for men than a return to the breast of nature. It is so in the *Funérailles de Phocion* (*The Funeral of Phocion*) which belongs to the Earl of Plymouth. Here nature is the great All: the color deepens to interpret this sovereign unity from which all comes, to which all returns. The man's body is lost in the landscape, whereas that of the Christ looked immense. He is a miniscule figure being carried down a road that leads away. The funeral will pass, it passes. A funeral procession? There are only two men here; without cortège they conduct the vanished and abandoned hero to nothingness and oblivion. Everything blends into the monochrome omnipresence of nature.

How can some people see Poussin as an academic figure? He said that a painting should be an enjoyable thing, therefore less an object of intellection than sensory perception. This was well expressed when he wrote that painting has power (the word is a dynamic, not conceptual), "power to induce diverse passions in the soul of the beholder". "Induce" is a striking word. In a magnetic field induction can produce an electric current. Does the artist resemble such a current which, by a similar phenomenon of induction, irresistably engenders a similar current in the soul of the beholder? Because he used language beautifully – and Poussin was a very great writer – he discovered the expressive term "induce" before the scholars did. In a letter written November 12, 1647 to Chantelou, he explained that he tried to show different passions, suitable to their actions, on the faces of the subjects that he painted (something professed earlier by Leonardo and later by Lebrun[9]). Furthermore he said that he tried to excite and bring out (induce) similar passions in those who looked at his pictures. Sometimes artists are the bearers of great lucidity. It was possible for Poussin to write those words and for them to remain almost without significance for almost two centuries. Before their full meaning could unfold the appearance of a great artist inspired by Poussin was required, one who was able to reply to a clumsy admirer: "I am not a romantic, Sir, I am a pure classicist." This was Delacroix.

And Delacroix was certainly in the tradition of Poussin. He wrote a good article about Poussin and, like him, he admired the Venetians. He also admired Rubens and Rembrandt. A conjunction of all these distinct forces occurred in him, and that is quite conformable with the French genius. For the strength of France consists sometimes less in creating a totally new attitude, than in realizing a new synthesis which includes the views that others have affirmed unilaterally. Such a synthesis enables men to assimilate these scattered contributions and progress beyond them. From affirmation it advances to comprehension.

The strength of Delacroix's synthesis (of classicism, romanticism, spirit and passion) was reenforced, as I emphasized in my book about him, by a strain of Germanic blood transmitted through his mother's family and through his Rhenish ancestors, the Rieseners and the Oebens. Thus a fecund association was made relatively easy for him between the lucid, rational Latin spirit, and the German soul, which is so open to Romanticism. He assimilated the new ideas of the German writers very quickly.

We must remember, for example, that as early as 1825 Edgar Quinet had translated the *Ideen zur Philosophie der Geschichte der Menschheit* by Herder, who died in 1803. And Herder stressed the importance of the "inner feeling" that the soul lives out, that marks its character, its *Gemutscharakter*. One feels, he emphasized, as though by an electric spark (Mesmerism had made electricity fashionable and so helped the comprehension of phenomena like induction) one feels "the obscure and the ineffable flowing powerfully together in one's soul". Thus was superseded the world of intelligible ideas – "clear and intelligible", as Descartes says – of ideas that are forms: with the obscure and the ineffable, the field of unconsciously experienced emotional activities was opened up. The way to the unconscious was taking shape. For the unconscious was not discovered by Freud, as they still say sometimes, but by the Germans of the beginning of the XIXth century, and in particular by the painter and philosopher, Carus. As long ago as 1845 his book, *Psyche*, offered one of the first coherent theories of the unconscious.

From that time on the suggestive powers of color would have been understandable, if only through William James' theory of emotions. James showed that changes follow the perception of a stimulating fact, and that this perception engenders emotion. Similarly my predecessor at the Collège de France, the child psychologist Henri Wallon, insisted that emotion establishes immediate communication without any intermediary between individuals, and apart from any intellectual connection. That is just what color does; it creates a direct relation between the artist and the viewer with no intellectual connection. Phenomenologically it has even been called a case of contagion. But long before that, in his *Vorlesungen über die Aesthetik*, which was translated into French in 1852, Hegel stated forcefully that the inner life manifests itself directly through color in a primordial way. This explains why its action is comparable to that of music.

Delacroix adhered to this new current of thought. "The main interest springs from the soul," he said, "and goes irresistably to the soul of the viewer." And Baudelaire, standing before Delacroix's *La Chasse au Lion* (*The Lion Hunt*), repeated like a faithful disciple: "Never have more beautiful, more intense colors penetrated to the soul through the channel of the eyes."

From then on the idea that color had magnetic powers was established. But Delacroix's theory, although it had assimilated Poussin's, was different. Poussin suggested the passions he meant to represent. But Delacroix was more inclined to express an individual passion, its personal quality of being. In this we can see the mark of the XIXth century. Poussin's theory of modes took on a new resonance with Delacroix, who attempted not only to interpret the feeling inherent in his subject, but to render even the soul of its painter. In 1855 he invoked "only impressions that I experience in my way"; again he spoke of "that little world which man carries within himself", whose silence and secret he tries to break into. Color was to be the great instrument of this revelation: "Color," he said, was "a much more mysterious force than line". Elsewhere he wrote of "color from which we receive mysterious shocks" and again he spoke of "what the soul has added to colors and lines to to get to the soul". These are the terms that Beethoven used for music: going "from soul to soul". Delacroix transposed them to painting and that is why for him painting was above all, colors.

Now we will call upon Goethe again, but this time in reference to drawing. It is a pleasure to me, in the presence of Mme. Ania Teillard, who has so rightly demonstrated the relation between drawing and graphology, to recall Goethe's phrase which Delacroix quoted in the supplement to his *Journal*. "In drawing," he said, (and even more in coloring let me add) "the soul tells us a part of its essential being."

In the end Delacroix was able to say, "Colors are the music of the eyes. They combine like notes. Certain color harmonies produce feelings that music itself could not attain." And he concluded in his *Oeuvres littéraire*:

"Who speaks of art, speaks of poetry." And why does poetry get its name from the Greek verb *poiein*? Because it must before all "create" not only a work, as everyone understands it, but also create an emotion, a state in the soul of the viewer. In the broadest sense, through poetry one fashions the man one speaks to. Similarly in art not only the work is created, but also the beholder.

"There is a kind of emotion entirely special to painting, an impression resulting from that exact arrangement of color and light and shadow. This could be called the painting's music. Even before knowing what a painting represents – if you come into a cathedral, for example, and find yourself too far from a picture to see what it represents – its magic harmony may still seize upon you." It was Delacroix who said this. And Baudelaire repeated it in very similar terms. Let us go back to his celebrated poem:

> *"Delacroix, lac de sang, hanté des mauvais anges ..."*
> "Delacroix, lake of blood, by evil angels haunted ..."

At the Exposition Universelle in 1855 Baudelaire commented on this poem and explained exactly what the associations in it were by which he had been able to bring the suggestive forces of color into play. He explained that when he wrote, "lake of blood", it was to express Delacroix's ardent and dramatic red, and when he said, "by evil angels haunted", it was to express Delacroix's supernaturalism. If he spoke of an "ever-green wood", it was the green complementary to the red. When he wrote:

> *"Où sous un ciel chagrin, des fanfares étranges*
> *Passent comme un soupir étouffé de Weber."*
> "Where beneath sorrowing skies, strange fanfares
> Pass like Weber's stifled sighs."

he was referring to "ideas of romantic music that awaken harmonies of color". This lucid and divinatory handling of the resources of color is verified again and again in Delacroix's work.

In his youth Delacroix expressed sensuality and voluptuousness. The body of the *Nude* at Lyon is a carnal rosy color, the peach blossom color that Goethe spoke of and discovered in the prism where it had eluded Newton. Beside this there is a burst of fanfare, the plumage of a parrot. And Delacroix would further amplify his orchestra. He wanted to bring this voluptuousness face to face with drama, and therefore painted *Sardanapale*. There the rose turned to red; Sardanapale had himself burned on a pyre in the midst of his favorites and the horses he had ordered slaughtered; this extraordinary drama associated the rosy sensuality of the flesh with the tragic red of blood, and the blackness and smoke of the fire.

Mellowing as he grew older, Delacroix became calmer and disgusted with human frenzy. Then he painted *Les Croisés* (*The Crusaders*). Here conquerers lead their triumphal procession through a ruined town. What a useless victory! What a lot of blood, fire, and ruins! In the middle Baudouin's horse is refusing to go on, and the victorious warriors, seen against the light, are no more than shadowy statues, black phantoms. Everything sinks into the blue, the smoke, the grayness – colors of depression. Here Delacroix is acceding to Rembrandt, whose influence upon him has never been sufficiently recognized, it seems to me. Elsewhere, in *L'Evêque de Liège* (*The Bishop of Liege*) Delacroix recalls an historic drama: The Bishop is brought before his conqueror, the "*Sanglier des Ardennes*" (Wild Boar of the Ardennes) and slaughtered in the midst of some troopers having a drinking bout. Night is everywhere, but the Bishop is light, and there is that white cloth which, as in El Greco, bursts forth like lightening from the heart of a storm just when the drama comes to a head. One understands why Baudelaire said, "Many people ask what positive ideas are contained in sounds, or in colors, but they forget, or rather do not realize, that music – which in this respect is related to poetry – represents feeling rather than ideas. Although it certainly suggests ideas, it does not in itself contain them." The ideas, in fact, arise *a posteriori*. They are introduced by the commentators. But what colors do provide is the power of emotion. St. Thomas Aquinas said long ago: "Our cognitive powers do not simply seek what pertains to the true, but also, as truth is awakened in them by means of the ideal contact of contemplation, the satisfaction of, in a certain sense, finding themselves *in* it." Thus our feeling has an intimate association with the power of color, going far beyond ideas.

Gaugin was steeped in the ideas of Delacroix, whose recently published texts he had read. But he applied them to a plastic conception of art, with the intention of bringing back the sense of space. This was the beginning of Modern Art, with its conviction that a painting is before all, a design. Paint and image have to come into design and be registered there. From this time on, the line is reintroduced. As a result Gaugin was led to combine the color symbolism, inherited from Delacroix, with the re-establishment of the line. But it is important to note that the line of Gaugin was not a stabilizing line; it was fluid, like the lines of flexible, soft, or liquid substances. He excluded the straight lines and designs that dominate crystalline forms. In this way his art contributed to the creation of the

Modern Style in which sinuous lines mark the continuity of a development and are no longer intended to define a form. They recede, flee away, and escape. To be sure, they outline "flats" the way colors are outlined in stained-glass windows, but they no longer congeal them.

Like Delacroix, Gaugin painted *La Lutte de Jacob et de l'Ange* (*Jacob's Fight with the Angel*), as the encounter of earthly powers which are dominantly red, with the angel whose wings are light. Elsewhere he painted himself in the features of *Christ à Gethsemani* (*Christ at Gethsemani*), with the red running into an almost putrescent orange, surrounded by a blue, nocturnal world. Those two religious scenes, *La Vision après le Sermon* (Jacob and the Angel), and *Christ à Gethsémani* offer us entirely different color schemes because of the two different dramas expressed in them.

In his new effort to re-join with the sacred, Gaugin relied upon the power of color. That was where he was greatest. After he arrived in Tahiti, far from the traditional religion that no longer held anything for him, and encountered the cults of primitive people, he experienced a sacred presence that was new and virgin, and he understood that through color he could touch upon that divine world and even rise to its level.

In 1896 in his *Poèmes Barbares* (*Barbarian Poems*), the brown of the skin constitutes a mass of human clay, concentrated against the intensity of the red background which is combined with blue; and, mysteriously, in the very heart of that obscurity an idol opens eyes of light.

Gaugin stated in 1885: "There are noble lines and lying ones, etc. And colors, although they are fewer than lines, convey even more because of their power over the eye. There are noble shades and common ones, harmonies that are quiet and consoling and others that excite by their boldness." And he added, which reminds us again of Mme. Teillard's research: "In graphology one sees some traits of honest men and some of liars. Why should not colors show us similarly how important or unimportant an artist's character is? "

And Gaugin put his finger on the kind of action that takes place: "Color is vibration, like music; [and he was fully aware of the part that wave-lengths play] it has the same power of getting at what is most general yet vaguest in nature: its inner force." With this he explained that he believed he had invented a new theory of painting.

Gaugin brings us to the stormy, high-tempered Van Gogh, a friend of his who was filled with his ideas and symbolism. But whereas Gaugin was preeminently an egoist, a self-centered man, Van Gogh was entirely given over to love. Coming from a family of Protestant ministers, he was imbued with the gospel teachings, profoundly imbued; he thought that no life was worthwhile except a life of love; painting was therefore for him an act of love. This made it possible for him to be simultaneously the most individualistic artist I know of, and the most altruistic. Our period, reduced as it is to small egoisms, has too exclusively emphasized his individualism.

But what our time is quite unsuited to understand is that Van Gogh was actually devoted to obliterating the individual before the divine. The grandeur that we feel in Van Gogh, the fascination that he exercises, comes not so much from a passionate affirmation of his personal characteristics, as from his ability to bypass the individual, to carry the "ego" to the extreme point advocated in India where it becomes joined to the "self". Van Gogh's color reveals this slow struggle upward.

He began with dark, earthy pictures. He painted potatoes and boots. That was his first manner. He was in the blackness, the brownness, the earth. But he had a device taken from the scriptures: *per tenebras ad lucem*, and all his life he made enormous efforts to realize it. Like Icarus, he rose toward the light, but his terrestrial wings were too weak, they melted and he was struck by lightning.

When Van Gogh received Gaugin at Arles, he carpeted the whole room with sunflowers. Yellow. And why yellow? Emile Bernard reported that, "He was passionately fond of yellow, the color of divine clarity." And in her book *Colour and the Human Soul*,[10] Gladys Mayer suggests that "Whereas in blue we abandon ourselves to the Universe, in yellow we experience the radiant force of our own being." A luminous center arises within us from which the rays of light radiate into the darkness constantly.

But she did not add what Henri Corbin explained to us yesterday: that, according to Iranian thought, "God is in me and I am in God." The inner light which the individualist projects outward as the expression of himself, is a light that has been given to him and that participates in another light. So Van Gogh's effort was not just expressionistic, as is always said. In attempting to project outward the light that emanated from him, he tended to rejoin the light it participated in, the light he rediscovered all around him.

When he painted portraits, Van Gogh tried to find this radiance in others and to translate it by appropriate color schemes. In *La Mousme (The Young Japanese Girl)* painted in 1888, which is at Washington, he painted the psychology of youth. Love arises through the light blue background which is so pure, mixed with a little of the melancholy that makes youthful ardor so complex. But all the strength is in the red.

On the other hand, when he portrayed his friend, the painter Bock, he went back to yellow. Dressed in a yellow vest, he set him against the background of a night sky, an infinity, wherein the stars partook of the same yellow light as the vest, or the earlier sunflowers.

And concerning the suggestive power of color, it was Van Gogh who said: "for expressing the love of two lovers, use a marriage of complementary colors, their combinations and contrasts, the mysterious vibrations of colors coming together. For the thought behind a brow, use rays of a light color against a somber background; for ardor of being, a beam of the sunset; and use red or green in painting terrible human passions." And all these ideas he also owed to Delacroix.

Through his colors, through his painting, Van Gogh achieved a fusion with the universal. When he experienced his first attack of madness, his first crisis, it was because inner forces were killing him; they were too strong. But he felt that these interior forces were no more than echoing the forces of the universe, and in his pictures the universe appears buffeted by inner tempests. He said it was a kind of fury, a furious madness. (He wrote in a letter, "I saw something like a furious madness in those bushes.") His madness came from being carried away by universal forces that reached him through their terrestrial appearances, and also from experiencing the light that emanates from all things, which is the light of being. He was torn between inner forces partaking of the earth – Goethe's darkness – and the call of the yellow, the light that partakes of divinity.

Let us turn to his last, very tragic work on the eve of his suicide. The yellow there is exhausted, it has become the color of rotted grass that will be used for stable litter. The road goes on, thrusts into the grain, but it gets nowhere. To the right, to the left, there is no longer a path, and the sky is blue, an oppressive blue-black with a flock of crows flying across it.

So color has brought us back finally to the roads that were followed by the Oriental and Islamic mystics, roads that we too, thanks to Henry Corbin, have been enabled to follow. But since my study is concerned with the West, it seemed best to me to start in the Western spirit, with the experimental findings of materialism. I did so because I do not wish to be accused, as Monod[11] accused his adversaries, of starting from a metaphysical preconception. Also, having started from these material facts, I have the right to continue, and not to stop short like Monod, the right to testify (since that is what I am doing) to the upward development of color which, from its beginnings as a physiological, nervous phenomenon, has become a phenomenon of sensibility, of the soul; and which, pushed to the extreme of death by the creativity of Van Gogh, has finally provoked a confrontation between man's inner forces and the external forces of the physical world, and likewise a confrontation between the inner light of man and the omnipresent light that, for all of us, is God.

Translated from French by Jane A. Pratt.

NOTES

1 Winckelmann, J. *Histoire de l'Art.* Translated from German. Paris: 1766, 1789.

2 de Montabert, Paillot. *Traité complet de la peinture.* Paris: Bossange, 1829 (9 vols) and Delion, 1851.

3 Benoît, Jaques. "Actions des facteurs externes sur l'hypophyse et les glandes génitales des oiseaux", in *Les Hormones sexuelles.* Paris: Hermann, 1938; "Etats physiologiques et instinctifs de reproduction chez les oiseaux", in *L'Instinct dans le comportement des animaux et de l'homme.* Paris: Masson, 1956.

4 de Vulson de La Colombière, Marc. *La Science héroique, traitant de la Noblesse, de l'origine des armes, de leurs blasons et symboles.* Paris: Gramoisy, 1644.

5 Huyghe, René. *Formes et Forces – De l'atome à Rembrandt.* Paris: Flammarion, 1971.

6 Monod, Jacques (late Professor at the Collège de France). *Le Hasard et la nécessité, essai sur la philosophie naturelle de la biologie moderne.* Paris: Edition du Seuil, 1970.

7 Mayer, Gladys. *Colour and the Human Soul.* East Grinstead, Sussex: New Knowledge Books.

8 *Collection de Lettres de Nicolas Poussin,* Paris, 1824; *Correspondance de Nicolas Poussin, publiée d'après les originaux par Ch. Jouanny,* Paris, 1911; *Lettres de Poussin, avec introduction de Pierre Columbier,* Paris, 1829.

9 Lebrun, Charles (first painter of Louis XIV). *Méthode pour apprendre à deviner les passions.* Amsterdam: Van der Plaeats, 1702; *Expressions des passions de l'âme représentées en plusieurs testes gravées d'après les dessins de feu M. Le Brun.* Paris: Audran, 1727.

10 *Vide* note 7.

11 *Vide* note 6.

TOSHIHIKO IZUTSU

THE ELIMINATION OF COLOUR IN FAR EASTERN ART AND PHILOSOPHY

I

The general theme of the Eranos lectures this year, "The Realms of Colour", is, as it stands, an immense subject that can be channelled into almost an infinite number of directions in accordance with various possible angles from which one may choose to approach it. In order to deal with the theme in a consistent way, the vast field must first necessarily be delimited in some way or other so that the subject of discussion might properly be narrowed down to a concrete point or a number of relevant points closely interconnected with each other within the boundaries of some very particular and special problems.

In view of this fact, I have decided to set limits to the area in terms of two definite factors: firstly, the geographical division of the cultural traditions of the world (and I have chosen the Far East), and secondly, the positive and the negative attitude one could take toward the aesthetic value of colour (and I have chosen the negative attitude). Hence the title of my lecture, "The Elimination of Colour in Far Eastern Art and Philosophy".

The negative attitude toward colour is in fact characteristic of the Far Eastern aesthetic experience, whether it be in the field of painting, poetry, drama, dancing or the art of tea. I shall discuss in the present paper some aspects of Oriental philosophy that will theoretically account for the remarkable natural inclination that is observable in Chinese and Japanese culture toward the subdual or suppression of colour leading ultimately to a total elimination of colours except black and white. I shall try to clarify further that even "black" and "white" in such a tradition cease to function as colours, and that they function rather as something of a totally different nature.

Many Westerners who have had some real aesthetic acquaintance with the Far East tend to represent its art in the form of black-and-white ink painting. The art of ink painting in China and Japan is in fact the best illustration of the negative attitude toward colour which I have just referred to as being most characteristic of Far Eastern art. For in this monochromic world of artistic creation, the inexhaustible profusion and intricacy of the forms and colours of Nature is reduced to an extremely simplified and austere scheme of black outlines and a few discrete touches or washes of ink here and there, sometimes in glistening black, sometimes watered down to vaporous grey. In the background there may be a haziness of faint grey; more often than not the background is a blank, white space, i.e. bare silk or paper left untouched by the brush. There is consequently no titillation and gratification here of the sense of colour.

What then is the real charm of the paintings of this sort? We know that it is not only the Orientals themselves that are attracted by the special "beauty" of the black-and-white. We know in fact that many an art connoisseur in the West have shown an enthusiastic appreciation of Far Eastern ink-painting. How are we to account for this fact? This is in brief the main problem which I should like to discuss in this paper. In so doing, however, I shall approach the problem not from the technical point of view of an art critic, which I am not. I shall rather try to bring to light the basic ideas that underlie the elimination of colour. I shall deal with this latter problem as a problem of a particular type of aesthetic consciousness, as a peculiar spiritual phenomenon revealing one of the most fundamental aspects of Far Eastern culture.

Speaking of a peculiar type of Japanese poetry known as *haiku*, which is said to be the most reticent form of poetic expression in the world, consisting as it does of only seventeen syllables arranged in three consecutive units of 5/7/5 syllables, R.H. Blyth once wrote: "*Haiku* is an ascetic art, an artistic asceticism". [1] The phrase "an artistic asceticism" not only characterises *haiku*; as is clear, it applies equally well, or perhaps even better, to the art of black-and-white ink painting. It is important to remember, however, that this artistic asceticism, i.e., the suppression of externals and the reduction of all colours to black and white, manifests its real aesthetic function only against the background of a highly refined sensibility for colours and their subtle hues. In other words, the true profundity of the beauty of black-and-white is disclosed only to those eyes that are able to appreciate the splendors of sumptuous and glowing colours with all their delicate shades and tints. Otherwise, the ultimate result of the achromatisation here in question would simply be utter absence of colour in a purely negative sense, which would not be apt to excite any aesthetic emotion.

Due perhaps to the climatic conditions of the country and the colourful and picturesque appearance of its Nature, the Japanese had developed from time of high antiquity a remarkable sensibility for colours and hues which go on changing with the seasons of the year.[2] In matters of colour, as Y. Yashiro observes, Nature in Japan is comparable to a gorgeous brocade resplendent with infinitely varied colours. These colours of Japanese Nature, Yashiro goes on to say, are of a dazzling beauty; they are beautiful enough to intoxicate our aesthetic sense. Yet, on the other hand, the brilliancy of the colours is characteristically counterbalanced by what we might designate as a chromatic "reticence", a kind of natural restraint, quiet soberness (popularly known in the West as *shibui*), spreading like thin mists over the colours, matting their naked flamboyance and subduing their unrestrained external gorgeousness. These characteristics of Nature in Japan are said to have positively contributed toward the formation of the typical, aesthetic sensitiveness of the Japanese to colour and its delicate nuances.[3]

However this may be, the very fact that the Japanese in olden times were endowed with a very peculiar colour sensibility is shown by a number of concrete, historical evidences. I shall give here two remarkable examples. The first one is taken from the aesthetic culture of the Heian Period (794-1185).

The Heian Period (meaning literally a period of Peace and Tranquillity) in which the Fujiwara family stood at a splendid pinnacle of prosperity and domination around the imperial court in Kyoto, was the first peak in the history of Japan with regard to the development of aesthetic sensibility. It is to be remarked that the unusually keen aesthetic sensibility of the Fujiwara courtiers centered around the beauty of colour. They were extremely colour-conscious. The Heian Period was literally a "colourful" period. And during the tenth, eleventh, and twelfth centuries, the heyday of Fujiwara culture, the aesthetic sensibility attained to an unprecedented degree of elaboration, elegance, and refinement. This is best observable in the use, choice, and combination of colours for the robes worn by the court ladies.

Unfortunately no real specimens of those Heian robes survive, but the lack of material evidence is well compensated for by the innumerable references to the court robes and their colour in contemporary literature as well as by the pictorial representation of the gentle scenes of court life in the narrative scrolls of later ages, notably in the picture scroll of the famous *Tale of Genji*. Costumes were in most cases described with meticulous care both verbally and pictorially because the garment a person wore was considered in the Heian Period a most immediate expression of his or her personality. "The garment *was* the person; it was the direct symbol of his or her personality".[4] It is important for our purpose to note that this symbolic function of the garment was exercised almost exclusively by the aesthetic effects produced by colours and their combination.

The prose literature of this period – the romantic stories by court ladies, their diaries and essays – mention the names of different colours, the number of which amounts to more than one hundred and seventy.[5] It is no exaggeration to say that the prose literature of that period constitutes in itself a flowery field of colours.

All these colours used to be combined in various ways through the most elaborate and sophisticated combination of clothes and their linings, undergarments and upper garments, so that they might constitute layers of colour harmonies. The matching of various colours was in fact an art of highest refinement to be displayed within the limits of the well-established and generally accepted code of aesthetic taste. When silk robes are laid one upon another, the lower colours are more or less faintly seen through the colour above, which could result in the creation of an indescribably delicate new colour. Thus, to give a few concrete examples, the colour called *kôbai*, "pink-plum" was in itself an independent colour evocative of the pink colour of the blooming plum blossoms. But what was called "pink-plum-layer" was a different colour produced by two colour layers, the outer layer being pink or white and the inside layer the dark red of sappanwood. Further, the "fragrant-pink-plum-layer" was still another colour produced by an outer layer of deep "pink-plum" and an inside layer of very light "pink-plum". Or to give another example the *yamabuki*, "yellow-rose" was, as the appellation itself shows, bright yellow reminiscent of the natural colour of the flower of a Japanese plant known by that name. But the *hana-yamabuki*, "flowery-yellow-rose", also called "evening yellow-rose", was a compound colour formed by an outer layer of light dead-leaf-brown and an inside layer of bright yellow. And *yamabuki-nioi*, "yellow-rose-fragrance" was a standardised colour layer to be used for the costume of court ladies, the uppermost layer being bright yellow having underneath a number of layers of increasingly light yellow and the final undergarment being deep blue.

More important still for the colour-conscious women of the Heian Period, however, was the stratification of harmonious colours coming from the very make-up of their formal costume. The court ladies wore the so-called *jûni-hitoé* meaning "twelve-layer" garment. It consisted of an outer robe of gorgeous brocade and embroidery and twelve or even more silk undergarments of different colours and shades which were arranged in such a way that each robe was slightly smaller and shorter than the one below it, so that a beautiful colour stratification might be visible at the neck and the outer edges of sleeves.

Quite naturally the ladies themselves and the noblemen in the imperial court had as a rule an extremely sharp and severe critical eye for colour harmonies. Even the slightest fault in the combination of colours could hardly escape their notice. In a passage of the Diary of Lady Murasaki, widely known as the authoress of the *Tale of Genji*, we find an observation made by herself, which is quite interesting in this respect. One day, so she writes, when all the court ladies in attendance on the Emperor had taken special care with their garments, a certain lady proceeded to the Imperial presence. Everybody without exception noticed that there was a fault in the colour combination at the opening of her sleeves. It was not really a very serious error, Lady Murasaki adds, but the colour of one of her undergarments was a shade too pale. [6]

I have gone into these details about the Heian costume in order to show in the first place the degree of elegant refinement reached by the Japanese of those days in the development of sensibility for chromatic colours and their aesthetic value. Enough has been said, I believe, to corroborate the statement that I have made earlier that the Heian Period was literally a "colourful" period in the cultural history of Japan. In terms of the distinction, also made earlier, between the positive and the negative attitude toward colour, Heian culture may rightly be said to be characterised by the definitely positive attitude taken by the courtiers of that age. The observation of this fact will naturally be conducive to another observation which is of greater importance for our present purposes; namely, that the elimination of colour which is unanimously considered one of the distinguishing marks of Far

Eastern aesthetics is backed by a passionate love of the beauty of colours and hues.

We must also observe in this connection that even in the midst of this flamboyantly colourful world created by the aesthetic sense of the Heian aristocrats there is almost always perceivable a kind of soberness, quietude and stillness, coming either from the very quality of the colours chosen or from the peculiar ways they are combined one with the other – or perhaps from both – so that the colours in most cases appear delicately subdued and toned down.

In this sense we may say that in this early period a marked tendency toward the subdual of colours is already observable. But "black" itself was in the eyes of the Heian courtiers, a dull, gloomy, unpleasant, and ominous colour. It reminded them of death, and, at best, of abandoning the pleasures of the world and entering the monkhood. The effect it was apt to produce was generally nothing but dark emotions like sadness, grief, melancholy. Not infequently the black-dyed robe is described as something ugly, lowly and poor,or odious and abominable. Even in such a world, however, there were among people of the highest aesthetic sophistication some whose colour taste was refined to such an extent that they could go against and beyond the common-sense standard of taste and find in black the deepest stratum of beauty as the ultimate consummation of all colours or as the direct expression of the sublimation and purification of all emotions realised by one who had penetrated the unfathomable depth of the sadness of human existence. In the *Tale of Genji* we sometimes are surprised to find the aesthetic eye of Lady Murasaki already turned toward the supreme beauty of a dark, colourless world far beyond the "colourful" frivolities of sensuous pleasures. [7]

The Japanese taste for the exuberance of glowing colour and the splendours of sumptuous decoration reached its second peak in the Momoyama Period which lasted from 1573 to 1615. Lavish display of colours and designs had never been so boldly made before in the history of Japan. In contrast to the too delicate aesthetic refinement of the Heian court aristocracy verging on effeminacy, the Momoyama, a period of warriors, had its culture saturated with their robust and vigorous spirit. It was a culture of virile vitality. The aesthetic taste of the age, quite in keeping with this warrior spirit, and backed by the unprecedented material prosperity of the merchant class, found its most adequate expression in the magnificent structure of castles and palaces and in the gorgeousness of their interior decoration. In fact the creative energies of this period were most lavishly spent on the construction of huge fortress-castles and palaces.

Nobunaga (1510-1551), the first military dictator of the period, erected his famous Azuchi castle. Hideyoshi (1536-1598) who succeeded him and who brought the splendour of the period to its apex, built among others his most sumptuous castle on Momoyama (meaning literally Peach Hill) in 1594, known as the Peach Hill Palace, from which the period itself derived its name.

Both Nobunaga and Hideyoshi had the celebrated artists of the age decorate the walls and sliding panels of their castles in the most magnificent manner. At the head of those colourists stood Eitoku Kanô (1543-1590) who was asked to undertake the grand-scale decoration of these castles. Eitoku Kanô, the founder of what is known as the Kanô school of Japanese painting, with his bold brushwork, large designs, and the decorative use of patterns of dazzlingly brilliant colours, truly represents the so-called Momoyama style. As the result of the assiduous work of Eitoku and his numerous disciples, the broad surface of the walls of the huge audience halls in the castles and the sliding panels were covered by abstract areas and decorative patterns of crimson, purple, lapis, emerald and blue on backgrounds of pure gold, amidst which stood out trees, birds and rocks painted with a certain amount of realistic detail – a flowery mosaic of rich colours. The halls were further glorified by folding screens representing various aspects of Nature, animate or inanimate, painted in a profusion of sumptuous colours glowing with hues of lapis lazuli, jade, vermilion, oyster-shell white, etc..

Thus the Momoyama Period is predominantly a "colourful" age, even more brilliantly colourful than the Heian Period, equally characterised by the positive attitude toward colour, though in a very different way from the latter. And yet – and this is the most important point to note for the purposes of the present paper – just at the back of this gorgeous display of flaunting colours there was a totally different world of powerful black-and-white painting. We must remember that the Japanese by that time had already passed through the sober Kamakura Period (1192-1333) in which Zen Buddhism thrived, emphasizing the importance of realising the existence of a formless and colourless world of eternal Reality beyond the phenomenal forms and colours. After the end of the Kamakura Period and before the advent of the Momoyama Period the Japanese had also passed through the Muromachi Period (1392-1573) in which many a first-rate painter produced masterpieces of black-and-white painting in the spirit of the austere restraint which is typical of Zen, and under the direct influence of the poetic ink-painting of the Sung Period in China. Most of these Muromachi paintings, done by Zen monk-painters, were of such a nature that they roused in the minds of the beholders an undefinable but irresistible longing for the colourless dimension of existence which these paintings so well visualised.

Thus there is nothing strange in the fact that in the grandiose castles of the Momoyama Period there were private chambers of the non-colour style standing in sharp contrast to the lavishly ornate official halls and corridors. In fact most of the famous colourists of the age who usually painted in the gorgeous Momoyama style were also well-trained in monochrome painting, the most notable example being Tôhaku Hasegawa (1539-1610), originally of the Kanô school, who left masterpieces in both the colourful and the black-and-white painting and who ended up by founding a new school of his own.

Viewed in this light, the Momoyama Period may be said to have been an age marked by the taste for the display of colour, which was backed by the taste for the elimination of colour. Far more telling in this respect than the pictorial art is the very peculiar elaboration of the art of tea through the aesthetic genius of the tea-master Rikyû (1521-1591).

Under the passionate patronage of that very warrior-dictator, Hideyoshi, who, as we have just seen, liked so much the splendour of flaunting colours and gorgeous forms and who had his castle so luxuriously decorated, Rikyû the tea-master perfected a particular art of tea known as *wabi-cha*, literally the tea of *wabi*, or the art of tea based on, and saturated through and through with, the spiritual attitude called *wabi*. The tea of *wabi* was according to the author of the celebrated *Book of Tea*, "a cult founded on the adoration of the beautiful among the sordid facts of everyday existence". [8] The tea of *wabi* brings us into the domain of the elimination of colour.

Wabi is one of the most fundamental aesthetic categories in Japan, and its taste casts its greyish shadow over many aspects of Japanese culture; for *wabi* is not a mere matter of aesthetic consciousness, but it is a peculiar way of living, or art of life as much as it is a principle of aestheticism.

Wabi is a concept difficult to define. But at least it is not impossible to have a glimpse of its structure by analysing it into a limited number of basic constituent factors. For the sake of brevity I shall here reduce them to three and explain them one by one: (1) loneliness, (2) poverty, and (3) simplicity.

(1) The first factor, loneliness or solitude, living alone away from the

dust and din of mundane life, must be understood in a spiritual or metaphysical sense. The idea of fugitiveness which is suggested by the word, if taken in terms of ordinary human life, would simply mean being-unsociable, which is exactly the contrary of what is aimed at by the art of tea. For the art of tea is intended to be enjoyed by a group of men temporarily gathered together for the particular purpose of drinking tea together. The "loneliness" in this context must rather be taken in the sense so admirably illustrated by the Zen master Sengai (1750-1873) in his *Song of Solitary Life* [9] which reads:

> I come alone,
> I die alone;
> In between times
> I'm just alone day and night. (In classical Chinese)
>
> This I who comes to this world alone
> And passes away from this world alone –
> It's the same I who lives in this humble hut all alone. (In Japanese)

The meaning of "being alone" is explained by Sengai himself in another place as follows. "What I call alone/Is to forget both alone and not-alone,/ And again to forget the one who forgets:/ This is truly to be alone".

(2) The second factor, poverty, "being poor", must also be taken in a special sense. It means primarily living in the absolute absence of all ornate materials, one's existing in a vacant space far removed from the luxury of rich furniture. Physically it *is* a life of poverty. But this material poverty must be an immediate and natural expression of poverty in a spiritual sense. It must be material poverty sublimated into a metaphysical awareness of the eternal Void. Otherwise poverty would simply be sheer indigence and destitution having nothing to do with aesthetic experience.

(3) The third factor, simplicity, is most closely connected with the two preceding factors. The tea-room of the so-called Rikyû style, originally designed by this tea-master for the purpose of creating the art of *wabi*, is outwardly nothing but a mere cottage too small to accomodate more than five persons, or even less. The interior is of striking simplicity and chasteness to the extent of appearing often barren and desolate. No gaudy tone, no obtrusive object is allowed to be there. In fact the tea-toom is almost absolutely empty except for a very small number of tea-utensils each of which is of refined simplicity. Quietude reigns in the tea-room, nothing breaking the silence save the sound of the boiling water in the iron kettle – the sound which to the Japanese ear is like the soughing of

pine-trees on a distant mountain.

From the point of view of colour, the essential simplicity of the tea-room may best be described as the state of colourlessness. The tea-room is not exactly or literally colourless, for everything in this world does have colour. To be more exact, we had better in this context make use of the commonly used Japanese phrase: "the killing of colours", that is, to make all colours subdued and unobtrusive to the limit of possibility. It is but natural that the extreme subdual or "killing" of colours should ultimately lead to a state verging on monochrome and sheer black-and-white. The monochrome is here a visual presentation of the total absence of colour. But we should not forget that the absence of colour is the result of the "killing" of colour. That is to say, under the total absence of colour there is a vague reminiscence of all the colours that have been "killed". In this sense, the absence of colour is the negative presence of colour. It is also in this sense that the external absence of colour assumes a positive aesthetic value as the internal presence of colour. Thus there is something fundamentally paradoxical in the aesthetic appreciation of colourlessness or black-and-white, and that not only in the art of tea but also in Far Eastern art in general.

Nothing illustrates this paradoxical relation between the absence and the presence of colour better than a celebrated *waka*-poem by Lord Teika of the Fujiwara family [10] (1162-1241), which is constantly quoted by the tea-men as their motto. The poem reads:

> All around, no flowers in bloom are seen,
> Nor blazing maple leaves I see,
> Only a solitary fisherman's hut I see,
> On the sea beach, in the twilight of this autumn eve.

The tea master Jô-ô (1503-1553), who initiated Rikyû into the *wabi* type of tea, is said to have been the first to recognise in this poem a visualisation of the very spirit of the *wabi*-taste. It is to be remarked that the poet does not simply state that there is nothing perceivable. He says, instead, "no flowers in bloom are seen, nor blazing maple leaves I see". That is to say, brilliant colours are first positively presented to our mental vision to be immediately negated and eliminated. What takes place here is in reality not even an act of negating colours. For the negation of colourful words in this context represents a metaphysical process by which the beautiful colours are all brought back to the more fundamental colour, that is, the colour which is not a colour. And the Nature is poetically re-presented in the dimension of the colourless colour which is symbolised by a fisherman's hut standing all alone on the beach in the twilight grey of the autumn evening. Thus the desolate wilderness of the late autumn depicted in this poem does not constitute a picture in monochrome understood in a superficial sense. It is, on the contrary, a sensuous presentation of the spirit of *wabi* as understood as an art of "killing" colours in order to bring them up to the dimension of the absolute Emptiness.

That the above is not an arbitrary interpretation of the poem on my part is testified by a famous passage in the *Nambô Records*, [11] a book in which a monk called Nambô Sôkei, who was one of the leading disciples of Rikyû, gives us a fairly systematic exposition of the principles of the *wabi*-taste tea as he learnt it from his teacher. In the passage in question, quoting the *waki*-poem which we have just read, Nambô notes that, according to what Rikyû has told him,

> Jô-ô used to remark that the spirit of the *wabi*-taste tea is exactly expressed by Lord Teika in this poem.
> The splendour of colourful flowers and tinted maple leaves (mentioned in this poem) are comparable to the gorgeousness of the formal, drawing-room tea. But as we contemplate quietly and intently the brilliant beauty of the flowers in bloom and tinted maple leaves, they all are found ultimately to be reduced to the spiritual dimension of absolute Emptiness which is indicated by the "solitary fisherman's hut on the sea beach". Those who have not previously tasted to the full the beauty of flowers and tinted leaves will never be able to live in contentment in a desolate place like a fisherman's hut. It is only after having contemplated flowers and tinted leaves year after year that one comes to realise that "living in a fisherman's hut" is the sublime culmination of the spiritual Loneliness.

The paradoxical relation between the absence and the presence of colour is equally well exemplified in a somewhat different form in a different field, in the Nô Drama, a typical Japanese art that flourished in the Muromachi Period lying between the Kamakura and the Momoyama Period. The Nô costumes were and still are of the gorgeous kind, made usually of colourful brocades with glittering gold, shimmering silver, and brilliant colours. In terms of colour, the Nô drama is undeniably a world of chromatic exuberance. Under the surface of this polychromic splendour, however, the vision of a genius like Ze-ami (1363-1443), the real founder of Nô as an art, was directed toward the world of black-and-white. For him the flower of Nô drama and dancing was to bloom in its full in a dimension of spiritual depth where all these colours would be reduced to a monochromic simplicity. [12] For the ultimate goal of expression in the Nô drama is again the world of eternal Emptiness. In the metaphysical vision of Ze-ami, the last stage of training to be reached by the Nô actor after having gone through all the stages of strenuous spiritual discipline was the stage of what he calls "coolness" where the actor would be beyond and above all flowery colours, a world of Emptiness into which all phenomenal forms of Being have been dissolved.

The fantastic gorgeousness of colour in Nô costumes is also counterbalanced and effaced by the austere restraint shown in the bodily movement of the actor. The sobering effect of the extreme restraint in the expression of emotion, which is not lost sight of even for a moment, is such that all colours lose their nakedly sensuous nature and turn into exquisite tone of subdued richness – subdued to the utmost limit of reticent expression. On the Nô stage movement represents stillness, and the stillness is not mere immobility in a negative sense. For in the peculiar atmosphere of spiritual tension, silence speaks an interior language which is far more eloquent than verbal expression, and non-movement is an interior movement which is far more forceful than any external movement. Thus beyond the external brilliancy of colour which the Nô drama actually displays on stage, the unfathomable depth of the eternal Colourlessness is evoked before the eyes of the spectator.

What, then, is this Colourlessness? And why Colourlessness rather than Colourfulness? In the second part of my lecture I shall try to answer this question by explaining the inner structure of the world of black-and-white.

II

I have in the preceding tried to explain through some conspicuous examples culled from the cultural history of Japan that the black-and-white or colourlessness in the aesthetic consciousness of the Far East is not a mere absence of chromatic colours; that, on the contrary, it is directly backed by an extremely refined sensibility for the splendour of colours; and that the colourlessness must be rather understood as the consummation of the aesthetic value of all colours.

I shall now turn to the problem of the inner structure of black-and-white and the particular philosophy of beauty underlying the monochromic forms of art that have developed in China and Japan.

I shall begin by quoting a remarkable statement made by Yün Nan T'ien (1633-1690), a well-known Chinese painter of the 17th century, i.e., the

Ch'ing Period, on the significance of extreme simplicity in painting.[13]
He says:

> Modern painters apply their mind only to brush and ink, whereas the ancients paid attention to *the absence of brush and ink*. If one is able to realise how the ancients applied their mind to the absence of brush and ink, one is not far from reaching the divine quality of painting.

The "absence of brush and ink" may in a more theoretic form be formulated as the principle of non-expression. The principle stems from the awareness of the expressiveness of non-expression, that is to say, the expressive absence of expression. It applies to almost all forms of art that are considered most characteristic of Far Eastern culture. In the case of the pictorial art the principle of non-expression is illustrated in a typical form by black-and-white ink drawings done by a few brush strokes or some light touches of ink on a white ground, the serenity of the white space being in many cases even more expressive than the exquisitely expressive lines and glistening ink.

Of course a drawing, as long as it remains a drawing, cannot entirely dispense with lines or touches of ink. The "absence of brush and ink" is in this sense nothing but an unattainable ideal for those painters who want to actualise the principle of expression through non-expression. However, one can at least come closer and closer to the absolute absence of expression in proportion to the ever increasing inner accumulation of spiritual energy. Hence the great achievements in the field of ink painting in the Sung and Yüan Period in China and the Kamakura and Ashikaga Period in Japan, when Zen Buddhism attained its highest ascendency in the two countries. And hence also the development, in the tradition of this form of pictorial art, of the technique known as the "thrifty brush" and the "frugality of ink". These two phrases originate from the realisation of the fact that, in order to express the unruffled serenity of the mind in its absolute purity and in order to depict the reality of things as they really are – in their natural Suchness, as Zen Buddhism calls it – the painter must eliminate from his drawing all non-essential elements by using as little brush strokes as possible and by sparing the use of ink to the utmost limit of possibility.

As the result of the stringent application of this principle, many artists painted in soft ink watered down to an almost imperceptible vapour of grey. The outstanding painter in the Sung Period, Li Ch'êng, for instance, is said to have "spared ink as if it were his own life". The kind of ink painting represented by these masters is traditionally known as "mysteriously hazy painting" (*wei mang hua*). According to the testimony of his contemporaries

Lao Jung used to paint in such a way that the whole space was veiled in a dim haze; one felt as if something were there, but nobody could tell what it was.

This is perfectly in keeping with the spirit of Taoism which, together with Zen, greatly influenced the development of ink painting. Lao Jung's work is no other than a pictorial presentation of the Way (*tao*) as described by Lao Tzu. In the *Tao Tê Ching* we read:

> Even if we try to see the Way, it cannot be seen. In this respect it may be described as "dim and figureless".
> Even if we try to hear it, it cannot be heard. In this respect it may be described as "inaudibly faint".
> Even if we try to grasp it, it cannot be touched. In this respect it may be described as "extremely minute".
> In these three aspects, the Way is unfathomable. And the three aspects are merged into one.[14] (That is to say, the Way can be represented only as a dim, hazy, and unfathomably deep One).

> The Way is utterly vague, utterly indistinct.
> Utterly indistinct, utterly vague, and yet there is in the midst of it (a faint and obscure) sign (of Something).
> Utterly vague, utterly indistinct, and yet there is Something there.[15]

If the "mysteriously hazy painting" of a Lao Jung aims at a pictorial presentation of the Way, the Absolute, as Lao Tzu describes it here, the ink painting could theoretically be developed in two different directions: firstly toward depicting the absolute Nothing which the Way is in itself, and secondly toward depicting this absolute Nothing as it functions as the ultimate metaphysical ground of Being. The author of *Tao Tê Ching* himself describes the Way as a contradictory unity of Nothing and Something. Thus:

> Deep and bottomless, it is like the origin and ground of the ten thousand things....
> There is absolutely nothing, and yet there seems to be something.[16]

If the painter chooses the first direction, he will naturally end up by drawing the Nothing in its absolute nothingness, that is, actually not drawing anything at all. Then, a piece of white, blank paper or silk, untouched by the brush will have to be regarded as the highest masterpiece of pictorial art. It will be interesting to note that in fact there did appear some painters who put this principle into practice. As a result we have in the history of Japanese painting what is known as the "white-paper-inscription" (*haku-shi-san*) which consists in leaving the paper absolutely blank and only inscribing at the top some verses that are intended to interpret the picture which is supposed to be underneath. This curious type of "white painting" is said to have been inaugurated by a Japanese teaman in the late Tokugawa Period, Yôken Fujimura.[17] But going to such extremes is inevitably conducive to the suicide of painting as painting. For, as long as one depends upon graphic means, one cannot, by *not* drawing anything, aesthetically evoke the vision of the Emptiness of a Lao Tzu or the Nothingness (*shunyatâ*) of Mahayana Buddhism.

The only possible way to take for the painter appears thus to be the second one mentioned above; namely, to approach the absolute Nothing from the point of view of its being the ultimate metaphysical ground of the phenomenal world. The basic idea underlying this approach is suggested in the most concise form by the following two verses of the distinguished poet-painter of the Northern Sun Period, Su Tung P'o (Japanese: So Tô Ba, 1036-1101):

> Where there is nothing found, there is found everything,
> Flowers there are, the moon is there, and the belvedere.

The majority of those who paint in "water-and-ink" depict something positive in black ink on a white ground – a flower for example, a tree, a bird, etc., or often a whole landscape. In so doing, the painter sometimes seizes the precise metaphysical instant at which the figures of phenomenal things arise to his mind in the state of contemplation, emerging out of the depths of the formless and colourless ground of Being. It is in fact a spiritual event. A fine example of painting as a spiritual event of this kind is the celebrated landscape painting known as the *Haboku Sansui* (i.e., literally the Broken-Ink Mountain and Water) of Sesshû (1420-1506). Sesshû was an extraordinary Japanese Zen monk in the Muromachi Period, who was at the same time the most distinguished ink painter of the age. *Haboku* or "broken-ink" is a peculiar technique of ink painting which is more properly to be called the "splashed ink" technique.[18] Briefly explained it consists in that the painter first draws the main points of his motif in extremely pale watery ink, and then, before the ink gets dry, quickly and boldly flings over the wet surface vivid blots of black ink and draws a few lines of deep black.

Necessarily in this work of Sesshû nothing is depicted with a clear-cut outline. The whole landscape consists of indistinct forms, varying ink tones, vapours and the surrounding emptiness. In immense distances of the background, beyond veils of mist, craggy pillars of mountains loom against the sky, vague and obscure, like phantoms. In the foreground a rugged wall of a cliff with thick bushes (painted with a few brush strokes in rich and thick ink) is seen rising sheer from the river bank. Under the cliff a small house is discernible. On the water, which is finely suggested by the absence of ink, floats a solitary boat, perhaps a fisherman's boat. The remaining surface of the paper is left entirely bare. But the empty areas obviously play in this landscape a role at least as important as – if not more important than – the splashed blots of ink. For it is only amidst the surrounding cloudy space that the positive side of the picture (consisting of a few black strokes and splashes) turns into a metaphysical landscape crystallising a fleeting glimpse of the world of phenomena as it arises out of a realm beyond the reach of the senses. It is, on the other hand, by dint of the figures actually depicted in black ink that the blank space ceases to be bare silk or paper, transforms itself into an illimitable space, and begins to function in the picture as the formless and colourless depth of all phenomenal forms and colours.

As another excellent example of the use of a wide blank space of a similar nature we may refer to the equally celebrated ink painting attributed to the Chinese painter Mu Ch'i (Japanese: Mokkei) of the 13th century, "The Evening Bell from a Temple in the Mist". It is a rare masterpiece of ink painting. A wide, dim space – a suggestion of the Infinite – occupies the greater part of the paper. The depicted forms are reduced to a minimum: a small corner of the roof of a house, the faint silhouette of a temple in the aerial distance, the shadowy woods emerging and disappearing in the mist, the lower parts of the trees entirely lost in the twilight. In contrast to the dynamism of ink splashes in the Broken-Ink Landscape of Sesshû, the equally hazy landscape of Mu Ch'i is of a static nature. A profound cosmic quietude reigns over the landscape. One might say that the dynamism of Sesshû's painting depicts the very instant of the forceful emergence of the phenomenal world out of the eternal Emptiness, whereas Mu Ch'i depicts here the essential stillness of the phenomenal world reposing in the bosom of the all-enveloping Silence. But in either case, what is evoked by the blank space is the same Great Void which is the ultimate source of all things. The blank space, in other words, visualises a metaphysical or spiritual space which is absolutely beyond time. It evokes a timeless space, the timeless dimension of things. And this is true even of the Broken-Ink Landscape of Sesshû in which, as I have just said, the "emergence" of the phenomenal world is depicted. For the emergence here in question is not a "temporal" emergence, but it is the metaphysical and a-temporal emergence of things in a spiritual

Space which in Mahayana Buddhism is often referred to by the word Mind.

Not all ink paintings, however, are done in such a vaporous and diffused manner. Quite the contrary, the contours of the things are often very clearly delineated with expressive lines, now heavy and thick, now agile and light. But the fundamental relation between the depicted figure and the empty background remains essentially the same. For the heightened impression of the positive presence of an object enhances, in its turn, the impression of the illimitability of the cosmic and metaphysical space which would engulf into its depths the phenomenal form that has emerged out of itself.

The peculiar relation which I have just mentioned between the heightened presence of an object depicted and the blank space enveloping it is most easily observable in paintings done in the "thrifty brush" style. Look at the famous "Mynah-Bird on a Pine-Tree" by Mu Ch'i, a monochrome picture of a solitary bird in deep black perched on the rugged trunk of an aged pine-tree which is drawn in extremely dry and astringent ink. The background is again a blank space which, by dint of the forceful presence of the black bird in the foreground, turns into the cosmic Loneliness of ultimate reality itself. And the piercing eye of the bird – which is the very center of the picture – seems to be penetrating into the deepest dimension of reality lying beyond the very existence of the bird itself.

This picture of the "Mynah-Bird on a Pine-Tree" will remind us of the oft-quoted *haiku*-poem of Bashô (1664-1694) who is in Japan popularly known as the peerless "*haiku*-saint". The poem reads:

> On a branch of a withered tree
> A raven is perched –
> This autumn eve.

This is indeed a verbal painting in black-and-white, the black figure of a solitary raven perching on a dead branch against the background of the illimitable Emptiness of an autumn eve. Here again we have an instance of perfect visualization of the cosmic Loneliness out of which arise the lonely figures of the phenomenal world – not through brush and ink this time, but by the evocative power of words. The externalized forms of Being are essentially lonely, no matter how brilliantly colourful they might be as pure phenomena. This essential loneliness of phenomenal things is best visualised by black-and-white. This must be what was in the mind of the *haiku*-poet Bashô when he characterised the basic attitude of verse-making peculiar to his own school in distinction from that of all other schools, by saying: "The *haiku* of the other schools are like coloured paintings, whereas the works of my school must be like monochrome paintings. Not that in my school all works are invariably and always colourless. But (even when a verse depicts things beautifully coloured) the underlying attitude is totally different from that of other schools. For the matter of primary concern in my school is the spiritual subdual of all external colours".

It will be only natural that *haiku* poetry whose basic spirit is such as has just been explained, should attach prime importance to the "absence of brush and ink", to use again the Yün Nan T'ien's expression. In other words, *haiku* – at least that of the Bashô school – cannot subsist as a poetic art except on the basis of the clear awareness of the aesthetic value of empty space. For a *haiku* is a poetic expression of a fleeting glimpse into a trans-sensible dimension of Being through a momentary grasp of an illuminating aperture that the poet finds in a sensible phenomenon. The latter can be sketched by words, but the trans-sensible dimension, the Beyond, allows of being expressed only through what is not expressed. *Haiku* expresses these two dimensions of Being at one and the same time by positively depicting the phenomenal forms of Nature. Hence the supreme importance of the blank space which is to be created by non-expression.

The artistic use of blank space is observable in almost all forms of art in the Far East. The technique of non-motion in the Nô drama to which reference has been made earlier is an apt example. Non-motion, or the absolute absence of bodily movement is nothing other than the empty space actualised on the stage by the actor through the cessation of motion. It is an instant of external blankness into which the entire spiritual energy of the actor has been concentrated. The technique of non-motion is considered the ultimate height to which the Nô dancing can attain. To express intense dramatic emotions through the exquisite movement of the body in dancing is still comparatively easy. According to Ze-ami, only the perfectly accomplished actor after years and years of rigorous technical training and spiritual discipline, is able to actualise on the stage the most forceful expression of emotion by the extreme condensation of inner energy into a sublimated absence of action. The actor does not move his body. He remains absolutely still, as if crystallised into an image itself of Timelessness. In this extraordinary density of spiritual tension, without dancing he dances; he dances internally, with his mind. And against the background of this non-action, even the slightest movement of the body is as expressive as a tiny dot of black ink on the surface of white paper in ink painting.

Much more could be said on the significance of dramatic blank space in the theory of Nô as developed by Ze-ami and his followers. Still more could be said on the role played by blank space in various forms of Far Eastern art as well as in other more practical fields of human life in the Far East. For the purposes of the present paper, however, enough has already been said on this aspect of our problem. Let us now turn to the more positive side of the matter, namely the significance of the positively depicted forms as distinguished from the empty background.

Let us recall at this point that the spirit of Far Eastern art in its most typical form consists in expressing much by little; it is an art which aims at producing the maximum of aesthetic effect by the minimum of expression verging on non-expression. Thus in ink painting just a few brush strokes and the resulting summary lines and ink washes can evoke the weighty presence of a thing far more impressively than a minute, faithful reproduction of its colour and the details of its external form. What is the secret of this type of art? The right answer to this question will be given by our elucidating the inner structure of the things as they are pictorially represented with the least possible number of lines and strokes, and with the elimination of all colours except black.

It will have been understood that monochrome ink painting in China and Japan is a peculiar art centering round the aesthetic appreciation of the spiritual atmosphere which it evokes. In this art Nature and natural objects play a predominant part. In fact the most typical form of brush-and-ink work is landscape painting. And the pictorial representation of landscapes and various natural objects is done by means of lines and ink tones.

The word "landscape painting" in this context, however, needs a special comment. For the word "landscape" does not necessarily mean a whole landscape. It is to be remembered that there is no *nature morte* in the traditional conception of painting in the Far East. [19] The concept does not exist. Many pictures that would in the West normally be put into the category of *nature morte* are regarded in the East as landscape paintings. It is of little importance here whether a "landscape" painting represents a whole landscape or only a flower, grass, or fruit. What is actually drawn may be a single bamboo, for instance. It is in reality not a single bamboo. Before the eyes of the beholder, the single bamboo expands itself into a dense grove of bamboo, and still further into the vast expanse of Nature itself. It is a landscape painting. Or, to give another example, a solitary autumn flower is seen quietly blooming on a white background. It is not a mere picture of a single flower, for the depicted flower conjures up the presence of Nature infinitely extending beyond it. And by so doing, the flower discloses to our inner eye the cosmic solitude and quietude of all solitary existents in the world. Even a fruit or vegetable can in this sense constitute the subject of a landscape painting. The most celebrated picture of "Six Persimmons" attributed to Mu Ch'i is a good example. In its extreme simplification of the form of persimmons drawn in varying tones of black ink, it is a pictorial representation of the vast cosmos. The underlying philosophy is Hua Yen metaphysics which sees in one thing, in every single thing, all other things contained. R.H. Blyth gives this philosophic view a brief but beautiful poetic expression when he says that each thing "is with all things, because ... when one thing is taken up, all things are taken up with it. One flower is the spring, a falling leaf has the whole of autumn, of every autumn, of the timeless autumn of each thing and of all things".[20]

As we have noted earlier, monochrome painting depends exclusively on two factors: (1) line and (2) ink tone. By definition it eliminates all chromatic colours that go to make Nature flamboyant in the dimension of our sensory experience. Necessarily and inevitably Nature becomes transformed in a peculiar way when it is represented as a world consisting only of lines and ink tones.

In the tradition of Oriental ink painting, drawing a natural object in brush-lines is directly conducive to the spiritualisation of Nature. The Oriental brush made of hard and soft bristles is of such a nature that it faithfully reflects the varying moods of the man who uses it and the various degrees of depth of his mind. Furthermore, it must be remembered that in China and Japan the brush-stroke technique is most intimately related with the technique of drawing spiritualised lines that developed in the art of calligraphy – the most abstract of all Oriental arts, exclusively interested in an immediate expression of the depth of the spiritual awareness of the man. Thus in drawing pictures by brush-lines the painter is able to infuse the object he has chosen to depict with the inner energy of his own, just as he does in writing ideographic characters.

The brush-strokes can be sudden, rugged, and vehement. They can also be soft and supple, serene and quiet. The painter sometimes draws an object with a fluid sinuous line of an indescribable suavity and sweetness. Sometimes his lines are alert, quick and fiery; sometimes, again, slow and heavy. Each line has its own speed and weight. The weight of the line is determined by the amount of power with which the brush is pressed against the paper. The pressure of the brush, coupled with the speed of its movement, faithfully reflects the spiritual undulations of the painter.

As for the ink tones, another basic factor of monochrome painting, sufficient explanation has already been given in an earlier section of this paper concerning its spiritualising function. Thus the Far Eastern art of ink painting is definitely a spiritual art.

It will readily be admitted that, as an essential spiritual art, this kind of painting requires the utmost concentration of the mind. The concentration of the mind is required first of all by the peculiar nature of Oriental paper used for this art. Oriental paper is no less sensitive than the Oriental brush in the sense that it absorbs water and ink easily and quickly. Even the slightest drop of water, not to speak of ink, soaks instantaneously into it and leaves an indelible trace on its surface. Strictly speaking, "painting" is here impossible. Unlike Western oil painting, in which colours can be piled up in layers, an ink painting is a work that must be finished once and for all. Every stroke is the first and the last stroke. Absolutely no retouch is possible. If a line gets broken in its flow, for example, it is broken forever; it cannot be continued, for the movement of the spirit has stopped as the line has stopped. There is thus no time for deliberation in the process, no room for subsequent corrections and alterations. As Chang Yen Yüan (9th century, the T'ang Period) remarks in his famous and important book on the fundamentals of Chinese painting, "He who deliberates and moves the brush, intent upon making a picture, misses the art of painting, while he who cogitates and moves the brush without such intentions, reaches the art of painting. His hand will not get stiff; his heart will not grow cold; without knowing how, he accomplishes it".[21]

The intense concentration of the mind is demanded of the painter not only for the technical or practical reason coming from the nature of Oriental paper. It is required also for another important reason, the discussion of which will directly lead us toward the more philosophical aspect of our subject. As in Western painting, Oriental ink painting starts from, and is based upon, a close observation of the things of Nature. The observation, however, does not consist here in a strictly objective, scientific and methodical observation of Nature. The observation of things which is demanded in the typically Oriental type of painting is a complete penetration of the eye of the painter into the invisible reality of the things until the pulse-beat of his soul becomes identical with the pulse-beat of cosmic Life permeating all things, whether large or small, organic or inorganic. Such an observation of things is possible only by means of an intense concentration of all the inner forces of the soul – a state of mind in which observation is identical with introspection, that is to say, in which the observation of the external world is at the same time the act of penetration into the interior of the mind itself.

In a passage of "Scattered Notes at a Rainy Window" (*Yü Ch'uang Man Pi*), which is considered the most important writing on Chinese aesthetics in the Ch'ing Period, the author, Wang Yüan Ch'i remarks:

> The idea must be conceived before the brush is grasped – such is the principal point in painting. When the painter takes up the brush he must be absolutely quiet, serene, peaceful and collected and shut out all vulgar emotions. He must sit down in silence before the white silk scroll, concentrate his soul and control his vital energy ... When he has a complete view in his mind, then he should dip the brush and lick the tip.[22]

It is important to observe in this connection that for the Far Eastern painter everything is inspirited; everything within this world has a spirit within itself. The painter concentrates first and foremost on penetrating into the "spirit" of the thing which he wants to paint. The "spirit" of a thing is the primordial origin of its phenomenal appearance, the innermost ground of its being, lying beyond its external colour and form. It is this inscrutable spiritual force, the life-breath, the deepest essence of the thing, that is considered to make a painting a real piece of art, when the inspired painter has succeeded in transmitting it through brush and ink. Even a single stone must be painted in such a way that its pictorial reproduction reverberates with the pulsation of the life-spirit of the stone.

This innermost spirit of things is variously called in different fields of thought in China and Japan. In the classical theories of painting it is called the "bone-structure". The "bone-structure" of stone, for example, is the depth-form which the stone assumes in the primordial stratum of its existence. It is the most fundamental form of the stone, which the painter must discover by years of close observation-introspection, through the painstaking process of elimination of all subordinate elements and external factors one after another until he reaches the utmost limit of simplification, at which alone is the "spirit" of the stone revealed to his mind in a flash of illumination.

In the theory of *haiku*-poetry, the "spirit" here in question is called *hon-jô*, the "real nature" of a thing. Explicating a central idea taught by Bashô,[23] one of his representative disciples says:

> Our master used to admonish us to learn about the pine-tree from the pine-tree itself, and about the bamboo from the bamboo itself. He meant by these words that we should totally abandon the act of deliberation based on our ego. ... What the master meant by 'learning' is our penetrating into the object itself (whether it be a pine-tree or a bamboo) until its inscrutable essence (i.e., its *hon-jô*) is revealed to us. Then the poetic emotion thereby stimulated becomes crystallised into a verse. No matter how clearly we might depict an object in a verse, the object and our ego would remain two separated things and the poetic emotion expressed would never reach the true reality of the object, if the emotion is not a spontaneous effusion out of the (*hon-jô*) of that very object. Such (discrepancy between the emotion and reality) is caused by the deliberate intention on the part of our ego.[24]

Likewise, in the same book:

> Concerning the right way of making *haiku*, I have heard our master say: As the light (of the deep reality) of a thing flashes upon your sight, you must on the instant fix it in a verse before the light fades out.
>
> Another way of making *haiku* is what the master has described as "shaking out of the mind the instantaneous inspiration onto the exterior form of a verse". This and all other similar ways taught by the master have this idea in common that one should go into the interior of the thing, into the spirit of the object, and immediately fix through words the real form of the thing before the emotion cools down".[25]

Thus, to come back to the art of ink painting, the most important point is that one should penetrate into the innermost reality of an object or a whole landscape, and seize the life-breath which is animating it. But the penetration of the artist here spoken of into the spirit of a thing cannot be achieved as long as he retains his ego. This is the gist of what Bashô taught about the art of *haiku*-poetry. One can delve deeply into the spirit of a thing only by delving deeply into his own self. And delving deeply into one's own self is to lose one's own self, to become completely egoless, the subject getting entirely lost in the object. This spiritual process is often referred to in the East by the expression: "the man becomes the object". The painter who wants to paint a bamboo must first become the bamboo and let the bamboo draw its own inner form on the paper.

What I have referred to in the foregoing as the "inner form", "innermost reality", "bone-structure", "spirit" etc. of a thing corresponds to what is called *li* in Chinese philosophy. The term *li* played a role of tremendous importance in the history of Chinese philosophy, first in the formation of the Hua Yen metaphysics in Buddhism, and later in the philosophical world-view of Neo-Confucianism in the Sung Period. The philosophy of Chu Hsi (Chu Tzu, 1139-1200), for example, may best be characterised as a philosophical system developed around the central concept of *li*.

For lack of time and space I cannot go into the discussion of this concept now. Suffice it here to say that for Chu Tzu the *li* is the eternal principle transcending time and space, immaterial, indestructible, and supersensible. In itself the *li* is meta-physical ("above form", *hsin êrh shang*), but it inheres in everything physical ("below shape" *hsin êrh hsia*); i.e. every physical object in existence, whether animate or inanimate. That is to say, every sensible object that exists in this world has inherent in it a metaphysical principle governing from within all that is manifested by the object in the dimension of its physical existence. The *li* of a thing is, in short, the deepest metaphysical ground of the thing, which makes the thing what it really is – the "is-ness" or "such-ness" of the thing as the Buddhists would call it.

In a famous passage of his "Commentary on the Great Learning" (*Ta Hsüeh*), Chu Tzu emphasizes the supreme importance of our realising the *li* of everything by means of what he calls the "investigation of things". He says:

> If we want to bring our knowledge to the utmost limit of perfection, we must take up all things and thoroughly investigate the *li* of each individual thing one after another. This is possible because, on one hand, the human mind is endowed with a penetrating power of cognition and because, on the other, there is nothing under Heaven that is not endowed with *li*. Our knowledge usually remains in the state of imperfection only because we do not penetrate into the depth of the *li* of the things.
>
> Thus the foremost instruction of the "Great Learning" consists in urging every student to go on deepening the cognition of the *li* of all things in the world, taking advantage of the knowledge of *li* which he has already acquired, until his cognition of the *li* reaches the limit of perfection. After years of assiduous and unremitting effort, the student may suddenly become enlightened in a moment of illumination. Then everything will become thoroughly transparent to him: the outside and inside of all things, the fine and coarse of every single object, will be grasped in their reality. At the same time the original perfection of the reality of his own mind and its magnificent activity will also become apparent to him". [26]

Thus according to Chu Tzu, the *li* exists in the interior of every individual man, but the same *li* exists also in each one of all physical objects under Heaven so that in the most profound dimension of existence man and Nature are one single reality, although in the physical dimension each thing is an independent entity separated from all the rest. Because of this structure of reality, man is able – at least theoretically – to return to the original unity of the internal *li* and the external *li*, through sustained effort in combining introspective meditation and a searching investigation into the *li* of each individual object in the world. The very moment at which this unity of the internal *li* and the external *li* is realised is for Chu Tzu the moment of supreme enlightenment corresponding to *satori* in Zen. A man who has achieved this is a "sage" in the Neo-Confucian sense.

Later, in the Ming Period, Wang Yang Ming (1472-1527), the celebrated philosopher of that time tried out this method of attaining sagehood advocated by Chu Tzu. The interesting incident is related by Wang Yang Ming himself in his *Ch'uan Hsi Lu*, "Record of the Transmission of Instructions". He and one of his friends decided one day to carry out Chu Tzu's teaching. As an easy and practical starting-point, the two friends agreed to try to grasp the *li* of a bamboo that happened to be there in the courtyard. They set to work at once. Day and night they concentrated their mind upon the bamboo, trying to penetrate into its inner spirit. The friend fell into a nervous breakdown in three days. Wang Yang Ming himself who held out longer than his friend could not continue the "investigation" of the *li* of the bamboo more than seven consecutive days. His body became completely worn out, his mental energy exhausted, and the bamboo had not yet disclosed its *li* to him. He gave up in utter dispair, murmuring to himself: "Alas, we are not endowed with the capacity to become sages!".[27]

In fairness to this remarkable thinker I would add that Wang Yang Ming later achieved enlightenment by means of pure contemplation and meditation. But to go into this subject would lead us too far away from our present problem.

It is in any case clear that the failure suffered by Wang Yang Ming was due to his inability at this earlier stage of his life to "become the bamboo", to use again that peculiar expression. In the field of painting and poetry we know the existence of many artists who could accomplish this spiritual feat.

The remarkable painter-poet of the Sung Period, Sung Tung P'o, to whom reference has earlier been made, has, for example, left a number of interesting accounts in both prose and poetry of his friend Wên Yü K'o (Wên T'ung, 1018-1079) who was widely acclaimed by his contemporaries as a rare genius in the art of painting bamboos. In a short poem which our poet composed and inscribed over a picture of bamboos by Wên Yü K'o, he says:

> When Yü K'o paints bamboos,
> He sees bamboos; not a man does he see.
> Nay, not only is he oblivious of other men;
> In ecstacy, oblivious of his own self,
> He himself is transformed into bamboos. Then,
> Inexhaustibly emerge out of his mind bamboos, eternally fresh and alive. [28]

In another place, a prose essay in which he describes the art and personality of Wên Yü K'o, he says:

> In order to paint a bamboo, the painter must start by actualising the perfect form of the bamboo in his mind. Then taking up the brush, he concentrates his inner sight upon the bamboo in his mind. And as the image of what he really wishes to paint clearly emerges, he must, at that very instant, start moving the brush in pursuit of the image like a falcon swooping at a hare that has just jumped out of the brush. If the concentration relaxes even for a moment, the whole thing is gone. This is what Yü K'o taught me. [29]

The image of the bamboo which Yü K'o says the painter must follow in a fiery swiftness of execution is the essential form that manifests itself in his concentrated mind out of the *li* of the bamboo. Quite significantly Sung Tung P'o uses the word *li* as a key term of his aesthetic theory. Everything in the world, he says, has in its invisible depth an "eternal principle" (*ch'ang li*). [30] A painting which is not based on the intuitive apprehension of the "eternal principle" of the object it depicts is not, for a Su Tung P'o worthy to be considered a real work of art, no matter how minutely and faithfully the picture may transmit the likeness of the external shape and colour of the thing.

It will have been understood that in this kind of pictorial art, the elimination of colour is almost a necessity. Colour-sensation is the most primitive form of our cognition of external things. In the eyes of the Far Eastern artist or philosopher colour represents the surface of Nature. For one who wants to break through the veils of physical exteriority of things and concentrate his mind on the eternal *li* existing in their interior as well as in his own mind, the seduction of colour is a serious hindrance in the way of his apprehension of the innermost nature of the things, and in the way of his realisation of his original unity with all things in the most profound layer of spiritual life.

From this becomes also understandable the very special function of black in Oriental painting. In coloured paintings, black functions ordinarily as the obstruction of chromatic colours. It indicates the end of all other colours, and consequently the end of the life-breath pervading Nature. In ink painting, on the contrary, black *is* life; it is the infinite possibility of expression and development. Black here is not sheer black. For in its negation of all colours, all colours are positively affirmed.

When a red object is actually painted red, the object becomes immovably fixed in that particular colour. According to the typically Oriental way of thinking, however, red contains in itself all other colours; and precisely because it contains in itself the essential possibility of being actualised in any other colour, it is here and now manifesting itself as red. Such a world, in which every single colour is seen to contain in itself all other colours, so that each colour appears as the point of convergence of all colours, such a world of infinite colour possibilities can best be painted in black – at least, in the view of the Far Eastern painter.

In the latter part of my lecture, I have exclusively dealt with the problem of the positive aspect of ink painting, that is, the problem of the positive representation of natural objects in this kind of Oriental art. In bringing this paper to a final close, I would recall once again the importance of the negative aspect of "painting without painting anything", the aspect of expressing by nonexpression what is not actually expressed.

Ike-no Taiga (1723-1776), a representative Japanese painter in the Edo Period, was once asked: "What do you find most difficult in painting? " "Drawing a white space where absolutely nothing is drawn – that is the most difficult thing to accomplish in painting" was the answer.

NOTES

1 R.H. Blyth: *History of Haiku*, vol. I (Tokyo, 1963). H. Blyth known as the author of a number of works on Zen Buddhism, *Haiku*, and some other aspects of Japanese culture, had a good understanding of the spiritual tradition of Japan. He died in 1964.

2 See Yukio Yashiro: *Nihon Bijutsu-no Tokushitsu* ("The Characteristic Features of Japanese Art"), (Tokyo, 4th ed. 1954), p.235.

3 *Ibid.*, p. 236.

4 Yoshio Araki: *Genji Monogatari Shôchô Ron* ("Symbolism in the *Tale of Genji*") in the Journal *Kaishaku to Kanshô* (vol. 142, Tokyo, 1948)

5 See Aki Ihara: *Heianchô Bungaku-no Shikisô* ("The Chromatic Aspects of Literature in the Heian Period"), (1967, Tokyo), p. 8.

6 *Murasaki-Shikibu Nikki* ("The Diary of Lady Murasaki"), Iwanami Series of Classical Japanese Literature, No. 14, (Tokyo, 1961), pp. 507-508. This passage is more fully quoted in English by Ivan Morris: *The World of the Shining Prince – Court Life in Ancient Japan* (a Peregrine Book, Oxford, 1969), p. 206. This latter book gives a fine description of the general characteristics of Heian culture. On the textile arts and costume decoration in Japan, Helen B. Minnich's *Japanese Costume* (Rutland and Tokyo, 1963) is the best work available in English.

7 On the special aesthetic significance of black in the *Tale of Genji*, see Aki Ihara, (*op. cit.*; cf. Note 5), pp. 203 to 235, a chapter entitled *Sumizome-no Bi*, "The Beauty of the Black-Dyed Robe"; also p. 23.

8 Kakuzô Okatura: *The Book of Tea* (Dover Publications, New York, 1964), p. 1. The book was originally written and published in 1906.

9 Daisetz T. Suzuki: *Sengai, The Zen Master*, ed. by Eva Van Hoboken (Faber & Faber, London, 1971), pp. 23-24.

10 Fujiwara Teika, son of Fujiwara Shunzei, was a *waka*-poet of the highest rank in the early Kamakura Period. His work represents the very spirit and style of the *"Shin-Kokin" Anthology*. The poem here discussed is found in this Anthology.

11 The authenticity of *Nambô Roku* has been very much discussed. But the importance importance of the book as a theoretic treatise on the *wabi* art of tea remains the same, whether it be a real work of Nambô or not. The passage is quoted from *Kinsei Geidô Ron*, Iwanami Series of Japanese Thought, No. 41, (Tokyo, 1972), p. 18.

12 See Shôzô Masuda: *Nô-no Hyôgen* ("Expression in Nô") (Chûôkôron Books No. 260, Tokyo, 1971), pp. 27-28.

13 The statement is in reality an inscription on a picture. I quote it from Oswald Sirén: *The Chinese on the Art of Painting* (Schocken Books, New York, 1936), p. 199. The italics are mine.

14 *Tao Tê Ching*, XIV.

15 *Ibid.*, XL.

16 *Ibid.*, IV.

17 See Yukio Yashiro: *Nihon Bijutsu-no Tokushitsu* (*op. cit.*), pp. 143-144.

18 For more detail on this problem, see Ichimatsu Tanaka: *Japanese Ink Painting – Shûbun to Sesshû*, Heibonsha Survey of Japanese Art, No. 12 (New York and Tokyo, 1972), pp. 173-174.

19 See Shôgo Kinbara: *Tôyô Bijutsu* ("Oriental Art") (Kawada, Tokyo, 1941), pp. 102-103.

20 Blyth: *Haiku*, vol. I, *Eastern Culture* (Hokuseidô, Tokyo, 5ed., 1967), Preface p. 8.

21 Quoted from Oswald Sirén, *op. cit.*, p. 24.

22 *Ibid.*, p. 203.

23 Dohô Hattori (1657-1730), author of the *San Zôshi* ("Three Notebooks") in which he noted down Bashô's remarks on *haiku* and its spirit.

24 *Aka Zôshi* "Red Book" (one of the "Three Notebooks"), quoted from the Iwanami Series of Classical Japanese Literature Series, No. 66. (Tokyo, 2nd., 1972) pp. 398-399.

25 *Ibid.*, pp. 400-401.

26 "Commentary on the Great Learning", Chapter V.

27 "Record of the Transmission of Instructions", Part III.

28 Translated from the text given in *So Tôba*, Shûei-sha Series of Classical Chinese Poetry, No. 17, (Tokyo, 1964), pp. 249-250.

29 Translated from the text given in *So Tôba Shû* ("Collected Writings of Su Tung P'o"), Chikuma Series of Chinese Civilization, No. 2, (Tokyo, 1972), p. 131.

30 *Ibid.*, p. 88.

INDEX

ABBREVIATIONS

iBA = in Black Africa; iCVE = in Christian Visionary Experience